Walter Macken (1915–1967)

Walter Macken, novelist, short story writer, playwright and actor, was born in Galway on 3 May 1915, the youngest of three children. His father, also named Walter, was a qualified carpenter who also worked as an actor in an old theatre in Middle Street called the Rackets Court; in March 1916 he was killed in the trenches at St Eloi, France.

The young writer spent all his childhood in Galway, growing up in St Joseph's Terrace and Henry Street. He first began to write at the age of eight and acted while still at school at the 'Bish'; on leaving in the 1930s he became a member of the company at the Taibhdhearc, the Irish language theatre in Middle Street. It was there he met his wife, Peggy Kenny, daughter of the founder of the *Connacht Tribune*. They worked together in the theatre until their marriage in 1937, after which they lived in London for a while.

Returning to Galway in 1939, Walter Macken took up the post of theatre manager with the Taibhdhearc, where in nine years he staged over seventy different productions. At this time he also began to write for publication both in Irish and English; in 1946 his first play in English, *Mungo's Mansion*, was successfully staged at the Abbey Theatre in Dublin and his first novel, *Quench the Moon*, was accepted for publication, while he was already working on the short stories which would constitute *City of the Tribes*.

He joined the Abbey for three years in 1948; a year later his second novel, *I Am Alone*, was published, and in 1950 his third novel, *Rain on the Wind*, brought him international recognition with the Book of the Month Club in the UK and the Literary Guild in the USA. His successful US theatre tour with the M.J. Molloy play, *The King of Friday's Men,* gave him the impetus to return home to Galway to establish a career for himself as a full-time writer.

In 1957 he embarked on his most ambitious writing project: the three historical novels, *Seek the Fair Land*, *The Silent People* and *The Scorching Wind*. He did extensive historical research for this trilogy, setting out to show in them how the ordinary people survived the battles and tribulations of those troubled times. In 1964 he turned his hand for the first time to writing for children, and his first children's novel, *Island of the Great Yellow Ox*, proved to be one of his most popular books. In all, he produced a body of work which finally came to ten novels, seven plays, three books of short stories and two children's books; most of his novels have been translated into many languages. His last novel, *Brown Lord of the Mountain*, was published just a month before his death on 22 April 1967.

CITY OF THE TRIBES

Walter Macken

CITY
OF THE
TRIBES

Walter Macken

BRANDON

Published in 1997 by
Brandon Book Publishers Ltd
Dingle, Co. Kerry, Ireland.

British Library Cataloguing in Publication Data
is available for this book.

ISBN 0 86322 228 5

Cover illustration and design: Steven Hope
Typesetting: Seton Music Graphics, Bantry, Co. Cork.
Printed by ColourBooks, Baldoyle, Dublin.

Contents

Editor's note

In late 1996 I received typescripts of over thirty stories by the late Walter Macken, which he had apparently written in the 1940s, and many of which he had intended should be published as a collection cohering around the character of the city of Galway, under the title of *City of the Tribes*.

A few of the stories were present in two different versions, and we have made our editorial choices; a few stories seemed incomplete, and these we have omitted. Some of the stories were more polished than others, and in editing we took a few liberties, such as omitting some repetitious material and changing the author's spelling of 'Citie' to 'City', but we sought always to respect Macken's characteristic style. Some of the typescripts were annotated in the author's handwriting, and in a very few instances in which words were illegible, we guessed. In general, we tried to be as true as possible to the original intentions of the author.

In addition to the stories now published in this volume, there are also some ten other unpublished stories by Walter Macken which do not seem to belong in *City of the Tribes*; we hope to publish these in a separate volume at a later date.

I wish to thank Ultan Macken sincerely for making these stories available, Fr Walter Macken for kindly providing the photograph of his father, and Terry Fitzgerald and Winifred Power for their editorial assistance. Most of all, I want to express my deep appreciation of

Editor's note

the late Walter Macken; in editing these stories I have been privileged to encounter at close quarters an exceptional storyteller.

Steve MacDonogh
March 1997

Ambition

BUSINESS WAS BAD with Bill. He stood in front of the church door with his hand stretched out and a most pitiful look on his dirty face. It was a raw gusty day, and the wind blew coldly about him.

He was impervious to the wind, since his body was covered with three waistcoats, two cardigans, a black frock coat, a half-frieze coat, and three pairs of trousers, the holes in one covered by the places where there were none in the next. A raincoat tied with a piece of cart rope held the whole outfit together, and his toes peeped blackly and coyly from gaping shoes which were tied to his feet with lengths of twine.

He thought of the single penny in his pocket and raised a hand to scratch at the hole in his bowler hat where his hair came out. He was very hairy, with long whiskers and hair to the shoulders matted and streaked with grey. It should have been a good drawing card, but Bill was beginning to realise that he must be losing his appeal. Not even the poor who were the best touches seemed to have spare pennies in this hard weather. 'I will have to think of something else to do,' Bill thought, 'because if I don't I won't see the colour of a pint until next summer.'

He saw a young man, sprucely dressed, coming towards the church, and he cheered up a little. As the young man dipped his fingers in the holy water font, Bill commenced his tale. He had said it so often that he never listened to it himself now. It was a harrowing story about a wife and nine children, with a dash of TB and starvation and cruel landlords thrown in. It should have softened a bank manager, but the young man merely looked directly at Bill and said, 'Why don't you go and get a job?' and went into the church.

Insults. The terrible things people do to the poor nowadays. Wouldn't give you the itch or if they did they'd cut your nails.

'The curse a God on the bosthoons,' said Bill out loud. 'I hope I'll see them in the pludder and I'll be passin' in me moty car, and I'll spit in their faces so I will, I will indeed, the paupers.'

'Now, now,' said the voice of the sacristan behind him. 'How many times must I tell you to keep away from the front porch of the church? If you must beg, do it outside the gates of the church. Off with you now!'

'All right, all right, all right!' said Bill, shaking a shoulder impatiently, glaring at the brother from narrowed eyes. He turned at the gate to look back at the black-cassocked man with the white hair. They were all the same, in or out of the church. 'Up and up and up!' he muttered back at the sacristan. 'The pludder for the poor, the pludder for the poor. Christianity, Christianity, hump the lot a ye!'

The brother waved his hand at him, ordering him away, and then turned back into the church tsk-tsking.

Bill shuffled along the pavement dully, his head down, muttering. It was a hard life. What was a man to do? The aroma wafting to his nostrils from the pub at the corner brought him back to reality again. He stopped at the door, like the Bisto Baby grown old and hoary, and he sniffed the air. He felt a great thirst at the smell. He could see his hand tightening around the cold pint glass and imagine only too well the feel, the velvet feel of the porter sliding down his throat. He opened the swing door cautiously and peered into the gloomy interior. Only two customers there and the buxom lady behind the counter leaning bare fat arms on the polished wood. He sidled in and went to the gloomy part of the counter. He saw the woman looking up from her talking and making a face and then continuing the conversation. There was a round globule of spilt porter on the counter where he stood. He dipped the tips of his fingers into it and sucked the porter off them. It nearly sent him wild.

'Well, what do *you* want?' she asked finally. He didn't like the way she underlined the *you*.

'Give's a pint,' said Bill.

'Where's the money?' she asked.

'Tomorra,' said Bill.

'Simple Simon,' said one of the men, a sailor man with a peaked cap and a blue jersey with words in red written on the front of it. The two men laughed and finished their drinks. Bill watched agonisedly as their glasses emptied.

'Tomorra,' he said to the woman again.

'Get to hell out of here,' she said, coming over with a cloth and wiping the spilt porter from the counter. Even that she wouldn't leave him.

'Stand's a drink?' he appealed to the two men. 'G'wan.'

'I would,' said the sailor man, 'if I thought you'd take a wash in it.'

Bill tried to smile at their laughter. 'G'wan,' he said feebly again.

'G'out a here; you stink,' said the second man holding his nose.

'Off with you now, off with you now,' said the woman, 'or I'll get the Guards.'

Bill gave up hope and shuffled towards the door. 'A mane crowd a gawks,' he muttered, 'suckin' maneness from their ould wans' dugs, them and dirty porter and bitches.'

He closed the door on their laughter and cursed his way around the corner and into the dusty small market-place. He bent into the mass of hay wisps and dirt that had been collected by the wind and extracted a cigarette butt. While he was bending, a small perky boy with a shopping basket running for a message paused to look at him. He gave up trying to remember what message his mother had sent him on to throw out a friendly feeler.

'How y', Bill?' he asked then.

Bill looked at him furiously and raised his arm in a threatening gesture. The boy felt hurt, so he stuck a red tongue between thin lips and made a noise with it. It infuriated Bill. He bent again grabbing for a stone to throw, and the boy took to his heels, went around the nearest corner, put his red head back again to shout, 'Bowsey Bill from Ballinasloe! Bowsey Bill from Ballinasloe!' and then he was gone.

Bill searched his pockets and found a match. The butt tasted rank and sour, but Bill sucked it into his guts and went along the narrow lane leading out of the market-place. The butt lasted him the length of the lane, and then he came into the place where long streets stretched away, crisscrossing each other, the houses built in long rows, their fronts half-way rough cast and halfway smooth plaster, the doorways opening on to the concrete footpaths.

He heard a voice singing and he paused to look. In the centre of the first street, he recognised the Boogie Man, a man with a club foot and a tall supporting walking stick. He held himself straight and wore a green moulded coat that fell almost to his heels, a green bowler hat on top, his coat lapels held across his neck with a safety pin. He had a small clean face, and his greying moustache, close cropped, crept down the sides of his mouth, giving him an Asiatic look. This is what he was singing:

> Whang, whang, whang,
> I am the Boogie Man.
> All the whopsie, popsie, topsie,
> Catch me if you can!
> Whang, whang, whang!

Housewives stood at their doors listening to him, leaning on the handles of their sweeping brushes, and the kids kept a respectful distance from him. Parents often frightened their children to bed with the threat of the Boogie Man, and here he was in person. He always got a fair hearing and modest rewards. Bill stood there watching the scene. He saw an insignificant looking man who wasn't even able to sing standing in the centre of a long street, just saying, 'Whang, whang, whang, I am the Boogie Man,' and the next second kids were cautiously approaching him with their parents' offerings. It dawned slowly on Bill, like unused machinery starting up, 'Here is a way to make the price of many pints. Just this. Why didn't I think of it before? This fella has no voice at all. Only standing talking. I have a voice. If I let a roar outa me I can be heard in the Aran Islands, so if me man is able to get money from just talkin' what'll I get for real singin'?'

He felt excited.

It was all so simple, when he thought of it like that. 'That's what a fella lacked. Ambition. Trust in yourself. Amn't I a block of a man with a chest like a bull and great noise in me if I wanted. It's only the courage that's lackin'. Them kids! What about the kids?' Bill suffered from the kids. 'But look at the way the Boogie Man can quieten them – a small weenshie man in a green coat. A look from his eyes and they are paralysed. A small fella like him. And me? A stump of a man like me. One look and they'll be transfixed. They'll be quiet as fleas in a frost.' He was all urgency now. He would go down the back of this street and go into the next street from the Boogie Man. He thought of them coming out with the pennies. One song, just one song, and he would have the price of one pint, or maybe two and a packet of Woodbines. He shuffled off, skirting the backs of the houses, not pausing as he might have done before to search the dustbins for discarded scraps. He did not halt until he emerged from the backs of this row of houses and darted across the bottom of the street to the next street. He paused there and poked his head around the corner.

He sighed with satisfaction. It was as empty of kids as the womb of a virgin. Maybe all the kids were dead or dumb or dying. It didn't matter. He would stand in the middle of the street, up there under the electric light standard, and he would draw air into his lungs and he would startle them out of their senses with the volume of his song. Nobody to be seen except the right people, the housewives sweeping the dust of their red-tiled kitchens into the street. He went bravely to the pole and stood there, frantically searching his tattered memory for a song. Any song. He dug out the scattered words from his slow mind. They all started with an O anyhow. So give them an O.

He opened his mouth, drew air into his lungs and howled at the sky.

'O-O-O-O-O-O-O-O-Oh!' Bill roared, closing his eyes to the volume of it. When he opened his eyes he got a severe shock.

At the beginning of his 'O' he was alone; at its completion there was a legion of children standing in a ring around him like magic creations from the street dust, looking at him solemnly, waiting for him to continue. All sorts of kids. Little girls with tattered skirts, clutching dolls and hoops. Little boys with tattered trousers and bare feet and running noses, summing him up with shrewd eyes.

'Go on, Bill,' said one youth to him kindly.

Another turned and screeched to a figure at the top of the street. 'Jimjoe! Jimjoe!' he roared, a small dirty hand encircling his call. 'It's Bowsey Bill from Ballinasloe. He's goin' t' sing.' He turned back to Bill then. 'Hold it until Jimjoe comes, Bill, 'at's a man!' Bill was a bit daunted. If he had a flail he would have swept all the children into the sky. Many parents had come to doors and were leaning there idly. Smiling. Have to be nice to the kids.

Jimjoe approached slowly, leisurely, and Bill was horrified to note that he was the little boy he had met in the market-place, the boy with the red hair who had made rude noises. Jimjoe came close and smiled sweetly at Bill. The smile of an innocent child. It made Bill feel a bit queasy. But Jimjoe still smiled, wrinkling the freckles on his small snub nose under the blue eyes.

'OK, Bill,' he said then, 'let's hear you.'

This might have daunted a great tenor, but Bill cleared his throat and spat and emitted his noise.

> O, Docthor, O Docthor, O dear Docthor John, (sang Bill)
> Your cod liver oil is so pure and so strong,
> I'm afraid a me life I'll go down in the soil,
> If me wife won't stop drinkin' your cod liver oil.

It was a pretty bad effort. If you have ever heard the moanings of a corncrake with a sore throat or a boy scraping the inside of a two gallon can with a rusty nail, you have heard Bill singing.

'Hey, Bill,' Jimjoe roared. Bill looked at him out of eyes that were misted with the effort he had made. His lower lip dropped blankly.

'Wha'?' he asked.

'Lookit,' said Jimjoe, 'would yeh sing that again? We didn't hear the words.'

The other kids chorused him. Bill looked around and then bent low so that he was talking at their level and couldn't be seen by the parents.

'Here,' he said viciously, 'g'wan away ou'r that an play, ye bees ye!'

Jimjoe immediately turned towards one of the occupied door-ways at the end of the street and shouted, 'Mammy! Mammy! Bill is after callin' me a bee. What's a bee, Mammy?'

'S-s-sh, s-s-sh, for God's sake,' implored Bill, 'I didn't mean nothin'.'

The parents were smiling and laughing to one another. Bill smiled at them and waved a hand. This made them smile all the more. It wasn't the first debut they had seen in the street.

'Well, sing it again,' said Jimjoe.

Bill sang it again. It was the only verse he knew anyhow. He was pleased with the effort this time. He thought he had rendered it well. The kids seemed to have enjoyed it also. They were con-vulsed with mirth. They were doubling up, laughing uproariously, staggering around in a pantomime of convulsions, their shrill laughter reaching for the sky. Doubt now entered into Bill's mind. Could it be as funny as all that? The people in the doorways were laughing, too, at the kids laughing. They couldn't have heard the words at that distance, so what were they laughing at?

They were mainly laughing at the red-head, he saw then. The kids were really laughing now at their own exaggerated gyrations and at Jimjoe, who was down on his back in the street kicking his legs in the air and holding his stomach with the laughter.

'That song is killing me, it's so funny,' he gasped, turning on his stomach and beating his hands in the dust. The long street was a cacophony of convulsions.

Bill stood there, bewildered, doubt gnawing at him, knowing something was wrong, holding on desperately to the tail of disappearing ambition, seeing in his eye the galling figure of the Boogie Man standing in a street alone with the kids at a respectable distance, just panting to hand him the hot pennies from their palms. And here now they were crucifying him; making a bloody laughing stock out of him in front of the world; and he with not another song in his head or a verse of a song that would silence them. He felt tears of frustration at the back of his head. The red-head had pulled himself to his knees and was laughing away, one hand up to his side, so in a moment of forgetfulness and madness, Bill raised his foot and kicked Jimjoe on the behind. He was a big man and there was weight in the kick. The body of Jimjoe rose a few feet in the air towards the circle of children, who scattered, and the falling body embraced the gravel.

There was a deadly pause.

Bill moved futilely towards the boy saying, 'You're all right now! You're not hurt, so you're not now!'

Jimjoe screamed and hugged and cupped his scraped knees until he squeezed a few drops of dark blood from the cracked skin. Then he ran towards his house howling, holding his knee with one hand, the back of his britches with the other, and all the time roaring and forcing tears from his screwed up eyes.

'Mammy! Mammy!' he was screaming, 'Bowsey Bill from Ballinasloe kicked me in the ah. Oh, Mammy, Mammy, I'm bleeding. Oh Mammy, Mammy, I'm dyin'.'

'Yeer all right, I tell yeh, yeer all right,' said Bill, following him hopefully.

And then the other kids scattered towards their houses howling.

'Mammy! Mammy! Bowsey Bill from Ballinasloe kicked Jimjoe on the ah.'

Bill halted then and looked around him.

He saw the kids spreading and he saw one or two furious looks on grown-up faces. He saw one woman who had been sweeping out a path coming towards him with a brush in her hand which she was waving threateningly. She was screaming something from the middle of a red face. He saw other mothers, too, debouching from their doors, making for him in a scattered phalanx, and overwhelmed by this evidence and disregarding the rights and wrongs of the whole matter, Bill turned and took to his heels.

When the kids saw him fleeing they raced after him whooping. Even the mortally wounded Jimjoe, miraculously cured, raced after him, too, picking up a cabbage stalk and hurling it after him. The women made for Bill, their brushes waving, and the lethargic dogs awoke and followed on the heels of the throng.

Bill fled on, leaving one of his gaping shoes behind him, his hardened sole biting into the hard ground, his rags laying out on the breeze. He had to run the gauntlet, his arms up to cover his head from the blows of the brushes of the women who ran from the doors in front of him, their screams loud in his ears, the thump of their brushes heavy on his armour of clothing, snapping white teeth of dogs at his heels and flying stones and cabbage stalks and offal from dustbins whistling and flying around his ears or landing with dull clops on his body.

The weight of his clothes had him sweating. His breath was coming in gasps from his chest. There was the sour bile of disillusion in his breast. He cleared the corner. His attackers weeded out behind him, only the kids keeping up with his speed. His heart groaned and his blood pounded as he raced up the other street, and he cast an agonised glance at the man in the green coat regarding him from widened eyes.

> Whang, whang, whang,
> I am the Boogie Man . . .

'They don't give you a chance,' Bill thought. 'The whole wide world is agin the poor.'

Battle

H E WAS STANDING in the doorway of the barracks watching the kids hitting the cock-standard against the walls of the big ball-alley in the yard. They were very intent about it and even though there was a nip in the March wind they had their coats off and their shirt sleeves rolled up on their thin arms.

'It is a good thing,' he thought, 'to see children playing handball in the alley of the police barracks.' There was a time, not so long ago either, when they would no more have gone near the barracks at all than they would have gone into the gates of hell of their own accord. 'All that now, I hope,' he thought, 'is going. I hope, at last, that the people will begin to look on the police as their guardians instead of men to be defeated in every possible way through lying and trickery.'

It was no wonder that they had regarded a blue coat as being the brand of an enemy. So often the blue coat was covered by a revolver belt, and cruel antagonistic eyes gleamed under peaked caps. People had come to hate the police, because they were no longer protectors of the citizens, but fearsome men, who came at night in lorries and took away your father or your brother. And many tales had been told of the bad days before the police became the Garda Síochána, when every barracks was sandbagged and guarded by machine-guns; of those same barracks, too, where men had come from the lorries and gone into rooms, emerging later with tottering steps and their eyes blackened and their lips torn to pieces from the blows of fists and truncheons.

'All that,' he thought, 'would take many years for the people to forget.' In those days a wrongdoer might have been a hero. You sympathised with him and made rude noises with your lips at the police. Apart from that, the people had been taught that to gain their freedom they must look on the police as their jailers.

It was hard for them to adjust to the new police. But they would, in time, if the police for their part were sympathetic to them, and instilled kindly into their minds the fact that the bad days were gone and that law and order once more roamed the land and should be encouraged. 'They will learn,' he thought; 'they will learn in time.'

So it was good to see the children of the citizens playing handball in the alley of the police barracks. It meant that they, at least, knew that the police were on their side, knew it instinctively, instead of having to pause and remind themselves of the fact.

'Hey, Sean,' said a voice behind him, 'the Sergeant wants you.'

He turned.

'All right, Paddy,' he said. 'What does he want me for?'

'Maybe you didn't clean your teeth today,' said Paddy with a laugh, going into the orderly room, the batch of official-looking documents in his hand.

Sean laughed and made towards the stairs, automatically smoothing the blue tunic stretching tightly on his big chest and pausing to level off the jaunt of his peaked cap. He was a big man, Sean was, and he looked very well in the uniform; tall and broad, his waist was slender. Young he looked, but of course you couldn't avoid that. He was new to the Guards and he liked it. Behind him was a small country town, school, the examination for the police and six months training in the depot in Dublin. Hup, One Two. Left right, left right. Left, left, I'd a jolly good job and I left. The dull clomp of bullets in sand at the targets. The weary days of drill. The lecture rooms. And the fatigues. The one he hated most: gathering leaves in the autumn from the great parade ground. Then the going out. The small country village where nothing happened. Just sheep-dipping inspections and forms and regulations and the travelling District Court, somewhat like Duffy's Circus – 'one day and one day only'. A weary year of that before he had been brought in here to the city, where he could be with people and deal with people and work it all out for himself. He liked it here: he was happy and he thought the people liked him. That, he thought, should be the aim of every policeman, that the good people should like him and feel that they could depend on him.

The Sergeant soon disillusioned him.

There were many sergeants in the barracks, but there was only one Sergeant. When they said 'The Sergeant wants you,' you knew whom they meant. It wasn't Sergeant Smith or Sergeant Brown, but *the* Sergeant. Some of them didn't even know he had another name. Sean didn't. In the city, the boys had a very obscene name for him. It was purely a double name from the Irish and it was very alliterative, short and pithy, and it summed up the bigness of him, the crudeness of him and the coarseness of him. He was a dying duck was the Sergeant, a throw-back to the old peelers. Brute strength personified, he was the iron hand. No finesse. The Sergeant always settled everything with his own colossal size. It worked, of course; you would have to hand it to him. All knew him, and the sight of the size of him appearing amongst them was enough in itself to end many things that could have become dangerous. 'Here's the Sergeant' meant the end of rows and the end of pitch-and-toss schools, and comparative calm at political meetings.

Sean faced the Sergeant now, and knew that he didn't like him.

He was sitting there on his hard bench, overflowing.

His hair was sandy and grew in short-cut bristles. His head was very big, yet it wasn't as big as his jowls, which were red and smooth in appearance. His nose was small, and his forehead low, yet his eyes were set wide apart and were the colour of steel. His sandy grey moustache stuck out from his face, its ends waxed. Very typical of a gone age, Sean thought. Sitting down he was damn near as tall as Sean, who was six foot in his socks. His shoulders were mighty, and it was virtually impossible for him to sit down without opening his tunic. No cloth spun would have been able to bear the strain of the huge chest and the terribly muscular stomach.

He looked up from his papers now, the pen looking very out of place in a huge hairy hand.

'Martin,' said the Sergeant, his voice vibrating the floor, 'I don't like you.'

He watched the effect of this pronouncement on the smooth face opposite him. 'A nice country face,' he thought, 'with strength in the chin and a hint of stubbornness in the mouth,' the thin sensitive nose tightening now and the big brown eyes staring steadily into his own. 'Like a calf,' he thought, 'a big country calf.' I don't like you either, these brown steady eyes said back to him, and to hell with you. But the lips didn't speak, they just waited.

'It's not that I dislike you yourself,' he went on, 'but I dislike your way of doing things. How many summonses have you brought into court since you came here?'

'Very few,' said Sean in a tight voice.

'Exactly,' said the Sergeant. 'But why don't you ask me,' said Sean inside, 'how many affairs I fixed up for permanent good where you would have summonsed and left rancour and canker after you? Ask me that can't you!'

'Now, you can't tell me,' the Sergeant went on, pounding the wooden table with his free fist, 'that this is a community of angels. For a town of its size it contains some of the greatest criminals in the universe. So when a policeman is not bringing people to court in this town, then there is something wrong with the policeman, not with the people. The people are as bad as ever; the leopard doesn't change his spots.'

'Maybe,' said Sean, 'they're not as bad as you make them out to be.'

'Are you giving me impertinence?' the Sergeant asked, with a roar.

'No,' said Sean, 'I'm not. I'm just telling you that I don't agree with you, that's all. I'm just telling you that I have a different way of working than you, and if you expect to judge my worth as a policeman on the number of applications for summonses I make, then you can say I'm a bad policeman and be done with it.'

'I knew it,' said the Sergeant, banging his fist on the table again. 'I knew it. You're nothing but a lily-livered son of a bitch. You love the people, don't you? You want to be kind to the people, don't you? You want to reform the toughs don't you? Preach the Gospel, why can't you, when you're at it? It's a priest you should have been, my lad, not a policeman. And I'll tell you something now, and let you never forget it. God is your baton. Do you hear that? Your baton is to you what the ass's jawbone was to Samson. You don't rule people by charity. You rule them by fear and respect. Samson finished them with the jawbone of the ass. Christ tried to teach them sense with gentleness and look what happened him. They crucified him, didn't they? And they'll do the same thing to you in the morning. So now! You hear. Go and do likewise, and don't have them going around saying you are a pansy. Sure, they listen to you! And then you turn your back on them and they say "Who ever heard such a soft eejit." I know. I hear things. I hear everything. You are to acquire backbone, Martin, do you hear, or I'll have you out of here so quick that you won't know whether you are coming or going. That's all now!'

He went back to writing again diligently.

Sean paused, the bile pouring into his mouth. He turned to go, holding on to the iron of discipline that had been carefully layered into him. He walked to the door and then he paused there, and he turned back and his face was red. He took the cap from his head and he came back and he banged it on the table.

'That's not all,' he shouted. 'I don't agree with you! What do you think of that, Sergeant? I'll tell you what I think. Would you like to hear what I think?'

The Sergeant looked up calmly into the furious brown eyes.

'Go ahead and tell me,' he said warningly, his big face on his fist.

'I think,' said Sean, 'that your days are numbered. I think that you are the last of your kind. Everybody in town knows that. They are only waiting for you to die or retire. The day you retire on pension, there will be a sigh of relief so loud that it will lift the clouds over the town. That's what I think. You're like a great ape that was born without anything to think with, except that the solution of all difficulties is the use of force. That belonged to the old days when you could crack a man's skull with your baton and be commended in court for doing it, by men who didn't belong to the country at all. You stopped living, Sergeant, when the English left. You still think you are way back there. But you are not. You can't rule a people by force now. This country belongs to them and they belong to it, and they'll grow up with it because it's their country, and when they have learned to respect it and its laws you will be as much an anachronism as an Irish elk at the fair in Eyre Square. That's what I think, Sergeant, and you can take me now, and you can fire me out of this office. You can take me, too, and fire me out of the Guards if you want to. I don't give a damn! That's what I believe and I have said it and now you know, and to hell with you!'

He leaned over the table, his face thrust close to the face of the unreasonably calm Sergeant. And Sean was thinking, 'He will rise now to his great height and he will give me a crack in the puss. I will let him strike me, and then I will go for him, and I will damage him considerably before we are separated and I am thrown out of the Guards.'

'Have you anything else to say now?' the Sergeant asked.

Sean was discomfited at the calmness of him. He stood back.

'No,' he said.

'Fair enough,' said the Sergeant. 'You will carry out your patrol in the Eyre Square direction since you happened to mention it. There's a fair there today, I believe. You will patrol it for six hours. It's Tinkers' Thursday. Since you have such a great disregard for the use of the baton, you will hand it over to me now,' holding out his hand.

Slightly bewildered, Sean reached automatically for his baton case, opened it and handed back the heavy ebony baton to the Sergeant.

'It's against regulations,' he said reluctantly.

'Hand it over,' the Sergeant roared. 'Now get to hell out of here. I want to think about you, Martin. I want to think about all that's coming to you.'

Sean looked at him once and then went quickly and stiffly.

The Sergeant looked after him for a while, ruminating like a great bull. And then he chuckled, a great grumbling chuckle, like a volcano with indigestion.

Sean went down the rickety stairs, his heavy boots clumping on the bare boards. Blind with anger and a seething helplessness, he pulled on his cap passing the door of the orderly room. He didn't notice the silence within as the occupants watched him leave. Poor old Sean, their eyes said, as they watched him going out the door, his shoulder almost taking the jamb with him in his rage. Hearing the noise of the Sergeant descending the stairs then, all of them became busy, ringing phones and writing charge sheets and talking importantly. The Sergeant surveyed the hive of industry with a lack-lustre eye, bending his great head to come in the door.

'Martin is to patrol the square by himself today,' he said. 'All the men are to keep away until they are told to go there. Do ye hear that? The first man that goes up the square for the next few hours, I'll pulverise him.'

Paddy, a tall man from Cork, was the only one to speak.

'But, Sergeant,' he said. 'What about the tinkers? There'll be trouble up there today.'

'That's the point,' said the Sergeant. 'That's just the point. I myself personally will take over the square today and I will go there in my own good time, and since you are such a great talker Paddy, it might be a good idea if you took a turn of duty out to Salthill and back a few times. You are full of energy. A walk would do you good.'

'But, Sergeant,' said Paddy, 'I'm oney after comin' in.'

'Well,' said the Sergeant, 'in two minutes you'll be oney after going out.'

Sean was blind to his surroundings as he made his way towards the square. He was thinking redly about what he'd like to do to the Sergeant if only he was able. He felt his muscular fist sinking into the Sergeant's belly, and he felt his knuckles ramming at the Sergeant's lips and the blood of the Sergeant flowing over them.

As he made his way through the crowded streets, towering over the citizens, ignoring the odd friendly 'Hello, Sean?' from here and there, his anger began to wane, and his regret came back. It would mean having to leave the Guards. He knew that. You couldn't talk like that to a superior and hope to get away with it. Especially a martinet like the Sergeant, who was nurtured and reared on obedience and discipline. 'Ah well, to hell with it,' he thought. 'Who wants to be a policeman anyhow? Small pay and no thanks, that's all that's in it! A lot the citizens cared anyhow. One Guard was the same as another to them, whether he was hitting them on the head with a baton or whether he wasn't. Maybe the Sergeant was right that they were calling him a soft eejit and a pansy behind his back. Well, let them! He didn't care anymore. He'd go back and help his brother on his farm, and he would save the hay and cut the turf, and he wouldn't see people from one end of the year to the other. He wasn't really all that keen on being a good policeman. Nobody wanted you to be a good policeman, so what did it matter?'

He found then that it was becoming difficult to make progress through the crowds, and his seeing came back to him.

The roads leading in to the square were simply jammed with people and animals, all milling under the cold glare of the March sun. He had never seen such a sight before. But then he had never been in town before on a Tinkers' Thursday. Nobody had ever told him before about Tinkers' Thursday, the March fair when all the tinkers of Ireland came to sell their horses. Like rivers flowing to the sea, they came from their mysterious places with their horses to buy and sell them with all the rest of the country. Such a clamour as was going on now. And the colour of it. Shouts and the neighing of horses from away in front there where the fair was taking place. Over all the smell of horse, and under all the leavings of the horse. As far as the eye could see, there were bobbing heads in all sorts of headgear and the noble horse heads raised above all, with flaring nostrils and foam at the bits between their teeth. White and grey and brown and black and speckled, the young fillies clearing the crowds from them as they pranced around with beautiful long flowing manes and uncut tails. Ponies from Connemara, barely as tall as the shoulder of an average man. And the placid mares with lifted foreleg, bored, they had been here before so often, and the foals having their dinners from under them. Grand little yokes, that stole your heart with their long legs.

Sean felt his good humour returning as his interest was aroused.

He was a countryman after all, and a horse meant as much to him as to any other man in Ireland.

He came in useful too, a bit up the square where the flood of people and horses and carts and cars was like the meeting of two great rivers which had become blocked. He got in the middle of it all and began to sort them out. It was difficult and it made him sweat, but it restored him completely to good humour. What a sight and what smells! All the countrywomen, sitting on the sides of their ass-carts, urging them on, stupidly getting in the way of everybody else. Everybody talking. The cars honking furiously. And the drivers of them talking in loud voices about wasn't it time the Urban Council did something about getting the so-and-so, such-and-such, what you may call 'em shaggin' fairs taken out of the town to a field somewhere. What were they paying rates for, I ask ye? Is it take the fairs out of the town indeed? What about the pubs? Look at them! What would the pubs do if the fairs were taken away from the square? What indeed, the so-and-so's. I've been here two bloody hours now trying to get my car through this mob, here, Guard, for the love of Christ, can't you make an opening here and get me through? All right, all right, all right, sir, just a moment now. Here, mother, for the love of God, won't you take the ould ass that way to hell. You're holding up the life of the city, so you are. The old face looking up at him, smiling. Give the poor oul ass time to pee, can't ye? What hurry is on me man with the moty-car anyhow. Dangerous things thim same motys are. Killed a duck a mine last June out near Furbo. Frightenin' the cows so that they lose pints a milk a day. That's right, roared a big country man dressed in bainins, waving a stick above his head. Take the good outa the bulls even too, they do, the bastards. Honkin' and fartin' like something outa hell. God never meaned the carts to be run be engines, he didn't. They'll have us all killed off, so they will.

Cajoling, threatening, using force to turn the ass-carts, lifting the asses by the bellies and by the tails to turn them the way he wanted them to go, Sean finally reduced order from chaos, so that a space was cleared at the junction and things could move along. He could feel the sweat under his cap and in his armpits and flowing down his legs. It was a terrible job. Abuse on his head and on other people's heads, roaring above the tumult. Keep back there, can't ye? Can't ye wait a minnit until me man has his cart past? If you don't stop honking that bloody horn I'll fix it for you. The drunken countryman with his arm about Sean's neck. No, dammit, I can't go and have a drink now. I'm on duty. Can't you see all I have to do? All right, all right so, I'll be over after yeh. I will indeed, on me oath I will! All right, the pub at the corner.

Two hours passed him by here before order was restored and the crowds eased off, so that he could stand in a grand cleared space and look around him with his hands on his hips. He licked his dry lips and thought how grand it would be to feel a pint glass of porter in his hand. Not that he could have got in for one anyhow. For, all conquering, above the smell of horses' urine, there flowed triumphantly the smell of porter. It was being spilled in barrels. Choked with custom, the pubs were, so that men over-flowed on the sidewalks, the porter spilling from the glasses in gesticulating hands.

He left then and went over towards the fair proper.

It was then he noticed the tinkers. They were everywhere. The women all looking the same nearly, with the shawls around them and their black hair pulled back into tight buns at their necks, their flesh sallow coloured. Almost all of them seemed to have sucking infants hanging from their bared breasts, and in their free hands they held baskets from which they were trying to sell things: red scapulars of the Sacred Heart and bits of lace and long strings of elastic. The most pleading looks on their faces and the heavy smell of drink from their breaths. Their menfolk were there, too. Sallow men also, wearing all sorts of picked-up clothes and caps and hats. Their faces black from the sun and the drink and unwashed time. Big men in the main, or small thin muscular men, all of them nearly with coloured bandanas around their throats and heavy ashplants or blackthorn sticks in their hands.

Sean wandered into the thick of the buying and selling.

After a while he came to the conclusion that there were only two types of horses at the fair: the worst horses that ever lived, broken-winded, spavined, decayed corpses; or gigantic, virile, healthy, full-blooded steeds that Finn Mac Cool would have been proud to mount. It depended on whether you were buying or selling, which class you castigated or praised. Sean thought all of them were grand-looking animals. But it was fun to hear the bargaining, the lies and the deceit and the flow of rhetoric and the obscenities. It was well after midday, and by this time everybody in the square except the children appeared to be half drunk. The fine smell of porter was being wafted from all directions. All good-humoured though. No hint here of anything angry. Everybody was enjoying themselves.

It was too good to last, of course. Everybody knew that – except Sean who hadn't been here before. In fact no Tinkers' Thursday had ever passed yet without the flowing of blood. The people all knew this, so it was the custom to parade to the fair in the afternoon to see the fun. Everybody expected it. Not now, they don't, in the more civilised days when you'd want to be a millionaire to get decently drunk. But then. Just after the Freedom when it wasn't so awful dear, a good drunk and a good fight was the epitome of a successful fair.

It was Big Peadar started it. Just the time that suited himself. Everybody knew – except Sean – that Big Peadar was bound to start it. It was a sort of ritual that Big Peadar should, and he always did.

He came from a public house now, tightening the belt on his trousers. He was a magnificent man. Big, with the shoulders of a stallion and the long legs of a filly that reared him above everybody there. Brown pants on his legs, a dirty grey shirt with all the buttons missing to disclose a great chest, brown and black and covered with curling hair. A sort of an arched thick neck like the middle part of a tree and a red handkerchief, dirty and stained, wound around it. His teeth glittering white in his black face, his mouth decorated by a lusty black moustache and his big face covered by bristles. Small narrow eyes and a big blob of a nose and his face marked very obviously with the healed scars of many fights, like a battling cuddy.

His hair was black and tangled as he came from the pub, took the cap from his head and threw it into the dust of the street, danced on it and then roared at the sky: 'I have a horse! I have a horse!' A great yell it was that soared over the noises of the fair and drew most heads in his direction. He had a blackthorn stick in his hand, and quick as a flash he danced around drawing great swipes with it, clearing a ring for himself and his small son, who stood there with his eyes gleaming, hiccuping from drinking the dregs of his father's porter glasses. His hand held on to the reins of a grey pony, fat and full enough, but nothing to shout about.

The crowds milled around Peadar's magic circle, straining their necks and leaning and grinning and nudging one another.

'I have a horse,' Peadar roared again. 'He's the greatest horse that ever put a hoof on the grass of Ireland. His father was the stallion of Mahomet of Arabia and his mother was the mare of Granuaile. Who wants a horse? He's as fast as the bullet from a gun and as sturdy as the pillars of the courthouse. A horse fit for a giant he is! He can carry more on his back than a ship on the sea or four other horses under a dray. Who wants the greatest horse that was ever seen at the fair of Galway? Stand back, let ye, and have a look at him. Thomasheen, prance the bastard!'

Thomasheen, grinning, pranced the horse. He was all right, but there were about four hundred horses at the fair that day that were better than him.

'Who wants him?' Peadar roared. 'Who wants the finest horse in the province of Connacht?'

One man rose to the bait and came into the circle. He was a big man, a countryman with a heavy *breidín* coat on him and a home-spun waistcoat and trousers. Heavy hobnailed boots. Broader than Peadar, but not as tall, and he carried an ashplant. The bottoms of his trousers and his boots were caked with dung. He rubbed his chin and moved around the horse in a circle with Peadar following him roaring, 'What'll you give for him, man? There hasn't been a horse bred like him since the one that took Oisín to Tír na nÓg. He'll live for ever, so he will. He'll be alive to carry the children of your grandchildren. As true as God he will!'

Unperturbed, the countryman bent and felt the horse's fetlock, then raised himself and lifted the horse's jaws to look at his teeth.

'Ivory, it is!' roared Peadar. 'As sound as the womb of a virgin. Every tooth in his head could bite a bar of iron. The greatest two-year-old horse that was ever bred.'

The countryman straightened himself and looked at Peadar.

'That horse is five years of age,' he said calmly.

Peadar danced.

'D'ye hear him, God?' he asked the sky. 'D'ye hear what the bastard said to me nag? Did you deliver him, you so-and-so?' he asked, pushing his face into the face of the farmer, bending to do so.

'It's a five-year-old horse,' the farmer replied unperturbed, 'and I'll give you eleven pounds for him.'

'You'll what?' Peadar asked. 'Say that again about me darlin'.'

'He's five years of age,' said the farmer, 'and I'll give you eleven pound for him.'

'You gouger!' said Peadar then, raising his stick and bringing it down solidly on the skull of the poor man. A most surprised look came on his face before he fell. The bulk of his hat saved him from the worst, but a trickle of blood shortly made its way down the side of his face. Then Peadar raised his foot and kicked him.

'Here!' Sean roared from the ring of the crowd, where he had come to watch, trying to push his way through. He saw the farmer rising to his feet and aiming a blow at Peadar. But Peadar dodged, and Sean heard the sound of the blackthorn hitting against the side of the farmer's head.

He felt sick and furiously angry as he tried to force his way through the crowd. It was the same as if he had got the blow himself, to see the innocent man with the ashplant getting it. As if at a signal, the whole crowd around him became a vortex of fighting. The tinkers appeared by magic and started to hit out left, right and centre, while the friends of the farmer who had been stricken down waved their arms and their feet and their sticks or anything at hand. The tinkers fought them and they fought one another, because here at last was the chance not only to beat the townsmen and the countrymen but to get a bit of their own back in a bout of intertribal warfare. Even the women with the sucking infants joined in, using their baskets of Sacred Heart scapulars as weapons, with their shrill screaming curses and their black nails to scratch, falling back from the other tinker women to roar, 'Hit me now with the child in me arms!'

Sean lost his hat first to the sweeping blow of a stick swung by a tall young tinker. Sean caught him close and took the stick from him and threw it far away and then flung the man from him. He was sorry. A raging woman came at him with her nails and he shouted as he felt the skin of his face being torn, so he caught her arms and held her down and turned her and flung her gently away. Then he got a blow on the side of his face from a closed fist. It rocked him so that he fell on one knee. He saw the boot coming for his face then, and fell further so that he just missed it, and after that he roared and raised himself and caught at the foot and pulled, and the man fell on the ground, and Sean planted a fist in his face and tried to get at Big Peadar, the instigator of it all. He could see him in the centre of a cleared space waving his stick and bringing it down, roaring curses and boastings like something out of a story. 'If I can get near him,' Sean thought, 'I'll kill him.'

He got near him, but it was a hard fight. His tunic was torn up the back and the collar of it was torn away, too, and hung down his chest. The bright silver buttons, many of them were missing from him when he finally got within hitting distance of Peadar. That was as far as he got. The great stick swung and Sean felt the sickening thud of it against the side of his own skull. Half conscious, he fell to the ground, and then he felt Peadar's boot biting into his stomach and he groaned.

Peadar danced around then boasting, tearing the shirt from his chest to expose it and shouting in the arc of his swinging stick.

'I'm a lion!' He roared. 'I'm a bull! I can lick any man in Ireland! I'd let the blood a Finn MacCool, so I would. Let ye all come! Let ye come from north, south, east or west and I can lick ye! I'll lick ye with me arms tied behind me back. I'll lick ye with me legs tied around me. Ah! Come on, any man in Ireland that wants it, let him come!'

Nobody wanted. There were too many of them either stretched bleeding on the ground or crawling away. So Peadar turned again to deliver another kick on the body of the Guard, but to his surprise the body of the Guard wasn't there. Instead, he got a puck in the kisser that rocked him on his heels. Sean put everything he had in the punch, but there wasn't enough in it. Peadar came for him again, his stick waving, his little eyes red. 'I'll crucify yeh!' he roared. 'I'll drain ye as dry a blood as a stone be the side a the road.' The stick swung. Sean caught the numbing blow of it on his arm and closed with Peadar, winding his arms around his body. Peadar raised his knee and brought it into his crotch. Sean fell with a groan.

He lay there, and he saw the stick being raised again, but he couldn't do anything about it. Oh, for a baton, he thought! He felt the ridged handgrip of it in his palm. 'If I had the baton now,' he thought, 'I would beat him into a clot of blood.' The stick was beginning to rise, and he tensed himself helplessly for the blow, but it never fell. There was a commotion in the outer fringes and then a great shout: 'It's Magairle Mór, men, it's Magairle Mór!'

Peadar raised his stick and danced around again.

'I'm Magairle Mór, too!' he roared. 'I'm a better man than Magairle Mór! I can lick a hundred Magairle Mórs!' And he danced around there, swaying, his great chest barely panting from his endeavours.

The Sergeant came through the throng like a scythe through a sward of hay. He just raised men in each hand and flung them aside. When the women came to scratch him, he raised them in one hand and smacked their faces with his other and threw them away. Sean raised himself to watch him coming. He thought he had never seen a nicer sight than the big face of the Sergeant and his waxed moustache ends standing out. The Sergeant cleared the ring and stood there with his hands on his hips.

'So you're at it again are you, Peadar?' he asked pleasantly.

'Come and get it now, Magairle,' Peadar roared. 'I'll give it to yeh now, so I will, so that yer children wouldn't recognise yeh for the rest of yer days.'

The Sergeant moved towards him slowly.

Peadar swung the stick and darted in towards him.

The Sergeant took the weight of the stick in his palm and then his fingers curled about it. He held it. Peadar held his end. They strained, and then the Sergeant started pulling Peadar towards him. He reached his free hand for him, caught him by the collar and hit him in the face. Peadar went back as if he had been hit with a mallet. The Sergeant took the heavy blackthorn stick then in his hands, and there in the sight of all of them broke it in two in his hands. Then he moved towards Peadar. Peadar was game. He was fighting mad indeed. He wanted no invitation. He tried the boot. It didn't work. The Sergeant caught the heel of it and turned it so that Peadar had to turn too. Then the Sergeant caught him around the neck and sprung him with his knee like you would an arrow from a bow.

Peadar came up again though. You had to hand it to Peadar. If he could dish it out, he could take it.

Sean was standing by this time.

'Sergeant,' he said. 'Please let me at him.'

'Go on,' said the Sergeant, 'take him.'

Sean took him. It took him longer to take him than it would have if the blood from his head wasn't blinding one eye and if his belly wasn't paining him and his crotch. But he took him. People will remember that fight as long as there is a fair in the square of Galway. It was a near thing, though, but he beat him, Sean did, and then bloody and torn and assisted by the Sergeant, they took Peadar, lolling between them, down the back way to the barracks, because this was the time before the police were going around in V8s. But when they locked the cell on the unconscious Peadar, Sean collapsed there in the cold draughty corridor outside the cells.

When he woke again he was lying in his bed under the white quilt.

He woke to a screaming pain and a throbbing head. It was a long, long time before his eyes could focus themselves. He was bandaged and cleaned and aching, and the Sergeant was there, sitting by the side of the bed with his tunic open, and funnily enough with his eyes anxious.

Sean looked at him.

The Sergeant looked at Sean.

'I'm sorry,' said the Sergeant then. 'I didn't think it would be that bad. He was mad with drink. He must have got bad whiskey. I only wanted to show you. I didn't think you would have gone in like that. I just wanted to show you. I wanted to have you coming running back to the barracks for help. That's all. Just so that you would come running back and you would have to come to me, the iron fist, the dying duck, to get you out of a fix. That's all. I never thought you would wade in like that.'

There was a pause as Sean closed his eyes.

The Sergeant's eyes fell to his hands.

'Maybe you are right, son,' he said then slowly, 'about me being the last of my kind. But you wanted my kind up to this. Things are not as rosy yet as you think. And they won't be for a long time. You say when I die people will celebrate. Maybe so. But I wouldn't like to think they would, because I have always been on the side of the decent people. You think maybe that many things can be settled with peaceful means. That may be true of the future, but I have also found that force settles many things peacefully as well. It's just that we didn't agree, that's all. I'm a bad Sergeant to let you in for all this in order to show you a lesson. But, honest to God, I didn't think it would turn out like that.'

'Sergeant,' said Sean, focusing his eyes on him painfully, 'it's me that has to ask your pardon. I should never have spoken to you like that. No other Sergeant would have taken it from me. I realise that now and also I realise that I have to make one great concession to your thinking. It's this – there are occasions on which it is essential to use force. If I'd had a baton today I would have played "The Siege of Ennis" with it on Peadar's skull.' He grinned.

The Sergeant laughed, loud and free.

'Ah, that's great,' he said. 'So you have learned something all the same.' He moved to the door then and paused there.

'You know,' he said, fiddling with the knob of the door, 'there's this difference between our thinking. You see me, all my life devoted to the police. I worked hard, too, and I always did what I thought was right. I'm a sergeant. One day you will be a chief superintendent, and you will be a good one. Believe me now, I know.'

Sean thought that over.

'Maybe so,' he said, 'but then I think that chief superintendents are made, and that good sergeants are born.'

It was worth it, to see the look on the Sergeant's face.

The door closed behind him.

The Passing of the Black Swan

IT WAS LATE afternoon when she started for home.

The sea was ruffled, and heaved like a sleeping giant under green blankets.

There was just sufficient wind to fill the old brown sail. It caught the sail and billowed it, and the black boat sidled over the waves, gently, like her namesake. Her black breasts were gently rounded, like the bows of the Viking boats of long ago on which she was modelled.

She was nearly a hundred years of age.

From a distance she looked just the same as all the other black puckauns which sailed the bay after the elusive fish, and even when you came nearer to her, she belied her age. She sailed so sweetly, *The Black Swan* did, and she looked stout. It took a keen ear to hear the groaning of her tarred timbers, the odd lurch of the ageing keel, and the hidden places where the implacable sea-water had found a crack and seeped to destroy. All that.

There were three men manning her at this moment as she headed for home.

Three generations.

The father, his son, and his son, too.

The father was very old.

At the tiller he was, sitting there holding the worn stick in his old hand. A very old hand. The flesh was loose on it, but still firm.

His fingers were gnarled from decades of weather. His legs in the rough blue cloth of his trousers were bent and thin. His body was curved, and he looked small in the blue high-necked jersey and the navy-blue reefer jacket. Only the eyes in his head under the black broad-brimmed Connemara hat were still young. They were blue and startlingly clear in his old face, a worn face, a sort of ivory brown from exposure, and looking delicately brown behind the short snow-white beard and moustache and the jutting white eyebrows.

His eyes were wistful and his lips were tight. He avoided meeting the eyes of his son or his son's son.

They were uncomfortable and unconscious of the contrast they presented to the old man, showing in themselves and their dress the slow march of civilisation.

The son was a fine man in his prime, over forty. He leaned his body against the side of the boat, his feet resting on the fish boxes, one strong arm across his chest and the elbow of the other arm resting on it, to hold the bowl of the brown pipe he was smoking. He was dressed just a little differently to his father. The same-coloured clothes, but he wore a plain double-breasted mac and the cap on his head was a peaked sailor's cap. But the high-necked jersey swelled on his great chest. He had a big face. The muscles on the sides of his jaws were prominent, and his skin was the colour of teak, and there were weather wrinkles around his eyes. Grey eyes. Very firm.

He was idly watching his son, who was just as idly coiling rope on the forecastle.

Even bending, the young son was promising bigness. You could see that from the swell of his thighs pressing against the cloth of the overalls he wore. Yes, overalls. Of blue cloth, of course. And over that an ordinary tweed jacket, much the worse for wear, shiny with washed fish-scales and tarred ropes, and on his head he wore a plain tweed cap. He had the blue eyes of his grandfather and the shoulders of his father, and he was smoking the butt of a cigarette.

His lips were red and his skin was clear, the down of his teens barely left behind him.

He was uncomfortable, too, and cast a look now and again at the old man at the tiller, a worried look.

And for some time they sailed, no sound within but the swish of the water being pushed aside and the creak from the swinging sail on the blackened mast and the wind in the ropes and the cry of the wheeling seagulls above them, attracted by the glint and smell of the dead and dying fish.

It was a particular evening.

Late August it was, the season of sunsets and hunter's moons. The sky above was clear, and all around a pattern of small clouds girdled the world. Behind them the sun was blazing to death behind the islands, and the clouds were coloured, multi-coloured, and if you had been on the sea ahead of them and looked back you would have seen the boat and the men in it as black silhouettes. Ahead of them, where at the end of the bay the land had shaken itself free of the clinging town, in the east there, the moon was about to poke its way into the twilightened sky. You could just see the tip of the top of it, gigantic. Where the sky wasn't coloured from the sun, it was green, crab-apple green, and green-grass green lower down. The evening star was beginning to glint, too, and the winking light of the lighthouse ahead of them was beginning to take on significance.

Oh, a very lovely evening indeed, one for contemplation, and wonder, too, at the glories that God could create from a blank canvas. Had things been different, they would have been sunk in contemplation, because most men who go to sea have learned while at sea to talk only the minimum, and not about silly material things. They have to leave that for the land and the pub in the evening with the mumble of mens' voices, or the clatter of crockery in their own homes.

But things were not different.

33

They were all tightened up inside with the things that were unsaid and had to be faced now. Every wave that the boat rode brought them nearer to the end of it, and the decision of it. The two younger men were surprised that the old man hadn't talked sooner. Maybe he wouldn't talk at all, they were thinking. That would be good, or it might be worse in a way, because concealed suffering only festers. So, although outwardly calm enough, the stomach muscles of the three of them were very tight.

And then the old man spoke, just as they were coming up on the small island where the lighthouse was built. The sun was gone at last, and their faces were in shadow, unlighted as yet by the climbing moon. He spoke then because perhaps he wanted them not to be able to look at his face and see the emotions working on his countenance. It is a fallacy that helps all of us, believing that darkness can conceal emotions.

'I remember,' said the old man, 'the first day I ever went out in her, so I do.' He had to clear his throat then, to get a frog of rust out of it. They waited tensely for him. 'Oh, a long time ago, maybe over sixty years ago, I was very small then, and I remember my father, and he putting the long line into my hand, and the drag of the lead was almost too much for me. I could feel the bite of the twine in my palm. But I held it, so I did, and when I felt the twitch at the end of it, I hauled, hand over hand, and I will never forget, ever, the sight of the green mackerel there on the water. I had caught him, be meself, and I thought then that there was not a greater man than me in the length and breadth of Ireland.'

They listened as he paused, and for a moment they thought, too, of the times they had gone and first felt the bite of a fish-loaded line.

'I loved her then,' the old man went on. 'You can love a boat more than you can love a woman or your own child. As true as God is there, you can. You can love a boat more than you can anything else in the world after God. People will tell you that a boat is only seasoned timber fashioned by the hands of man and ballasted by the even limestone blocks.' He slithered his boot over the blocks now. 'But that's not so. If ever anything living had a soul, it is a boat. It was me called her *The Black Swan*, from the sight of them in the river, the white ones, sailing sweetly and without seeming to put any effort into it. She was the *The Black Swan* to me, and we in Ireland know that a swan is a precious thing, that inside the white feathers there is a human shape; everyone of us knows that. You would no more kill a swan than you would kill your own mother. Well, she to me is like that, too.'

His voice ceased and they could hear the lapping waves.

'She often talked to me. Often when a great sorrow would be on me, when my father died and I was young and I had so many to provide for, when I took her out to sea then for the first time on my own. She talked to me then. She took me to the right places where the fish would be that meant so much to me. As sure as God is in heaven, she did! I wanted in my foolishness to go places other than where my father had gone, thinking like all young people that I knew better than he, but when my hand would turn the tiller to go in my direction, she would go the other way. This is as true as the tiller is in my hand now. I cursed her, too. I hammered at her sides with my hand and my nailed boots, but she wouldn't go. I gave in to her in the end and followed her. That day I took more fish than I had ever done before. You know that, even though you are young, that she would know better than myself. Even though you don't like her now and you are about to kill her, you know that what I say is true.'

The son stirred, and took the pipe from his mouth.

'Father,' he said, 'that's wrong. We don't want to do that. But she is like all other things. She gets old. She has lived longer than a man even. And times are changing. There are different ways. We must move. We have to have an engine. You know she wouldn't take an engine on her now. Listen, listen, can't you! You can listen if you want and you can hear the groaning of her keel.'

'She is beyond repair,' said the son's son, flatly but kindly.

The old man swallowed his futile anger.

'If you tried to put an engine on her tail,' he said, 'I would take an axe to her myself and chop her into a million pieces. By Holy God, I would.'

The son shrugged and put the pipe into his mouth again. His own son turned away. It is useless, they told one another, useless to argue with him.

'Why can't you let me have her?' the old man asked pleadingly. 'I can run her. I know every twist and turn of her, ever caulk and baulk of her. She would answer to me, I tell you. I would just tell her and she would go where I wanted her to. Can't you see that? When your mother died and the light went out of the sun, I went down to the quay and I went away in her, far far away, and we were alone and she talked to me, and even then it was deep winter and the sea was very cross, but I was alone with her and I came back again, and then my heart wasn't as sore as before I left. She has been a wife to me when my wife died and a father to me when my father died. If I didn't have her those times, I would have died like them, and if you take her away from me now I will die, too. As true as God, I will. What else have I left in life but her?'

'You are silly now,' said the son gruffly. 'You are speaking like a character in a fairy tale. We cannot run two boats. We cannot afford to run two boats, and you can't handle her alone.'

'But why not, why not, why not?' asked the old man.

'Because,' said the son, 'you are an old man. You won't admit it. You are nearly eighty. The sea is no place for you. Not any more. You see yourself all the time through the wrong eyes. You are looking at yourself as you were one time, not as you are now. You see yourself still as a tall man, powerful and big chested, but you are not, and that's the truth of it. For your own good and to save the worry that's on us thinking about you, can't you see that you are an old man? That you can't handle a heavy old boat like this alone, not any longer? I don't wish to be brutal, but I must tell you out clear like this, to try and make you understand.'

There was a stricken look on the face of the old man.

The son's son spoke then, too, kindly, his voice deep like his father's, but not as strong.

'It's because we like you, Grandfather,' he said. 'It is no ease to us to have you out here in the cold sea with us. We are too fond of you, so we are. We like you to be waiting on the pier for us when we come home in the evening. When we are out in the cold and the wind and the rain, it is very peaceful to realise that you are at home near a fire, warm and smoking your pipe over the ashes. We want you to live with us for a long time. We don't want to have your death on our minds.'

There was a long silence, as they looked at him. Both of them felt that what they had said was totally inadequate, that they hadn't pierced his thinking at all. Because they did love him and they were proud of him. He was the King of the Claddagh, and all men respected him for his goodness and the kindness of him, and for the deeds he had done in the past, and for his great honesty. He was a model on which other fishermen tried to fashion their own sons. That was true. They knew it, and they knew it was a great thing to be his son and his grandson, because all men became respectful when they heard that you belonged to him, but it was so hard for them to explain what they felt.

The old man was going to speak. They awaited his speech anxiously, and then he dropped his head on his chest, so they sighed and turned away.

This is the end then, the old man thought. The end of *The Black Swan* and the end of me, too. He knew that they were doing what they thought would be for his good. He knew what he wanted, too, but he couldn't come straight out and tell them there. In the first place, he would find it hard to put into words, and in the second place, he was misty about it himself. He just had a dim picture of himself and *The Black Swan*, just the two of them, sailing sedately over the water. It never struck him that it would be difficult for him to hoist the weight of the brown sail or to hold the heavy boat in heavy seas. He didn't want to think of that. All he wanted to think about was the two of them alone, on the sea. If the rough came and proved too much for them, two ancients like them, then what did that matter? They would go under the waves, and the water would close over their heads. He would prefer that.

That was the trouble.

He couldn't say to them, 'I want to die out there, on a rough black night with the waves vicious.' He couldn't say, 'I do not want to stay at home warm and smoke my pipe over the ashes. I do not want to go home and wither and rot away to old death under your kind eyes and the eyes of your wife and children. All is tranquil and peaceful, but that is not what I want at all. I want violence and fight even at the end.'

He wanted to say to them, 'Wouldn't it be far kinder to shoot me, instead of keeping me warm at home and bringing me home a pint of porter in a jug because you thought the walk too much for me? What am I to do all day, while I am drooling over the ashes smoking my pipe? Give me *The Black Swan* and the sea if you want me to live for you. Not the other, not the smothering kindness of your house and the weary waiting, sitting on the capstan at the pier waiting for you to come home again.'

All this, he thought vaguely. How can you tell it to them? How can any man fight against the awfulness of well-meaning kindness?

The boat veered towards the gaping mouth of the docks and turned up where the river and the sea became one. His hand unconsciously guided her in, skilfully avoiding the flow of the river, feeling the rising tide on her tail and taking her across in a sweep towards the fishing boat pier, hearing for the last time the musical creak as the sons lowered the sail, the blocks sighing mournfully.

The moon was shining strongly now, and all over the mouth of the river away from the race, the white swans, hundreds of them, were sleeping with their long necks tucked under their wings.

The boat scraped against the granite wall. The young man leaped for the steps, raced up them with the rope in his hand and tied it swiftly to the stone bollard nestling above in the green grass. The boat shuddered a little and then lay placidly.

The old man sat there, listening to the low, seemingly disembodied voices of the men above questioning them about their fishing fortunes, and he sat there as his son and grandson returned and took the boxes of fish from the belly of the boat, and he sat there as, with the help of the others, they started to strip her.

They took the sails from her, and they took the mast from her, and they broke off her forecastle with their axes, and with crowbars they levered off the iron braces and cleats of her, and they took the tiller-shaft from his hand, and they raised the big wooden rudder from the water, and then with their crowbars they took the ballast rocks, so neatly laid, and they tore them from her womb, so that shortly she was riding the water, high and unrecognisable, a hulk of a thing, with the exposed water gurgling inside her, water that was seeping through her wounds.

So quickly it was all done.

The side of the pier was piled high with her guts.

They did it in silence now, too, as if the pain the boat was suffering was being transmitted to them from the slouching despondent little figure of the hunched old man at the back of her.

They consulted then, quietly, and they tied a rope to her bow and connected that to the stern of a heavy rowing boat, and they slowly pulled her over to where the earth rose from the sea in an incline. An old black shed there and rails and a rusty capstan. They lowered the trolley, and they fixed the wheels under her, and they pulled her from the water with little effort.

After that they lifted the old man out of her, gently, and left him standing while they heaved her from the trolley and left her lying on her side, forlorn, useless, on the coarse sea-grass.

The son put his big hand on the old man's shoulder.

'Come on home now, father,' he said.

'You could do with something warm inside you, I bet,' said the son's son on the other side of him.

'I'll be up in a while,' said the old man. 'I'll be up in a whileen after ye.'

They looked at one another worriedly.

'Don't be too long,' said the son.

'No,' said the old man, 'I won't be too long.'

They left him then.

When the crunch of their boots on the ground ceased, there was no other sound except the gentle hiss of water escaping from her, that and the muted sound of traffic on the town streets away in the distance and the scream of a mother calling a recalcitrant child home to bed.

The old man stood a while dazed, looking at *The Black Swan*, who had been so lovely. And look at her now! He went closer to her and rubbed his hand along the part where the seaweed and small barnacles and winkles clung to her under the waterline, such a contrast to her body above where the heavy tar gleamed and shone in the light of the moon. He picked at her side with the nail of his finger and the soft rotting wood came away in his hand.

Aye, she was old all right, and withered like himself, but now she was dead and he was alive.

'What have they done to you at all, my lovely black darling?' he asked as he walked around her, resting his white beard on his arms as he looked into her gaping interior. Blackness and rusty nails and nothing, and he saw her as she had been, and as he had been, and a terrible bleakness came over his heart, and he sat down on the wet ground close beside her, his shoulder hugging her rounded breast, and his head sank on his arms then resting on his knees, and the senile tears poured from his eyes.

'Oh God, oh God, oh God,' he said then to the night.

The moon shone on them.

The shadows merged them as if they were one and as if in answer to his weeping, the water came from her sides, too, and poured down them. Was it water?

Or was it tears?

The moon climbed high, ageless, and the white swans slept with their long necks under their wings.

New Clothes for the Giolla

THE GIOLLA WAS a nice person. He had a soft heart for young children.

It was often I saw him myself, sitting at the side of the street mending broken toys for them, or laughing and he going around hand-in-hand with them in that game Ring-a-ring-a-roses, and he falling on his behind so hard that he would damage the foundations of the houses. The children liked him very much, anyway.

But it wasn't the same way with their parents.

For he had faults. He was as dirty as an unringed pig, they said. He was seldom cleaned in a hot bath, it is true, but nobody had a bathroom in those days. It was usual for the people to bath themselves in front of the fire each Saturday night in one of those tin baths that would put a hump on a leprechaun. Although he was fairly old, they said he hadn't done a handful of work since the day he was born. That was a big fault, I suppose, when the rest of us had to work from dawn to dusk to earn the food of our mouths.

He was never seen in the chair of a barber, they said. This was also true, for if there was little hair left to the rest of us, the Giolla had plenty and to spare, and although it bore the colour of age, it was as thick and heavy as a field of good hay. His whiskers likewise. When it grew too long, it was his custom to pay a call on a housewife with a new scissors in his hand, and she would have to bring him into the kitchen to cut his hair and whiskers. Well, they

43

weren't very pleased with this – but they were Christians. Believe me, they made no delay in cutting the Giolla's locks, putting him out on the street and throwing his shorn cairn of hair into the fire. He chose a different housewife each time, and when she had the work done, he would leave the scissors after him. Maybe he stole the scissors, I don't know, but I do know this: that there wasn't a house in the street without a new scissors on the dresser.

It was my own opinion that the Giolla was a man with real freedom, and I was often in envy of him. He ate when he was hungry. When it failed him to steal food, he went from house to house until he got it. If this failed him (sometimes the women were in a red anger with him), he would go with the dogs searching the house-wrack in the garbage bins at the back doors. In the summer he would sleep in the fields, and in the winter he liked stables or one of the old tenement houses closed up by the city councillors.

At the time I am referring to, he was very hot in the mouths of the people, and every one of them saying, 'We will have to do something about that Giolla. It's not right to be letting him run free in this manner. Look at him! He'd put shame on a Protestant!'

I admit he didn't look handsome at this time. You couldn't praise his clothes. The trousers were torn, worn, holed. And the shoes and the coat – well! He had no shirt. He didn't need one, he said himself. 'Let the slaves wear shirts,' he would say. 'I'm free from the tyranny of that piece of clothing.'

The women were very hard on him, as I have explained before, and in the end they began to give dirty talk to the men. Isn't that the way with them always? So something had to be done, and in desperation we, the men, called a meeting together in O'Flaherty's pub one certain Saturday night. We had to drink a lot of porter, and it was near midnight and a half-barrel empty before we found the solution of the question. Some thought he should be drowned, and some thought he should be taken in a motor car and let loose in Belfast. If the meeting was costly, we all thought it was worthwhile.

Since it happened that I was the only one present who was favourable to the Giolla, it was delegated to me to put the fruit of the meeting into action – that was, that I was to take the Giolla with me to the parish priest, so that he would talk to him.

I told a sort of lie to the Giolla. I said that maybe he'd get new clothes from the priest.

The priest was a nice man, a tender-hearted person. So when I spoke to him first he was very high-minded. 'We must be careful,' he said. 'We must think of the freedom of the individual. That's a very important point.'

'Speak to the Giolla yourself then, Father,' I answered.

'Ah, bring the poor fellow in to me,' he said.

I did this. Well! The priest's eyes opened wide. He never saw the like before. Also, the Giolla smelled a bit.

'God in His glory!' said the priest. That's all, and then he called the police.

Then they came and we had a conversation. They got a man to sign a paper saying the Giolla was loose and wandering and it was only just that he should be sent to the old people's home. (There was a time and this place was called the poor house.)

The Giolla had no word to say except, 'Hey, where is me new clothes?'

I borrowed a veteran van from a friend. I put the Giolla sitting beside me and said, 'Come now with me, Giolla, to a place where you will get new clothes.' And off with us.

After a time we reached the place, and I went in with my papers.

'Ah, the creature!' said the Matron. 'Ah, the poor man, bring him in.'

I did this. She looked at him.

'Great King of Glory,' she said, 'we'll have to wash him immediately.'

Well, you never saw an adventure like it, ever.

On the word 'wash', the Giolla turned and ran out of the place with a high foot, roaring. I followed him, and four other men as well. He was gone a mile before we could lay a hand on him – and then we had to struggle back with him. The anger had him as strong as a bull. I never did such hard unpaid work before. 'Traitor! Bodach! Cripple!' – these were some of the names he called me that it is possible to quote.

When he saw the bathroom, he nearly lost his mind. Five of us it took to get him out of his clothes and wash him. In the end we succeeded, and he was quiet enough by the time we put the new clothes and the new shirt on his body. To tell the truth, he was quiet because he was half-drowned.

'Well, look at this now,' said the Matron. 'Isn't he a proper gentleman?'

It was true for her. You wouldn't recognise him. He nearly looked a real fashionable gentleman, without doubt.

'Where are you going?' he asked me then.

'I'm going home,' I said. 'Haven't you a wonderful place here? There will be joy on all your friends that you have such a marvellous home.'

'For the love of God, don't desert me,' he said, looking at me with wide eyes. You'd think there were tears in them.

I was suddenly sad. I thought, 'Our street will not be the same with the Giolla out of it.' But a man must not be weak. The neighbours were depending on me.

'You will be better off than anyone in the town,' I said. 'When the age comes on myself, I will follow you to this beautiful house. Well, that's that. Goodbye, Giolla. I will call and see you again sometime.'

'Don't abandon me,' he said.

I left him abruptly and jumped into the van. I had fulfilled my duty.

I was taking the road on myself when I heard the turmoil and noise and shouting behind me. I looked and there I see the Giolla fleeing from the place again like a greyhound, and four men on his heels.

'Oh, great God!' I groaned and left the van and took up the chase.

Wasn't he the devil? What did he do? Down to the pig-house he went, and before anyone could lay a hand on him, he jumped the wall and threw himself down and turned his body in the muck; turned and twisted around and around, like an ass on sand, until the new clothes and the man himself were dirtier than they had ever been before. Then he rose and looked at us over the wall with a smile on his mouth.

The Matron was nearly dancing with anger.

'Take him out of here!' she shouted. 'Don't let me lay an eye on him again! Take him! Out of my sight with him before I murder him!'

'But the papers, the police, the priest?' I said.

'To the devil with them,' she said, 'and with you, and the Giolla. Take him out of my sight before I lose my soul over him!'

And she went, and the men went, and I was left with the Giolla.

It wasn't my fault. What could I do with him? I could only take him back home again with me.

It's little regard anyone in the street has for me now. They hardly address a word to me. You'd think I was a Jehovah Witness. My own wife is not too kind to me.

All the same, the Giolla has new – if dirty – clothes. And even if he has cast off the new shirt, he has freedom – not like me. Free from every man's tyranny; the honey and sweetness of total personal freedom, he possesses.

And he plays games again with the children in the back streets.

Dad

'HAPPY THE CORPSE that the rain rains on.'
Many people were saying it that day at the funeral,
remarking how odd it was that there was no rain
raining on the corpse of Dad. A sign it was that if the rain rained
on the corpse that he was shooting up to Heaven practically jet-
propelled, and if it didn't rain, you just lifted your eyebrows and
left the fate of the corpse to the imagination. But all the citizens
said it now as a joke, knowing Dad as they did.

From the tall church where the last mass was being said for him
and from where his coffined corpse would be taken in the motor
hearse to the graveyard, from the church all the way to the bridge,
the road was lined with people waiting for the funeral to pass
them by so that they could join in. The footpaths on either side of
the road were jammed with the waiting people, and up above, just
outside the church, you could see the dull sun glinting on the roofs
of all the cars and the heads of the people with their hats off
following the coffin from the church. If you strained hard enough
you could see the tilted coffin down the steps on the shoulders of
the bearers and you could hear the screech of the oiled rollers as it
was pushed into the hearse with the glass sides. After that the
flowers went in. Such a lot of flowers. So many that in the end
they had to pile them up on top of the hearse itself, and the
enclosed coffin was practically covered with them.

'The whole city,' a writer in the local paper said this Friday morning, 'was thrown into gloom at the unexpected death of one of its most honourable citizens. Well known to one and all for his kindness and Christianity and charitable dealings with the halt, the lame, and the blind and the unfortunate, the death of the man that the whole town knew simply as "Dad" will leave a gap in our ranks which can never be filled. This town of ours will seem an empty place without the sight of his bowed figure, white hair and kindly face in the midst of us.' ('What the hell else,' the reporter had remarked to a colleague, 'you can say about him I don't know. It's utterly impossible to write anything but tripe about the very good people.') 'All that is left now for us to do is to join our tears with the sorrowing widow of Mervyn James Tender, and hope that the sorrow of the whole town at his loss may be a little comfort to her in her present affliction.'

The cortège left the church door and started the road towards the town. It started at nothing and ended up a very long procession.

By the time it reached the bridge, there were several thousand of the citizens walking behind the hearse, and behind the citizens were many cars. People who are given to those things made it their business to count the cars, and they counted 105. So with eight priests at the head of the procession, thousands of citizens walking behind, followed by 105 cars, that meant it was a big funeral. The enumerators of these things nodded their heads and talked to their neighbours, and it was agreed in the end by all that this was the biggest funeral since we had buried our last bishop, the Lord have mercy on him.

If you were a stranger who had come to town, and had never heard of Dad, if you joined with the people and moved from group to group, you would have learned the whole story of his life up to the present day, because it is the custom of all to walk at a funeral and talk about the dead. People who knew him tell this and that about him, mostly redounding to his worth. At some funerals, of course, there are always people who are willing to talk bad about the dead (even when they are walking behind his corpse they can't let him alone), but today you could travel from one end to the other of that long funeral and sorry man would you find who had a bad word for the man under the flowers.

You would see all sorts of people as the cortège wound its way to the main street: very well-dressed men, with cultivated stomachs covered with good cloth, with walking sticks and bowler hats, sturdy burghers with the mark of prosperity all over them and the polish shining on their shoes; and middlemen and working men. There were all kinds at the funeral. And women with shawls on their heads, holding them close to their faces and speaking out of them about him. And if you halted a little you would see the first car that passed, and in the back of it, sitting alone, you would see the widow, a small woman with white hair and a pale face, somewhat shrunken in appearance, with her eyes straining before her. 'Ah, the poor creature,' you would think, 'it's sad for her at her age to be left without a man that has been with her for so long.'

Up into the shops now, where all the blinds were pulled and doors closed for the passing of the hearse, and frowns from the burghers if a pub here and there hadn't the door closed to honour the dead, with harried assistants rushing out to close it when the funeral was almost on top of them.

You could see all that and you would immediately know that it was a man of some importance who was being buried.

Listen then to the talk about you and build him up from that.

Mervyn James Tender.

Forty years ago, at the age of twelve, you could have seen this man wheeling a little handcart on which he delivered messages for a shop in the main street. A diligent boy, as honest as the day. He was remembered by other men who in that time, too, had been pushing little handcarts and starting their careers as messenger boys. The career of Mervyn was brought up to illustrate their own cleverness in rising from messenger boy to 'my shop there, that we're passing now. Didn't do too bad, did I, in forty years. Big turnover, seven assistants. They don't know what work is. If they had to face the day's work that I had to face when I was their age, they'd be dead now.' Mervyn didn't wait long as a messenger boy. In three years he was inside the counter of the shop, and a decenter or more intelligent assistant would have been hard to find.

The woman with the black shawl around her face remembered him then. Always the kind word for the poor he had, so he had. Didn't matter a damn if you had a shawl or a fur coat, it was all the same to him. '"Yes, Ma'am," he'd say to you, and, "No, Ma'am" just as if you were a lady, not like some a them that wouldn't give you the time a the day, fawnin' on the fur coats, treatin' yeh as if yeh were somethin' nasty that crawled out of a box a oranges from one a them foreign places. Always a ha'penny off or two as well, and trust you until the pay day.'

Five years later he had his own shop.

'I arranged that for him,' you would hear a man say. 'I'd just started up as a solicitor at the time. I remember well, it was the first decent bit of commission I got on sales. He was good that way. He was always willing to trust his business to youth because he was young himself and didn't see why he couldn't help the young people. He was bound to prosper from the first. He had the manner you know.'

'He had, the bastard,' said a shuffling old man in very tattered clothes, and a very red nose and a pock-marked face. 'I gev that fella his first job with me. My shop then, and he turned around and sets up on his own around the corner, and before I know where I am, he has all me best customers whipped away from me, like thieves in the night.'

'He gave nothing away in business,' said a tall man with a smooth bowler hat. 'He was a very shrewd business man. Where would any of us be if we weren't shrewd? We'd be like old what-you-may-call-him, now, that wreck over there. Dad worked for him first before setting up on his own.'

'I remember well when he got married,' said the lady sitting in the back seat of a beautifully upholstered car, number twenty in the procession. 'I went to him for everything when he set up on his own. He was alone first and then he got her. She had been an assistant in some little pokey country shop somewhere and she came to him, and two years later he was married to her. He was very handsome at the time. Quite a few of the better-class girls of the town were setting their caps at him. We were all surprised when he married her. Nice and quiet and pretty in a mousy sort of way, but a country girl. Not quite, eh. . . .'

'I know, not quite out of the top drawer, my dear,' said her companion. 'He rarely brought her to anything. You remember those hops and that, long ago, and the dances in the Town Hall. So colourful. But she rarely came with him.'

'She was terrified. She wasn't brought up to that sort of thing you know. She never lost it either. She always dressed as if she had just come from the farm. She always had the look of it somehow. Pity they had no children.'

'Yes, he was such a fine man, and he absolutely adored children. I believe there was some talk of one early on, a miscarriage or something, and nothing after that.'

'You'd think that since she was from the country she could at least produce children.'

'Now, dear, that's hardly nice. She's a simple soul and she'll be lost without him.'

'If it was you or me, Jack, that was bein' put under,' said a tall man in a cap and frayed ends to his trousers, 'there'd be none a this fuss. There wouldn't be eight priests at our funeral. One curate they'd send up to fire a rock at your pine box and let the grass grow over yeh.'

'He was a very good man,' said the priest to his companion in the Franciscan habit. 'A very good man. A Christian man. He was a pillar of the sodality, you know. It will seem strange to have the processions now without his white hair beside you holding the canopy over the monstrance. I don't believe he missed a day in his life that he didn't go to nine o'clock mass. The Vincent de Paul Society will be lost without him, too. And he was good to the poor.'

'Indeed he was,' said his companion. 'Look at the two old men he has in his shop. If it was any other man, these two would have been thrown on the winds of the world long ago. But where another man would have got rid of them and brought in younger people, he kept them there year after year, paying them their wages, although they are practically useless to the business.'

The two old men walking behind the hearse had all the appearance of being twins who had aged in exactly the same way. They weren't. One had a white moustache and the other hadn't a white moustache, but that seemed to be the only difference in their appearance. Both wore bowler hats, old ones, which they wore every day anyhow. They had black coats, old coats, carefully darned and brushed to get the shine off the seats of them. And they wore dark trousers carefully pressed, the cloth worn thin. And their shoes shone, even the leather patches were barely distinguishable. They were thin men of a height and their shoulders were stooped. Their eyes were pale and of an indeterminate colour.

'He was a good man, John.'

'He was that, Peter.'

'He had to be a little hard in business to make it pay.'

'That's true, Peter.'

'He was a lonely man in a way, despite all his friends.'

'He was a lonely man.'

'Here he was born and worked and died well-off. He must have died well-off, John?'

'He must have died very well-off, Peter.'

'And yet, at his funeral there is no one much to walk behind his hearse, only two old withered men like us who were his servants.'

'And his wife, Peter, don't forget his poor wife.'

'Aye, his wife, John.'

'The Lord have mercy on him, Peter.'

'Amen, John.'

Into the square the funeral moved, the flood of people coming from the mouth of the street like water from a tap into a sink. They spread out, and some of the busier men dodged around a corner to let the funeral pass so that they could get back to work. Behind, the shops had raised their blinds again and opened their doors and life went on, the same as before, even though Dad was dead.

Up the long hill past all the houses with the people at their doors, their arms folded, looking at the marchers, gossiping about this one and that one, because they knew little of Dad and were quite used to the funerals passing their doors. 'Hey, Maggie,' a woman would say to a house next door. 'There's such a wan now. He'll be the next I'll say. Look at the way the poor oul divil is totterin' on his pins.'

'It'll be a bad day for the whiskey manufacturers when he goes,' her companion answered with a little whispered laugh. 'Look at the face of 'm!'

The bell in the graveyard started to peal as the hearse approached the tall iron gates. The rubber tires gripped the gravel on the ground protestingly as the car turned in, and the gears clanged a little so that drivers of cars shivered at the sound, and then it went into the graveyard walk smoothly, gently puffing carbon monoxide at the flowering bushes at the side of the walk. And the people followed and you could hear the peculiar crunch of leather on gravel, many feet, much leather. Some people glancing around saw away over the walk the yellow clay piled high in preparation, so they climbed up the grass beside the walk and took a short-cut towards the yawning grave, stepping carefully over the other graves, pausing to think, 'There's such a one. We put him away last year.'

Only the hearse and the widow's car came into the place.

The hearse stopped, and the driver lifted the gate at the back of the hearse and handed the floral wreaths around, and then four men caught the coffin and hoisted it out. The rollers under it were smooth. It glittered in the sun. It was a prosperous coffin, of good wood, you could see that at once, and made in the luxury class, with the silver handles at either side and the name written on the silver plate in black and outlined with a little touch of pale crimson.

They hefted it and six men took it in their arms and went towards the grave, down another gravel path, their feet raking the gravel in unison. The priest was there and the widow. The priest wore his stole, and the widow stood on a small hill backgrounded by the crowding people.

She looked very small and very forlorn.

Two planks were laid across the grave, and they placed the coffin on the planks. The priest opened his book, and taking the brass handle of the holy water sprayer from the urn, he shook it on the coffin. You could see the water landing in little globules on the painted timber, like water on an oiled cloth. Then they put two long canvas tapes under each end of the coffin, pulled the planks away and lowered it into the ground.

The graveyard was overlooking the city.

Down there, if you looked, it lay at your feet, and you could see out as far as the bay and the ships looking like toys on it and the mountains on the other side. The water was placid, and the clouds were rolling up from the west, white clouds edged with black as if they were mourning, and they would have been, too, only for the patches of blue sky where the sun shone through. The grass all around was very high here and very thick, and since it was early in the year, it hadn't yet started to get yellow, and many a man with land outside the town noticed this grass and idly thought what great grass it was and how it had the very best manure obtainable. Thought that, and then brought his mind back to the widow.

'It's killing her,' they said, as they saw her looking out to the sea. 'It's killing her to see them putting him away,' as everybody there waited for the three shovelsful of clay to fall and ring hollowly on the coffin from the unpractised hand of the priest. 'She can't bear that at all,' they said, thinking of how it had hurt themselves.

And indeed, tears were forcing themselves from her eyes as she regarded the vista in front of her. Her eyes were fixed on the sailing boats in the bay and on the seagulls circling lazily in the sky.

'They are free,' she was thinking. 'They are free, and only now, at last, can I feel free, too.' She was waiting with every nerve in her body to hear the soil clumping on his coffin. 'Because until I hear that,' she was thinking, 'I won't really believe that he is dead.' Even at home in the parlour when he was tastefully laid out on the table, stiff and silent, she couldn't bring herself to believe that he was dead at last. That it wasn't some gigantic joke that was being played on her by God.

Thump.

Thump.

Thump.

There it was at last, accompanied by the murmured Latin. She brought her eyes back at last to the ground at her feet, automatically answered the murmured responses to the priest's prayer, and then stood there and watched the men with their shovels, competently and practisedly filling in the clay and stones on top of him.

The tears were flowing very freely from her.

'Ah, the poor creature,' they said, 'the poor, poor creature.'

'It's true,' she was thinking. She raised her eyes then and she let them circle the many faces surrounding her. Kind faces, avid faces, cruel faces, speculative faces, honest faces, with not a tear amongst the lot of them. But they were kind in the main, she thought, and they were all filled with a transitory sorrow for her. 'What,' she wondered, 'was John thinking, kind old John over there, and Peter, their hats in their hands held in front of them and the gentle breeze raising the sparse white hair on their heads? They weren't crying, that was sure. But they had cause to cry,' she thought. 'They have just as much right to tears of unutterable relief as I have myself. What would happen,' she wondered, 'if I stood up now and talked to all those people? If I stood on the hill here and raised my arms to the sky and said "Listen to me, you fools!"'

No, you didn't do that.

But the fact remained that they were mourning a sham.

'Even his very name,' she thought, 'is a sham.'

There never had been any soul in the world named Mervyn James Tender. That was the name his inferiority had made him adopt because he had been brought into the world with no name at all. Even though he had been young, he had looked coldly at the world and he had said, 'If you want to be what you are not, then be it well.'

So he took a high-sounding name, so that people would say, 'Well, with a name like that he must have had good beginnings.' Nobody could suspect a bastard under the title of Mervyn James Tender.

She had believed in Mervyn James Tender when she was so young and so innocent and had come to work for him. He had pleased her, with his bustle and politeness and his ambition. To watch the way he got customers. Coldly and calculatingly, he had it all worked out. How to get them and how to keep them. 'You have to have a front,' he said. 'What pleases people? Well, when you know what pleases people, you just do it, and that's all that's to it. Success is yours after that. Find the formula.' He had found it, and it had worked for him. To the snobs you are servile, to the rich ingratiating, to the poor generous, but purposefully generous. That was it in a nutshell. It had worked with her. The kind employer, looking after the welfare of his staff. It was easy to look after her, a young girl from a small country town. He looked after her too well. There had been only one chance of freedom since she had come to him, the day she told him she was going to have a baby. A short struggle there. His pride against his good name. What will people say? So he married the girl. It was good for business.

'Why didn't some instinct let me go then?' she wondered. 'It was because I was so afraid of the disgrace, when if I had known I would have been only too glad to flaunt my disgrace in the eyes of the nation.' But she couldn't. She married him, and so began the terror.

At first words.

Then actions.

Even now, when there was no need for it, she felt her whole inside shrinking at the thought of him. It was the refined cruelty of the waiting that he practised. He would leave her alone for months, one time for even a year, and then he would pick just the smallest reason, and he would rise big before her with his eyes blazing, and she could see herself falling back with her hand over her mouth and all the incubated fear coming out of her eyes. He would take her by one arm and he would use the other with his fist knotted tight. It wasn't the beating. It was the fear of it. Knowing that it would come, as sure as one year followed another. And that there would be no end to it except death. Not even age. He remained vigorous to the end. Not even God. It happened sometimes when he had come home from Holy Communion.

The hardest thing to bear was that if she had gone into the streets and shouted her terror to the skies, nobody would have believed her. He was Dad. The town had an affection for him. He was perfection in all ways: to the poor, to his God, to all men. 'Look at John and Peter,' they would say. 'Two old men ridden with terror,' she could answer, if she would have been believed. Two old men, afraid of growing old. Afraid of what would happen to them in their useless old age. So they took the few shillings, enough to stave off actual want, and even to themselves she doubted if they said anything at all evil about him. 'What was the use?' she thought. 'You couldn't encompass in your thinking all that evil in a day. It remained for the years to sort it. Maybe he wasn't responsible.'

'Oh God above,' she thought then, 'let me become anything but a hypocrite.'

They patted down the grave in a rectangular tidy way, and they put the green swards on top so that you could see where they had been cut carefully from the heretofore virgin earth, 'polluted now,' she thought, and on top of all that they placed the flowers.

Then the people who remained got to their knees, preserving their knees from the cold touch of the grass with handkerchiefs and prayerbooks and folded newspapers, and they intoned a decade of the rosary for the repose of his soul.

'He will need it,' the widow thought, as she rose and turned and made her way back to the car.

She was delayed there for a time, accepting the condolences of people who came to shake her hand. She had to put up with the pompous men who lectured her on the goodness and greatness and kindness and generosity and acumen of Mervyn James Tender. And at last she was away, and the car nosed its way though the gates and into the main road.

She stopped it a little way down to pick up the two old men.

They raised their hats to her and thanked her in their soft apologetic voices, and they sat one on either side of her. She knew they were worried about what was going to happen to them. They didn't think that the widow knew them or anything about them, or would have any thought at all for their future.

'I won't tell them until we get home,' she thought, 'and they are sitting in front of the fire with a glass of port. It will be nice then, in the room of his house where they had never been, to give them their freedom and security.'

Meantime all she said now was, 'It's a very nice day, isn't it?' and nearly laughed at their startled faces.

Deputy Johnny

THE SMALL SQUARE was crowded.

It was a cut back from the main street of the town, an open place with shops all around where the people came once a week to sell their produce. It was dark, and light shone on them from the tall electric pole under which the platform was erected, and at the lip of the square there were two further lights, so you could easily see the face of the speaker. He had his hands in the pockets of his overcoat because there was no handrail, just planks laid on porter barrels with a pole at the back to which a tricolour was nailed. It hung in folds. There was no wind. Sultry and sweaty the night was, but the man on the platform remained cool looking and unruffled.

There was quite a crowd in the square. Some old people who remembered the deputy from way back and some young courting couples who hadn't the price of the pictures. Some drunks who hadn't the price of a drink and some sober citizens who always turned up to political meetings, always hoping that the next one would be different from the last, that they would surely hear something new that would stir them, that might send the little shivers of excitement up their spine. There were no shivers. So they stood apathetically in the lights and listened to the smooth voice of the deputy. There were several tall policemen with their hands behind their backs, just in case, but there was no need. One of them was openly yawning, bringing up his hand just in time to hide his gaping mouth. So they looked on at the deputy and, behind him, the party members, well fed and well groomed, sitting on a form. The red-faced one in the middle was the prospective candidate, moving a little uncomfortably, saying 'Shush, let ye!' to a few children who were playing behind the platform and who raised their voices occasionally.

The audience was bored. The deputy was bored, too, even though he didn't look it.

A few of the young girls admired him and clapped one or two of his sayings, and the other people clapped then as well, reluctantly, so that once or twice he lost the thread of what he was saying and had to seek for it frantically again, his hands clenching. Not that he didn't know it all by heart, but his mind wasn't on it. He wanted to be finished with it. He wanted to get back to the lounge bar in the hotel and feel the pungency of the whiskey in his nostrils.

He was handsome still. He had a square face, very smoothly shaved, and a square jaw, and his lips rolled out from his teeth. His nose was straight and well shaped, and although his hair was very grey, almost white, it was strong and virile still, thickly brushed back from a widow's peak from the parting on the left. That's why the young girls admired him, that and the broad shoulders under the dark coat. You could see they were thinking what a man he must have been. Even so clean and neat as he was now, you could see him with a gun in each hand and his jaw muscles leaping and he daring them to face his guns. Great tales about the deputy. What a gunman he had been. How many bullets he had in his body. He was a legend.

The young men envied him his clothes, as well as his reputation, that spotless white collar with the black and silver tie and the expensive wool coat and the grey double-breasted suit stretched across a massive chest. Even from here you could see the glint on his black shoes. 'Oh yes,' they might say, 'he did all right for himself, just as all the heroes did. And more power to him. If I was a hero, too, one time, I would do all right for myself now as well. Why wouldn't I? And can you blame me?'

'Up the Republic!' screamed a voice then from the shadows.

It startled them all. The deputy stopped speaking and looked over. He had to peer to see her near the pole, an old woman with a trailing shawl with her back to the wall. There were a few titters from the crowd. One lounger shifted the cap on his head and encouraged her.

''At's the girl, Mary Ann!' he said, nudging a friend.

'Up the bloody Republic!' shouted Mary Ann.

The crowd around laughed. The prospective candidate came forward a bit and waved his flat hand and said, 'Shush there! Shush now, let ye!'

'And we'll crown de Valera king of Ireland!' shouted Mary Ann in a sort of singing screech that trailed away.

The deputy saw the two policemen closing in on her.

'No, no!' he said and waved them away. They looked up at him, startled. 'Leave her alone!' he said.

He saw the eyes looking up at him and a few open mouths.

'As I was saying,' he went on, and drew their attention. All the time his mind was flaring. Some memories crowding back into his brain, set up by the shout of an old woman crying for the republic. 'How right you are, old woman,' his mind was crying; 'how right you are to want the republic, and not to accept the shadow for the substance.'

He remembered back a long time when he was in this town, oh, many many years ago. He had stood on a horse-cart on this very square and he had talked. Different talk then, by God. Oh yes. He set them alight with his talk then, holding a gun in his pocket because he didn't know what moment a lorry would pull in off the street and black-coated figures in it with their guns blazing. No apathy then, was there? By God, no. Tar barrels blazing and batons falling, crunching on skulls, and girls screaming with fear and some with defiance. 'Up the Republic!' then was something, like a trumpet call to heaven, and in a strange disturbing way there was something about the thin call of the old woman now that stretched back a tenuous thread through the years. The lean years. The hungry years. The great years.

He brought his speech to a close.

They clapped. The chairman rose and said just a few words in thanks for the busy deputy, the great man, who had come all the way from Dublin to address them on behalf of one of the city's sons who was going to the polls next week and who they were sure would sweep the opposition into the gutter where they belonged.

All the time the deputy was sitting behind him, bending forward, shading his eyes with his hand to get a look at her. Her head was thrown back against the wall of the shop. He could see grey hair and spittle at one side of her mouth, but he couldn't see her face. 'Up the Republic!' she had called, in a voice that had echoed inside him.

Why? Why? What was it? The deputy pounded his knee and felt a strange excitement.

Clapping and the people drifting away idly. He stood up and he shook hands. On the platform and going down from it to the long car that had hauled its gleaming length to the platform from a side road. 'It was good of you to come. You have done a great night's work. It's in the bag after that, wait'll you see. I'll never be able to thank you enough.' That was the prospective candidate, sweating, rubbing his hands, creases of worry on his forehead. The deputy smiled at him. He had seen them come before. Young and eager like this. Badly dressed. But they changed. They learned to get into the groove, the groove he was in himself. Lapped around in grooves, he was, and sick of it. Sick of it. You got what you wanted, and what was left after that? What more did you want?

But he smiled and shook hands with them. His hands were soft. He knew they were. The nails on his hands were manicured down to the half-moons. 'All right. We better get back to the hotel now. They'll have the dinner ready. We ordered roast duck. Do you like roast duck, Deputy.'

'Yes, sure I like roast duck, why wouldn't I? And a jar, for God's sake. I'm parched with the thirst.'

'Yes, yes. Sure. Sure. Come on now. We'll be away.' Climbing into the car, one on each side of him, two more in front with Jim. Didn't know them very well. They were after his time. New faces. Where were the dead now? Men from this town that should be sitting beside him in the luxury car going to the hotel to eat roast duck. Out on the mountains. Some of them buried where they had fallen so that the grey crows couldn't get at their eyes. They had little stone monuments anyhow. That should compensate them for the roast duck. 'What the hell has come over me tonight? Why should the cry of a drunken old woman disturb the even tenor of my ways?'

They swung into the street and the car hissed along. The deputy waved at a few, who waved and shook hands through the open window with hands that were stretched in. Hard hands. Work-worn ones. Maybe he knew those long ago, in the good days. But who could tell? Time dimmed all, even the memory of blood brothers. Time and success. Nothing more boring than success. Up a winding street and nearing a wooden bridge, he remembered. Yes. There used to be a police barracks there. How we passed it by with the sweat breaking out on our upper lips, sauntering as if we hadn't a care. What would have happened if the policeman with the cold eyes came over and found the Luger under your oxter? He laughed.

'Good form, Deputy?' said the prospective candidate.

'Yes, yes,' said the deputy, and then as a picture formed out of the past, he leaned forward and squeezed Jim's shoulder.

'Stop it, Jim. Stop it, for the love of God!' he ordered. 'I have to get out.'

He saw their mouths open.

'Something to do!' he said. 'Something to do! I must go back. Keep the roast duck hot. I'll be after ye!'

'But Deputy . . . !' they protested.

'Go on with ye, for Christ's sake!' said the deputy and banged the door. 'On, Jim!' and Jim drove on. Trust Jim.

The deputy raced back the way the car had come.

He remembered now all right. His heart was beating fast. His lips were pulled back from his teeth. His coat flew out. He brushed against the passers-by with mumbled words of apology. This is it. He saw every door in the street he passed. How many times had he pulled in there and crouched back after curfew from the searching lights of a Lancia lorry. He didn't see the amazed looks on the faces of some of the people who had been at the meeting as he pushed by, towering over them, his eyes gleaming. He broke into a run, and he didn't slow his pace until he came back to the small square of the meeting.

It was empty. All around, the ground was littered with handbills and cigarette packets and orange peelings, the excrement of politics. And Mary Ann was leaning still against the wall, the shawl trailing from her shoulders, her head hanging on her chest.

He stood in front of her. Yes, it was she. The hair was grey. Make that brown and gleaming brightly after it had been washed in lavender soap. God, how it came back now. The whiff of lavender soap all around her. The sunken brown eyes that nearly disappeared when she smiled. They were closed now. The narrow eyebrows were just two or three white straggling hairs. The even white teeth, a little big to match the shape of a generous mouth. Face fallen in now. She was tall if her head wasn't drooping. He went nearer to her. Saw the cardigan tucked into the faded patched skirt that was a sort of purple colour. The black stockings with white flesh through the holes and the rubber shoes, one of them held with a safety pin. But it was Mary Ann.

He stood directly in front of her, so that the light must fall on him.

'Hello, Mary Ann,' said the deputy.

He saw the head jerk and then rise slowly, slowly. The tightly shut eyes opened slowly, slowly. Yes, dear God, brown eyes, that seemed to have been washed in acid since he had seen them last. He saw them try to focus on him. Saw them squint and the tired head go to one side. And then she spoke. Sort of rusty it came out of her. And the lips pulled back from her teeth. Few teeth and what were there decayed.

'Hello, Johnny,' said Mary Ann.

'You knew me, Mary Ann,' said Johnny, reaching and holding her arm. It was a thin arm, but not to Johnny. He felt it like he had squeezed it in his fingers only yesterday. A fine arm, as firm as the body that bore it. All those years. All those years. She had looked at him and she had remembered like that.

'I knew you,' said Mary Ann, dropping her head again. 'Knew Johnny.'

'Come on, Mary Ann,' he said. 'I'll see you home.'

Her eyes came up again. Widened a little. A sort of titter came out of her. He put one arm around her and pulled her away from the wall. She came freely and then walked with him. He was surrounded in memories. He couldn't see the present at all. She wasn't this Mary Ann to him. Her hair was brown and her firm breast rubbed against his arm as he supported her. Too full for words. All coming back to him as he turned off from the square, down the narrow lane of poor houses that smelled of last year's leavings. Lights in them. Narrow unhealthy windows. A raised brawling voice coming from one house. A screaming tirade of obscenity.

Johnny didn't hear it. No. He knew the way home. He had walked it often with the big brown girl that was Mary Ann walking beside him, smelling of lavender soap and the whin bushes and all that was fresh from the country. In the danger of the red years, she had been the only milestone of peace. In the tortured, sleepless years. Because when he was with Mary Ann, he knew he had peace, and that he could rest for a time before he travelled on. That none could come near him with her there watching him. Waking from a dream to feel her long fingers pushing back the hair from his forehead. Great God, how could he have forgotten? So long. Being a success. She had slipped away like a ghost. When she shouldn't have. Always he would say, year after year, 'I must go back and see Mary Ann,' and the kind feeling would come into his heart and the peace of her flow over him. Soon. Soon. But soon is never. And the years had wiped it all away. Speeches and meetings and the famous deputy. Position in the land, that you work to uphold. No time for the frivolities. No time for the past.

He knew where she lived and he brought her unerringly there.

Cut off the lane and across another ill-lighted road and up by the canal, and there was the house, snuggling up against the towering wall of a factory. A small house, once it had been thatched, but they took the thatch away and built a slate roof on to it. With a skylight window above. He searched for it with his eyes. How many times had he seen the sun and the moon and the stars through it? How many times?

He pushed open the door. Not locked. Nothing worth stealing. There was a small glow from the almost obliterated turf fire. He left her at the door and went forward with a match. There was a candle on the mantelpiece over the fire. How well he remembered that. The yellow light hid the poverty of the kitchen.

'Didn't I remember, Mary Ann?' he asked her in a sort of childish wonder. The very house. She was sitting on a chair inside the door. It had no back. There was a small table beside it. Opposite there was a trestle bed with a patchwork quilt thrown on it. Another backless chair near the fire. And over there the staircase to the room above. He walked over to it quickly. There was no staircase now, just a black hole gaping above where he had had the whitewashed room with the trestle bed and the linoleum on the floor and the smell of flowers that she always had. Always. As clean as a room in a hospital. And now from it he could smell mice. Stale, rancid, the smell that came down from there, of mice and aged dust and the green rainwater that seeped in through the gaping slates. He didn't see the lack nor smell the change or wonder why the staircase had had to be burned for firewood. Not Johnny. He was way back.

'God, I was so tired when I found you, Mary Ann. Awake in my sleep, looking over my shoulder. Afraid of friends. Afraid of shadows. And then you found me and took me in. You remember, Mary Ann?'

She rose from the chair and helped herself over to the fire with a hand on the table. A skinny hand in which the dirt was ingrained. Johnny didn't notice. She left the shawl behind her. Her shoulders were pitifully thin.

'Johnny never came back,' he heard her say. 'Johnny never came back.' She put up one hand on the mantelpiece and supported herself there. The figure in the picture of the Sacred Heart seemed to be looking compassionately on her. Johnny didn't notice what she said. He was away in the years, waking up in the room above when the day was done.

'You remember, Mary Ann? You would wake me with the cup of tea. "Ah," you'd say, "you can take the air now. The night is fallen."'

He went closer to her. Looking down at her bowed head from his great height.

'And we walked, Mary Ann. I remember it now. The field of the whin bushes up above, you remember. Near a stretch of water, where the earth had collapsed and made a shelter, and we lay there and watched the moon. There was moss in it and it was as soft as the petals of a red rose.'

He put his hand on her hair at the thought. Coarse grey hair. He remembered up there so well. The feel of her hand, plump and soft, and her breath was fresh on his cheek, and her heart was as big as the inside of a cathedral. And as peaceful. His head on her breast. His eyes closed. Thinking, 'Why is there war? Why must I be like a rat running from hole to hole, afraid of my living life? Why can't I stay here forever with Mary Ann in the field of the whin bushes lying on the moss that is as soft as the petals of a red rose?'

'You were my first love, Mary Ann,' he said and his voice was very soft.

'Johnny never came back,' said Mary Ann. 'Johnny never came back.' She fumbled behind the picture of the Sacred Heart and she pulled out a small bottle. She pulled the cork with her teeth and put it to her head. There was liquid in it that gleamed a faint purple in the light from the candle. She shivered and threw it away. He pulled back from her.

'Alone. Alone,' she muttered. 'What they say. Names after me, names the children have for me and setting the dogs on me. The weary years. The weary years.'

She fumbled her way forward then and fell on the bed. It squeaked under her weight.

'Johnny is coming. Johnny is coming,' she told a ragged pillow that was stained and old. 'Up above in the small square. Johnny is coming. Hello, Johnny. Hello, Mary Ann.'

Johnny pulled back from her. The gleam faded from his eyes. He looked around him. From the old hag on the dirty bed to the kitchen gleaming palely in the light of a small guttering candle. 'What am I doing here at all?' was the thought of the deputy. He felt panic in his breast. He smelt mice from the gaping black hole above. Beads of sweat broke out on his forehead as his hands fumbled at the inside pocket of his coat. What would they say? Think of his wife, the svelte woman with the blue-white hair making speeches at the annual prize-giving of the school where his daughter went. Oh, God.

The wallet stuck in the corner of his coat. He pulled it free. He opened it. He grabbed the clean uncreased notes from it, went over to the bed.

'Memory of the old days. Your kindness to a fleeing gunman. Never forget, the republic is grateful to you.' Hating himself and the terror that was raping him. Suppose she went around talking about him. The deputy was pompous. She turned her head and looked up at him. Watched him standing there terrified and the crisp notes in his hand. What look came in her eye? Was it the slow clear look of utter disillusion? Were they tears of hurt that a hero could have feet of clay and currency hands? Were they maudlin drunken tears that started to pour down the wasted cheeks, or were they genuine hurt tears?

He didn't wait to find out.

He threw the money on the bed and turned and fled. He thought he would never get his hand into the air. He fumbled at the door. He felt panic that she would rise and come clawing after him, that the mice would come dropping from the room above. Will the door never open?

It opened and he burst free.

He ran. He was as terror-stricken now as he had ever been in the old days of the tight corners. He went up by the canal. The moon was bright and shone on the waters. The canal was bounded by iron railings. When he had run for some time, he slowed and put his hot hands on the cold impersonal touch of the steel. Then he bent his head and rubbed his forehead on them.

'Oh, Mary Ann! What has happened to you? In all the years, what has changed you so? What misfortune has torn the inside out of you and sucked you down to the skeleton that I saw just now? I should have come back long years ago and found out. It was up to me. I could have been useful. I could have staved off the horror of the misfortune that beset you. But I never came.'

Many times he had leaned on this canal and she had been warm and brown beside him. Her teeth shining and she laughing at the moon.

'You're no good, Johnny,' said the deputy aloud. 'You're no good.' And then he turned and walked slowly, pulling the collar of his coat about his face and sinking his hands into his pockets, walked slowly back to the lights of the streets, back into his own successful life, right ahead into the barren years.

Tale of a Kid

UNCLE TOM CALLED for John Willie on an evening in July. Staying with the neighbours he was.

Uncle Tom stood there in the kitchen and looked at him, a small boy, very thin in his jersey and his pants and the sandals on his bare feet. A clean little boy right enough, but Uncle Tom didn't think much of the pallor of him and the way the two eyes were starting from his head. 'Aye, he's like Julia,' he thought, 'with that thin nose and the generous mouth of his father that he might have been better without.' His body was too thin, because you could see the way his shoulder-blades were pushing though the jersey. There was fear in his eyes, too.

'Surely,' Uncle Tom thought, as he talked nonsense to the big woman with the white apron and the kind eyes, her red hand resting protectively on John Willie's brown hair, 'surely it isn't afraid of me he is?'

John Willie wasn't afraid.

It was just that at the moment big men meant fear to him, and Uncle Tom was very big. He always wore tweed suits and they bulged him. He had very broad shoulders, and the hands resting on his knees were huge, and even so they couldn't cover the breadth of his knees. His hat was off and showed up his head, a big head with grey-black hair clipped close, and his ears were big and hair grew out of them, and hair of his eye-brows jutted out over his eyes. Clean-shaven jaws moved massively as he talked, and now and again his hand would rise to push back the hairs of his virile moustache. He made Mrs O.'s kitchen seem very small.

'We'll be goin' now, so,' said Uncle Tom, rising, his voice rico-chetting off the four walls like a drum beaten in a confined space. 'It was very Christian of you, Ma'am, to keep him for the few days.'

'Indeed,' said Mrs O., moving her hand on his head, 'he was no bother, so he wasn't, God bless him. It was a pleasure to keep him. He wouldn't eat enough to keep a bird alive.'

'Say goodbye to Mrs O., now,' Uncle Tom commanded.

'Goodbye, Mrs O.,' said John Willie, obediently turning to her and holding out his hand, 'and thank you for all your kindness.'

It was too much for Mrs O.

She turned away towards the kitchen range, her apron up to her eyes, crying away quite loudly.

It embarrassed Uncle Tom, and even John Willie felt uncom-fortable, even though he was fond of Mrs O. and in the few days he had been with her he had found comfort in her big bosom and the all-enveloping love of her eyes. She was so big, Mrs O. was, that she poured sympathy out of her like water out of a tap, an eternal tap, because Mrs O. could never shut it off. She gave it to stray cats and dogs and particularly children, and more particularly John Willie.

'Because,' said she to her husband that evening over the fire when the kids were in bed, 'it'd go through you to see him standin' there holdin' out his hand like a little polite angel, and thankin' me. Oh God, and to think of all that has happened to him and he so young, and to be goin' off now to the other side of the town livin' with that big uncle of his, with no woman or nothin' in the house to look after him.'

'From what I hear,' said her husband logically, 'his uncle is better than any woman in a house. It's a lovely house he has up there by the river, shinin' like the sides of an aluminium pot.'

'Ah, but a child wants a mother,' said Mrs O., 'and a woman makes a difference.'

'Well, women like you mebbe,' said her husband, throwing the unconscious compliment to her across the smoke from his pipe. 'But mebbe, after all that happened to the poor little bastard, he'll be better off with a man as a change.'

They thought about it.

'Well,' said Mrs O. in a hushed voice, 'when I saw him there at me door on Tuesday mornin', with his face the colour of a sheet and his hands shakin'. Oh I never will forget it, not while I can see with my eye. "Mrs O.," says he, "would you come out quick, I think me mother is dead." Sweet God, me heart nearly turned over, I tell yeh. But I didn't think it was so bad, so awful bad as it was. When I went out and saw her lyin' there on the kitchen floor . . .' It started her off again.

'Now, now, for the love a God,' said her husband, patting her arm awkwardly, 'forget it, can't you? Can't you try and forget it?'

'It isn't meself,' she said then, blowing her nose resoundingly. 'It isn't meself at all, because I've seen enough things in me life that thim things only make for pity, but what was so terrible was the thought of a little boy like that walkin' into the kitchen and seein' his own mother lyin' on the floor like that. Ah God, it doesn't bear thinkin' about, so it doesn't.'

'He's young, he's young,' said her husband. 'He'll get over it, so he will.'

John Willie found his uncle's house very strange.

It was like going into a foreign country, this going across the city to a house on the other side of it. It was a small house of one storey, and it had two rooms, the kitchen with the fire in it and the bedroom off that, where his uncle had fixed up a small bed for him just under the window, where he could look out in the morning if he liked and see the river flowing to meet the sea. In front of the house there was a small garden with a wooden paling, rather drunk, around it, and another garden at the back where an apple tree grew. 'You can have apples off that,' his uncle said, 'when they're ripe, and if all the little so-and-sos leave them to ripen.'

He wasn't afraid of his uncle now. He was used to the bigness of him, and anybody could see he was a kind man, the way he patted the head of his gundog, as he called him. 'What's a gundog?' Uncle Tom told him. A big red-coloured pointer with knock knees, a friendly oul yoke of a thing that licked you and wagged his tail. Uncle Tom got the tea. A boiled egg, a brown one, and tea and bread and butter and strawberry jam. He would have loved to be able to eat it, but he wasn't. Uncle Tom didn't urge him, just sat back in his wooden chair and pulled at his moustache, his forehead furrowed.

'I'm all right,' John Willie was thinking, 'as long as it doesn't get dark.'

It was summer, so it took a long time to get dark.

But it did in the end, and when the time came for him to go to bed, just the mention of bed from Uncle Tom and he could feel the shaking beginning in his legs. Even though it was cheerful in this kitchen sitting on a stool in front of the turf fire with the oul dog's head on his knee and the light on and Uncle Tom in huge slippers watching him kindly, even then it started – a shiver in his stomach and his hands going cold. But he had come to accept it now, so when Uncle Tom said, 'It's time for you to go to bed, John Willie,' he said, 'It's awful good a you, Uncle Tom, to be lookin' after me.'

'Ah, to hell,' said his uncle. 'Amn't I your uncle, amn't I, your own mother's brother, and who has a better right to look after yeh?'

Taking off his clothes and getting in between the sheets. Lying on his back there, his hands clenched by his sides. Then it started. It was always all right while it was day and he was about (just a sort of grey mist all around him) but then when he went to bed, even in Mrs O.'s house with her two young boys in the same bed with him, it would happen like that. A blackness and then the blackness would be split by red, and he would have the picture of his mother lying there face down, and he could see her hand as white as flour lying in the blood that was spread all around her from somewhere under her face. Then he would feel a whimper escaping from his throat, and he couldn't stop back the words that came out of him, like 'Oh, Mammy, Mammy!' and no tears from his eyes, just the awful trembling that started at his feet and worked its way up so that he would be trembling all over. Then it would stop for a while and he would shiver and feel very cold, and then it would start again. All night. Until there would be grey streaks in the window, and then he would fall asleep and in the morning wake up again, with terror leaping at him. And it would go, and he would be ready then to carry on a day in the middle of a grey mist.

It started now again.

He shivered and clenched his teeth so that the immature muscles at the side of his jaws stood out and, if he would have seen them, were white. He forced himself to stop shaking when he heard his Uncle Tom coming in.

He closed his eyes, and he traced his Uncle Tom's going to bed: the rustle of bedclothes and the heaving sighs and the sagging and creaking springs under a great frame. And then the light going out, leaving the shaking to itself again while a small whimper burst from his lips.

Uncle Tom listened.

He was perturbed.

He heard the bed over under the window rattling. 'What is it?' he wondered. 'Is it that he's playin' a little game or somethin'?'

'If only the light was on,' John Willie thought, 'it might go away.'

Uncle Tom heaved himself out of his bed and went over to John Willie, his bare feet scuffling on the lino.

'What is it, John Willie?' he asked. 'What is it?'

'It isn't anythin', Uncle Tom,' said John Willie, the shivers in his voice now, even; 'it's just that I have the shakes.'

He felt Uncle Tom's big hand coming down gently on his shoulder.

'Wait a minute,' said Uncle Tom and left him, and then the light was switched on. He came back and sat on the side of the bed and looked down at him, the starting eyes and the face muscles and all his body trembling. The worst thing of all was the kind of brave look in his eyes, mixed up with a little horror and a little fear and a little of wonder as to what was wrong with him. 'Oh, the poor, poor little bastard,' Uncle Tom thought, keeping his face immobile. 'The poor, poor little fella.'

He felt a terrible surge of flaming anger against his sister. Why did she have to do it? Did she have no thought at all for the little chap she was leaving behind her? Could she not see him now, lying on a bed, shaking like an aspen leaf in a gentle wind, with the look of puzzled wonder and shock all over him? It was so bloody goddamned awful selfish of her to say, 'I'm going to die anyhow and to hell with it.' He would never understand how it could happen that a sister of his could be so weak as to die of her own wish. That was a great puzzle. But this was worse, looking at this frightened, shocked child trembling in a bed. 'Of course,' thought Uncle Tom, 'that's what's wrong with him. It's shock.'

'Come on,' he said then, bending down and taking the boy's body into his big arms. He walked across the room and put him on his own bed, and then he went back and switched off the light and put his own big body in beside him, reaching one great arm under his head and pulling him into him.

'Tell me about it, John Willie,' he said then, in the dark.

'It's the night, Uncle Tom,' said John Willie. 'It always starts at night.'

'Lookit, we'll beat it, won't we, John Willie?' the big voice asked. John Willie felt like laughing, a sort of glee.

'We will, Uncle Tom,' he said, his voice shaking with it.

'Your mother died, John Willie, because her mind wasn't right at the time. You know that, don't you?'

'She didn't mean it, Uncle Tom,' said John Willie. 'Everybody said she didn't mean it.'

'Of course, she didn't,' said Uncle Tom. 'And now she's dead and she's up in heaven lookin' down at yeh, and she'll take a poor view of me if I don't look after you proper. Do you know what, John Willie?'

'What, Uncle Tom?' asked John Willie, the trembling quiescent for a moment.

'Tomorrow,' said Uncle Tom, 'I'm not goin' to work, and I'm not goin' to work the day after or the one after that. Do you know what we're goin' to do, John Willie?'

'What, Uncle Tom?'

'We're gettin' up early tomorrow morning,' said Uncle Tom determinedly, 'and we're goin' to go down to the river and get out my boat, and then we're goin' off, the two of us, and we're goin' up the river, and from that we're goin' up the lake, and we're goin' to stay there, and you'll be surprised at the things I'll show yeh. Have yeh ever been up the lake, John Willie?'

'No, Uncle Tom.'

'Well, yeer goin' now,' said Uncle Tom.

He talked to him for a long time, and the trembling was spasmodic but it didn't stop, and John Willie slept when the grey dawn was in the sky, and Uncle Tom held him all the time in his arms, and sometimes he cursed and sometimes he didn't.

The sun was high in the sky next day as the grey fishing boat nosed its way against the sluggish current of the Corrib. Uncle Tom was behind the oars, and if John Willie had been feeling properly, if the grey mist of the bad business wasn't wrapping him around, he might have had the proper seeing. And Uncle Tom was a sight. He was only wearing a vest, and his great shoulders and arms were very brown and very thick, and the muscles were lepping in them, and the oars cut effortlessly into the water with a rhythm that would carry him for many miles. Most of the citizens envied Uncle Tom. He wasn't married. There was that. Then he never drank much and he had no family, on account of not being married, so he could afford enough to buy a fishing boat and all his fishing equipment, so that he was a notable fisherman and was a great adviser to the fishing fraternity. And in the winter he had a gun and he went shooting wild duck, so that it was seldom you would see him without rubber boots or flies on the band of his hat or a landing net hanging out of him or the cased rods.

Funnily enough they all meant very little to him now, looking back there at John Willie sitting on the seat with his thin hands grasping the sides of the boat and his face very pale and the eyes still starting in his head. For the first time in his life nearly, Uncle Tom felt some feeling stirring in him for a human being. Up to this they meant very little to him, and his dreams and thoughts were of flitting birds or leaping fish or humming flies or graceful mallard falling awkwardly from the sky. 'John Willie,' he was thinking, 'isn't much different really from a young animal that has lost its mother in a shockin' way, like a young duck that its mother has died, filled with shot. There's a way,' he was thinking, 'to get the kernel of hurt out of him, to soften it up so that it will melt away.' The first remedy, like now, was the fresh air and the things that were near to God and not shut away from him by four frightening walls of a house. He knew the way he was feeling now. He had a fear of the water. A fear of the insecurity of boards, thin boards, between you and river. All that. It was a start anyhow, to take the mind off what it was most full of. He could see that his mind was still haunted. 'Mustn't rush it now,' he thought. 'It will have to seep into him of its own accord,' so he forcibly stopped himself halting to point out to him the things that John Willie would be seeing for the first time.

So he kept silent. All that you could hear was the regular dip and swish of the oars, and the gurgling of the water as the bow cut into it, and the breeze rustling the rushes lining the route of the winding river. Or the seagull calling in the sky, or the squawk of the cormorant standing like an ugly black emperor on a rock. The whistling birds in the bushes, corncrakes croaking and clocks tick-tocking in the rough grass, the curlews winding away with their lonely calling or the peculiar whistle of the golden plover, and to the trained ear, over from behind came the plop of a lazily rising fish, and without looking Uncle Tom could see the rounding ripples of the water. All that he wanted to tell John Willie, and to distinguish the calls for him and to point out how very much more there was in life besides people, even though there were near and dear people who had died shockingly. 'But better be quiet,' he thought. 'Gradually, gradually, that's the answer.'

And John Willie was hearing and seeing all of those things. Strange calls were sounding in his ears and peculiar smells were in his nose. The smell of fresh flowing water and drowned ash leaves rotting and new-mown grass and rushes and disturbed bogland. And he saw the winding river and he saw the ruined castles and houses fringing it where once wealthy people had lived and died, scarcely believing that one day their big dwellings would be in ruins to provide shelter for cropping cows. It was all a strange humming and a strange smelling, and the only trouble he had was that they all seemed to be coming to him from behind a veil which he couldn't stretch a hand to draw apart. He saw the river going on and on and he saw the birds in the sky and after some hours he saw the river opening out into a wide stretch of water.

'This is the lake now,' said Uncle Tom.

That was the first word he spoke.

'I see,' said John Willie, feeling frightened at the great water, but thinking, 'Well, Uncle Tom is here and if anythin' happens Uncle Tom will fix it up.' That unconsciously, which was good. There was something to lean on now.

He was interested in a faraway way in the approaching island, looking like a dot at first and gradually assuming shape with the trees and the bushes with strange coloured flies and butterflies hovering around. A fairly big island shaped like an elongated O, with piled limestone rocks around it and then coarse grass and the trees and in the middle of the trees a sheltered place of grand green grass where Uncle Tom left him. He was mildly interested to see Uncle Tom putting up the white tent that surprised you when you went inside at the size of it. And he could admire the deft way Uncle Tom had it erected and all the doings stowed away in it, and faintly he felt that he should be more surprised at all the strange things that were happening to him.

Uncle Tom was disappointed.

From the small things he knew about boys, they would have by this time been in transports of screams and questions, of hundreds and hundreds of questions. But as he looked at John Willie's pale face and saw the dumbness and the tightness of him, Uncle Tom felt like cursing or crying, he didn't know which, because he remembered his own first day up the lake. It was engraved on a not very imaginative memory as a red-letter time. 'Ah God,' he was thinking, 'maybe this was the wrong thing for me to do? Maybe I should have brought him to the doctors and let them try and do somethin' with him?'

He had a fire going then, and the smell of burning wood in the open air that he always loved meant little to John Willie. Or the scalding tea made in the old black can, with thickly buttered bread and jam. 'I don't feel like atein', Uncle Tom.'

When that was cleared up it was nearly evening. The sun was going fairly low on the far side of the lake, going to bed over the city, and the mountains, miles and miles away from them were faint purple dreams – and Uncle Tom thought. And then he rose up and said, 'We will go now, John Willie, and we will chase the goats.'

'What's that, Uncle Tom?' John Willie asked.

'We'll go and chase the wild goats,' said Uncle Tom, 'and we'll have roast kid for supper. Have you ever et roast kid?'

John Willie searched a reluctant memory.

'We had it once, Uncle Tom,' he said. 'It's sticky. It sticks to your teeth when you eat it. It's nice.'

He had a picture of the butcher's down from his house, with the spitted carcasses hanging and the small kid stretched on wooden sticks and the sheet of perforated suet laid across his gutted interior.

'Come on so,' smiled Uncle Tom, thinking that if the running and chasing didn't do something for him, it was a poor look out.

Two hours they were chasing the goats.

Goats are very agile, but this was an island and Uncle Tom himself was nearly as agile as a goat, and once to his joy he heard John Willie screaming with breathless laughter. Just once, but that was something.

So they caught the kid.

All young things are very attractive. 'Indeed,' Uncle Tom was thinking, stalking back to the camp with the tiny kid in his arms, 'what difference is there really between John Willie and this kid in my arms? Think of a young calf or a young pup or a young foal or a young ass, the way they strike in at your chest. John Willie was walking along beside him raising a thin hand now and again to rub the head of the kid, a very frightened kid with a thumping heart and delicate convulsing legs straining fiercely for freedom.

'He's a nice fella, isn't he, Uncle Tom?' John Willie asked, breathless from the running.

'He'll be nice for supper,' said Uncle Tom, thinking, 'this might do the trick now.' He thought that John Willie's eyes weren't quite so startling. 'And God,' he thought, 'isn't it me that had to pour sweat for just that little!'

He laid the kid down in front of the tent.

'Hold on to him, John Willie,' he said then, 'until I go in and get the jack-knife.'

He delayed a long time getting the knife.

John Willie knelt on the ground with the young kid pressed between his knees. He could feel the heart of the kid going as fast as his own. The little neck of him was straining all the time, and now and again the immature mouth would open and a bleat would come out of it.

'My God,' John Willie thought, 'he's going in to get a knife to kill this little kid!' A small little thing like this. A wee helpless little fella. 'Here,' he said to the kid, putting his face down close to him, 'it's all right, it's all right.'

'Meig!' said the kid.

Away from the other side of the island there came a bleated answer. John Willie raised his head. It was a lonely call. 'God,' he thought, 'that must be the poor little fella's mother!' He looked down at the kid again and his own heart was going very fast, and suddenly he really saw the kid: brown and white and little whiskers beginning to sprout under his chin. 'He's going to kill him,' he thought with horror. 'Uncle Tom is going to kill him.' He looked up, and it seemed to him that the tent was very white and the grass was very green and there were vivid colours in the sky. And then Uncle Tom came out of the tent, bending, the wicked-looking knife clicking open, Uncle Tom feeling its edge with his thumb, and John Willie thought, 'Why, Uncle Tom's face is very clear for the first time, and he seems to be a kind-looking man.' Maybe he wouldn't.

'Here give 'm to me now,' said Uncle Tom, getting down on one knee. John Willie heard again the cry of a distracted nanny goat.

'Are yeh really goin' to kill 'm, Uncle Tom?' he asked.

'I love roast goat,' said Uncle Tom, stretching his hand but not raising his head.

'Uncle Tom,' said John Willie, holding on to the kid, 'please don't kill him, Uncle Tom. Please let the kid go.'

'What's that!' said Uncle Tom, raising his head and looking at John Willie, hiding the elation in him to see the eyes shining, even maybe on the verge of tears.

'Don't kill the kid, Uncle Tom,' said John Willie. 'Please let him go back to his mother.'

Uncle Tom looked at him closely and pulled a fierce frown on his face, concentrated heavily, and then said very reluctantly, 'Oh, well, if you want him to go.'

'Aw, I do, I do,' said John Willie.

'Very well,' said Uncle Tom, rising.

John Willie hugged the kid and then rose with him and pointed his head in the direction of his mother. The kid hesitated, disbelieving, and then darted away as if all the devils in hell were after him.

John Willie put his two hands between his knees and bent forward laughing.

'Look at him go!' he cried. 'Look at him go!'

Later in bed, on the blanket laid over the ferns and the rock moss, with Uncle Tom bulking largely beside him, and the moon over the tent lighting them palely inside, John Willie said, 'Would you have really killed him, Uncle Tom?'

'As dead as a doornail,' said Uncle Tom.

'I saved him so, didn't I?' John Willie asked, 'I saved the kid didn't I?'

'You certainly did,' said Uncle Tom, 'and I looking forward to roast kid for my supper.'

'What kind of a yoke is that screechin' outside now, Uncle Tom?'

'That? That's a curlew, John Willie.'

'And the other thing, the kind of a whistle?'

'That's a sandpiper.'

'And what was the big black yoke of a bird that was sittin' on a rock when we were comin' up the river?'

'That was a cormorant. They're terrible divils for killin' the fish.'

'D'ye remember the place we passed with oney the walls standin'? A kind of a oul castle? What was that, Uncle Tom?'

'Well, I'll tell you about that now, John Willie,' said Uncle Tom, but before he was finished John Willie was asleep; and lying there with his great arms under his head, Uncle Tom was thinking, 'Well, do you know, thank God, that's nearly better to me than catchin' a ten-pound trout, or a six-pound trout anyhow,' and he moved one of his arms to put it around the sleeping child.

Saga

THE PRIEST TINKLED the bell of his bicycle as he turned up the lane from the main road.

It was dusk and the evening was turning very cold. It pierced its way easily through the thin stuff of the black coat he wore, right the way through into his chest. He wasn't impervious to the cold, but it didn't mean all that much to him. His deep-set eyes were fixed in front of him, his thoughts allowing him just sufficient sight to see the road ahead of the wheel of his bike. It wasn't a very new bike, but it was well preserved, like an old car that has seen service with a good family. The priest's face was very thin. You could see the bones of his cheeks pressing against the white flesh of his face. His nose was a thin, straight line, and the hair at the temples under his black hat was white, making the shadows at his temples look deeper than they were. A thin, thoughtful face, like the death-mask of an emaciated saint, but then everybody said he was a saint. He didn't know that, and probably if he had he would have been angry with embarrassment, but it was just a saying amongst the poor, and few people there were to hear their voices or their comments on living. A strange thought: that if these people were permitted to edit the newspapers that were supposed to enlighten the people, that humbug and cant would end for ever, if they could remain poor and their comments accordingly remain truthful.

He raised his hand in a salute to a tall man who passed in the dusk and lifted a forefinger to the peak of his cap.

'I like them to do that,' the priest was thinking. He remembered an argument, if you could call it that, he had with one of his flock, a man who passed the priests and never saluted them at all. He wondered why. It came in the end to worry him. Not that the man wasn't saluting, but that he was making it so obvious that he just wasn't going to salute by the tense way he kept his right hand screwed to his side. He could guess in a way what it meant, the defiant attitude of the turned worm, saying, 'I will stop saluting the priests, just to show that I am a free man.' Shake off the priests today and the government tomorrow. In the end the priest had summoned sufficient courage to go and ask the man straight out why. It seemed the man had been waiting for just that question for a long time. It took him ages to explain, or to declaim, that the Irish had for too long been forelock slaves, going around to all the gombeen men in the country, the haw-haws and the Sir Launcelots and the gentry, touching their peaks to them and thanking them with sheep's eyes for their goodness in allowing them to walk the same earth as them. Now he was free. He was his own man. He would salute his betters if he could find them, which was very doubtful, but until he did he would keep his hand by his side.

'Do you think God is a better man than yourself?' the priest asked him then.

The man considered it for some time and then acknowledged that, yes, he thought God was a better man than himself.

'Well,' said the priest, 'I don't want you to salute me if you are a better man than I am, but I do want you to salute God, who is a better man than you.'

The man looked at him suspiciously. The priest looked back at him and said, 'Even now, here talking to you, did you realise that I have God in my pocket?'

'That was a nice phrase,' the priest thought now, dismounting outside number seventeen in the lane. 'A very nice phrase,' smiling fondly, 'that I have God in my pocket.' He always felt that way when he was carrying the consecrated Host to the sick who wanted communion. It made you want to walk cautiously, the conscious-ness of it all, what a terrible thing of greatness it was that you were permitted to walk the earth at all with God in your pocket.

He knocked gently at the closed door.

It was a two-storey house in a row of houses facing an orchard surrounded by a high wall. The lane was narrow between the wall and the row of houses, and the wind found it difficult to sweep into it. A sort of poor, secluded backwater from the mainstream of life. Small windows in the houses with awful red-brown paint on the door and window-frames. The paint of the poor, he had come to recognise it as. It would have been far nicer a pale green or even white, but then the red-brown paint was cheap and lasted longer, he supposed, God help them. There was a light behind the yellow blind of the window.

The latch of the door was lifted and it opened. A big woman was standing there, peering and then stepping aside to let him in, as he took off his hat, disclosing his thinning hair.

'Mrs Corcoran?' he enquired.

'She's back in the room, Father,' said the woman, thinking, 'Thank God it was him they sent. He's a great comfort, so he is, that man.'

'I'm Mrs Casey,' she went on, 'I do be lookin' after her.'

'How is she?' he asked, resting his hat on the table, summing up the kitchen with the red tiles shining and the plain wooden table scrubbed white and the small coal range, glittering and over-heating the small kitchen; the dresser against the wall with all the delf and the collected knick-knacks of a lifetime; the picture of the Sacred Heart with the small red-globed oil lamp burning in front of it and other pictures, faded enlargements of single people or family groups in old-fashioned clothes. 'It all speaks of poverty,' he thought, 'all this wonderful cleanliness added to devotion to God.'

Mrs Casey was closing the door.

'Poorly, I think, Father,' she said in a sort of penetrating whisper that he had also come to associate with his visits. 'Though I'm thinkin' she's pickin' up a bit now. Yesterda' she was terrible bad altogether. Weren't we nearly sendin' for the habit for 'r, but she perked up there at two o'clock this mornin' and et a bitta bread an' butter. The doctor has just gone a few minutes ago. He had to be off. Says to keep her comfortable. Advised 's to send for the priest, too, just in case, he says, not that we wouldn't have anyhow, but there, he's a nice man an' he does the best he can, though they have the feet run offa the poor divils sindin' for 'm to look after their corns nearly, the ungratefuls.'

She paused for breath, her large arms with the rolled cardigan sleeves held comfortably on her stomach.

'Are you a relation?' he asked.

'Oh, no indeed, Father,' she said. 'I'm oney a neighbour. Mrs C. hasn't a soul or sinner left to 'r on the face a the earth, so we do be helpin' 'r out like when she's under the weather.'

'Kind,' murmured the priest, opening his coat.

'This way, Father,' she said then, going towards the stairs at the back of the kitchen. She didn't go up them but walked past and opened a door on her left.

'She must be bad,' the priest thought out of his knowledge, 'or they wouldn't have her downstairs.'

'It's the priest, Bridey,' she whispered into the room then, standing inside to allow him entry.

He met the eyes of the woman in the bed. Her face was fixed on the door. There was a look of relief in her eyes as they met his own. He saw the eyes first, a faded blue, piercing because the whites of her eyeballs were showing, too, and her eyebrows had remained dark. It was a wasted face he was looking at, creased with suffering and the lines added with the years. Her hands lying on the white quilt were coloured ivory and the blue veins in them were startlingly apparent. That was all of her to be seen. The face and the arms and the rest of her barely discernible under the unruffled white quilt.

'She's going to die,' the priest thought, and he felt his heart sinking. It always did. He had come on those visits so often now in forty years that all he had to do on a sick call was to step inside the room and he knew if death was coming to it or not. It was a sort of feeling you got, that was unexplainable, a sort of muffled feeling in your head, and a faster beating of your heart. You never got used to it. It was like stepping into a great plain of loneliness stretching away to an unseeable horizon, that you were on the fringe of it and you had to stand there and watch some soul put a timid foot into it and walk away hesitantly with their eyes looking back at you over their shoulder, with a look of fear, or a look of terror or a look of calm or a look of peace or a look of anguish. It all depended on who was dying. 'This woman,' he thought, 'will look back calmly over her shoulder.'

He approached the bed and sat on the chair beside it.

'Hello, Mrs Corcoran,' he said.

'Why, I know her,' he thought then, looking more closely. Her eyes weren't piercing now. There was a look of shyness in them, with her head slightly averted. The flesh was slack on the bones of her face. Her forehead was broad and her hair that had once been dark, holding still a hint of darkness, grew thickly still from her head, outlining the face with the blue eyes and the Grecian look of her, where the bridge of her nose met her forehead. He closed his eyes for a second and saw why he knew her. Saying mass in the church at the side altar. That was it. He remembered the face and the head covered with a black shawl when he would turn with a blessing. Not that his eyes always saw on those occasions, but sometimes, for the fractional seconds that your mind flitted from your devotion.

'You were always at seven o'clock mass, weren't you?' he asked when the door had closed behind Mrs Casey.

She seemed to be barely breathing. Her eyes turned back to him again and looked at him and the sparse grey eyelashes fluttered over them.

'Yes, Father,' she said. The day she thought would never come had caught up with her, the day when she would have to have a priest coming to her. No matter what had happened to her in her sixty years of living, this was something she had never anticipated, that any day could dawn that she wouldn't be able to heave her body from a bed and dress herself in the early dawn and go to the church around the corner for seven o'clock mass. And when at last she couldn't and when she looked into the tired eyes of the doctor and knew what was happening to her, a terrible fear had taken her over, that she would go out to where she had to go and see no priest at all, a feeling that wanted to make her scream to the low white ceiling above her; and the hours since they had sent for him had seemed every one of their minutes like centuries plucked reluctantly from the maw of time. 'Because,' she said to herself, 'there was only one thing left to me, only one ambition, one end, and if that had gone as well, what was the use of all the rest? What was the difference between it all and the sight of a dead dog killed on the street by the wheels of a car?' But now that he was here, and she had silently prayed that if it was anyone it would be him, this tall, thin man with the emaciated face of a saint, who had the eyes of a kind heart and all the furrows of impatient suffering, and the frown of thought.

He took the thin purple stole from his pocket and put it around his neck.

'Not,' he thought, 'that the poor woman really needs all those comforts of dying.' He could nearly tell everything she would say to him in her confession. He could nearly recite it for her himself. In this room that seemed so familiar because he had seen so many of its like, the light brown wallpaper and the white quilt that had covered probably all the dying who had ever died in this lane of houses, and behind him the table with the spotless white cloth on it and the candles guttering in the polished brass candlesticks. So he leaned towards her, and the shadow of him was thrown big on the wall as she opened her eyes to the ceiling above and said, 'Bless me, Father, for I have sinned.'

Inside her then, at that point, she felt something rising. Up from her heart it came like a cloud of vapour, and she traced its passage from her chest to her throat and felt it lodging in the roof of her head, so that her thoughts were imbedded in it and the lightness made her feel as if her body was suspended, and from the midst of the vapour she brought out the things she wanted to tell him, to see them herself for the last time really more than anything else, to know that there was somebody listening to her, just one person in the whole world, to know that behind her when she left she would be leaving her voice, in a man's ears, on the air, like the faint notes of a long-dead trumpet.

'I met Joe when I was twenty-one.'

(Joe, of the tall rangy body and the big white teeth always grinning. She was working in a bar, a buxom brown girl she was then, and so light on her feet, so active in her mind, appreciating the joys of living, closing herself to the sight of drunken men and their cursing and lewd talk and silly talk, and Joe big amongst them with his laugh and the smile that would rise a quack from a dead duck. He had a widow's peak of black hair and that, with his big mouth and slanting eyebrows, made him look like a picture of the devil, but he was far from being a devil. He wasn't rich enough in the first place because he was a carpenter, and always you could smell timber from him. His hands were broad and powerful and it was a wondrous thing to see him rubbing smooth timber lovingly with the flat of his hand. A proud man, who would only work for men he liked and at jobs he liked, so that he was often not working at all, and the wait before they could be married was very long. It was too long.)

'I sinned with Joe.'

(Oh God above, even yet she couldn't feel sorry for it, not really sorry. So long ago and she could feel his arms around her, very strong arms with nothing on them but muscle, and his smile dulled, and all of him in his eyes.)

'I was very impatient with Joe.'

(When they were married and she at home with the three sons, and she would be there in the house shivering in front of the dying fire and Joe coming home so late, and her lips would be tight with anger as she sat and listened, and she would hear him as sure as shooting. His voice preceding him, a strong baritone voice that brought all the sleeping neighbours to cursing wakefulness at that Joe Corcoran, and then they would lie back with their arms under their heads grinning as they listened to 'I stood in a land of roses, and dreamed of a land of snow, where you and I were happy in the days of long ago.' His eyes like a dog, big and brown, beseeching her not to fight with him, that he didn't mean it, it was an accident and it wouldn't happen again. Helping him into bed, knowing that he would do it again sometime, but that he would be so sorry that you would have to forgive him.)

'I despaired. I turned my back on God.'

(Then Joe came home to his tea on a Friday evening, and said, 'I'm afraid I have a bit of a cold, Bridey,' and coughed and went to bed and was dead in this selfsame bed on Monday morning at eight o'clock. With what they called galloping consumption. It had been in his family, they said, else how could such a fine strong man not yet thirty with the body of a giant and the belly of an athlete go out like a snuffed candle. A black cloud over her mind here. A shiver at the sight of a black priest. Nausea at the thought of a bit of bread that was supposed to be God in a church. And the smell of some kind of spirit.

'Oh God, it was a bitter time, when you took Joe.' But she came out of it, a long time afterwards, and she was no longer young and her hair wasn't brown any more, and something had been burned out of her, but she lived and found God, and that's how she managed to live. Until the next time.)

'My three fine sons . . .'

(All gone, like a shower in the sun, a dash of water on a hot range, a delicate flower in a frost.)

'If only God hadn't let them live so long.'

(But live they did, to grow strong and tall, to see them coming home from school with the devilish look of their father. Mischievous boys, strong boys. The sight of football boots and hurley sticks and the smell of their sweat and the sight of the muscles rippling on their well built bodies and their laughs and the blood that flowed when they were cut and the iodine and the bandages torn from used sheets. And she working, working. Going to a house on the hill and another in the valley. Alternate days. Cleaning and eating and saving the bit for the boys. Two shillings and sixpence a day and a midday meal. Bits here and there. Crumbs from the table of rich men. Some of their cast-off clothes and their cast-off shoes tossed in a corner for Bridey. 'That'll do Bridey fine; don't throw it into the dustbin.' All that. And it was no good. The coming home, tired, to do for the lodgers she had to take in as well as going out to work in order to make ends meet.)

'I thought God was laughing at me.'

(One after another they went down. They said, 'I think I have a bit of a cold, Mother,' and they coughed and went to bed on a Friday and were dead, laid out in their brown habits on this bed, on a Monday morning. It never took longer than three days. Never longer than three days. And she could see her heart shrinking in her body each time it happened. Her arms blindly held out trying to hold off the blows of a cruel God.)

'God,' said the priest to her, 'is inscrutable.' So inscrutable indeed that it seems it is rarely the fate of man to get near Him. He thought of himself. He had a picture of himself kneeling at the foot of his own cot in his room illuminated only by the light from a street lamp outside the window, on his knees, his hands clutching his forehead and the sweat flowing from his body in rivers, trying to get near God, to stifle the terrible doubts that were racking him from inside and out, and afterwards, after the struggle, the perfect peace of lying back exhausted on the pillow, knowing that, after all, that everything was all right.

He looked at her now, at the pale ivory colour of her face and the wrinkles spread by the light of the candle, a small ordinary woman lying back under a white quilt with the mist coming over her eyes.

'Bridey Corcoran,' he said then, softly, 'it is through suffering that God comes to you, through suffering.'

'Not sympathy,' he thought. 'It is the hard apparent cruelty of it all that brings its reward.' He looked at her and he thought, 'She at this moment is nearer to it all than I have ever been.'

She barely heard him.

She felt terribly lonely. 'After all my life,' she was mistily thinking, 'what have I left at all? Nothing at all from it all, except a few sticks of furniture that have lived longer than myself. Nothing at all. My Joe and my lovely sons, all gone.' She heard the priest rising and then she felt the Host being carefully inserted into her mouth. It rested on her tongue and she held it there and she didn't want to think anymore. Just to think, 'Maybe not alone at all, after all.' And it ceased to be hard and melted in her mouth, and then she opened her eyes a little as she felt the thumb of the priest, with the holy oil on it, resting gently on her senses, on her hearing, her seeing, her smelling, her tasting and her feeling, the gentle touch of the warm oil of the anointing. And then she looked and she saw them in the doorway and all around her bed. People.

Real people.

Mrs Casey with her eyes red. You can always count on Mrs Casey, to mind the house while I run out to the job. To give the kids their tea because I won't be in in time. For the loan of an eggcup of tay, when you were short, or the loan of a shilling for a few fags before pay-day.

And big Mungo there, bulky and looking out of place in the small room. His hair grey, his eyes with pity in them and discomfort. When she had the troublesome lodgers living upstairs, that bullied her and wouldn't leave, and she down in the church praying that God would soften their hearts and that they'd stop crucifying her, God answered through Mungo. Taking her into the house next door, and saying, 'Stay there now and close your ears.' And the banging that went on next door and the loud cursing and the clatter of pots and pans being thrown from above on to the hard pavement below. Coming in after a time with bruises on his face along with a look of satisfaction: 'The lodgers have departed now, Ma'am.'

Tall Tim, too. 'I'll fix that pipe for you in a second.' Or 'I'll fix the leg of the table. Or put a bit of a new board in that door. What do I want money for, wouldn't Joe do the same for me if he was here? Joe was a great man. He had a voice like an angel.'

Many more.

All gathered there in front of her eyes. Some standing, some kneeling, men and women who had seemed to mean nothing to her, but now meant everything to her, because she saw, 'They were my life, all of my life.' And at the end, before her frail throat contracted, she thought, 'Now that it is all over, maybe it wasn't so bad after all, at all, and isn't it a great thing to believe that you will not be alone wherever you are going, wherever you are going. . . .'

It was a very small funeral, the priest saw.

In the street of the lane there were twenty-three houses and eighty-nine people. There were eighty-seven people at the funeral, along with himself.

In Rahoon they buried her. He liked it there. You went west out of the city along a second-class road from which the dust rose, and at the end of it you mounted a hill and went in an iron gate. All around nothing but the country: green fields and gorse bushes and tall trees, the smell of cattle and fresh milk, and the sound of churns rattling on ass-carts. Bathed in sunshine and rain and protected from the Atlantic storms.

He walked back the long white road alone, idly regarding his black shoes, grey with dust.

'Yes,' he thought, 'it is a saga.'

Not like the saga of the Fenians, or the Red Branch Knights and Cuchulainn or Tristan and Isolde. Not the saga of Tara and the High Kings of Ireland, or the loneliness of dead patriots, of movements and banners and blood bathed in glory. Just the saga of a little girl who comes to the city and meets a man and marries him and has three sons and loses them all, and struggles on blinded with pain and suffering and a faith in the intangible, who dies and is buried in a cheap pine coffin smelling of cheap quick-drying paint, a coffin that costs four pounds nineteen shillings after heavy argument with the builder, because that was all the collection amongst the poor neighbours would allow. That and the four horses with tossing black plumes and polished hooves and the man on the hearse with his red nose and white moustache and shining top hat polished probably with Guinness, as the song goes, and a white sash around his shoulder over the old green moulded coat. That, and six feet of yellow clay, carefully covered in with green sward, and blessed by a priest who really and truly meant it, who saw it all, the saga of Bridey Corcoran, who would rest in Rahoon, with nothing over her head to mark her passing except some flowers which would fade and her name written in ink which would also fade in the big book of the caretaker.

'Worthy of saga,' the priest thought, because it is saga sublime, because Bridey Corcoran was the salt of the earth to which she had returned. Because Bridey Corcoran and her like were the granite foundations on which society was founded, and if they were taken away, society would collapse. Simply because they were good people, and nobody in the world ever wrote a saga about a good person.

He turned up the collar of his worn coat as the shower of rain poured implacably from the sky.

Dovetail and the Turkey

IT WAS A select funeral.

Small, but select.

No cars, no cabs and the rather disreputable hearse had been hired at a reduced sum after much argument with the disgruntled owner-driver. As a mark of his aggrievement, he refrained from putting polish on the horses' hooves and he himself wore a cloth cap in place of the ancient polished topper. 'That'll show them, bargaining over corpses indeed!'

About two hundred people went to the graveyard on the hill, or roughly one in a hundred of the population, but they represented every grade from the tenement dwellers near the docks, who had to reach their rooms by climbing a rope like monkeys, to the sleek but sincere presence of two aldermen who had an affection for the deceased even though he had frequently borrowed money from them. And an odd thing was that they all praised him highly, at least one hundred and ninety-nine of them praised him. It was only Pludder Finnegan who held aloof, and since, in a way, he was the cause of Dovetail's demise, the other citizens took a poor view of him.

None was louder in wrath than Gaeglers, who had been the last man to speak to Dovetail alive, and he was an object of interest since his name had got into the papers at the inquest. He was a tall, powerful looking man with a collar and a blue suit and he always used large words when he was speaking.

He was fond of Dovetail. There was a large bunch of flowers on Dovetail's coffin which had been contributed by Gaeglers. He had borrowed the flowers from a convent garden a few miles outside the town, and when certain of Dovetail's mourners thought this was hardly fitting, Gaeglers said that he was sure they would like Dovetail to have them if they knew, since in a way Dovetail had died in the service of the Church, and all on account of the misfortune that had brought him to Pludder Finnegan's pub, which was a sort of half-way house fifteen miles outside the town. He had gone in there to quench his thirst on Christmas Eve, which was only three days gone.

'That's him now,' Gaeglers said, pointing at Pludder, who walked alone resolutely with his hands clenched and his mouth determined, as if he wanted to see Dovetail down to the bitter end. 'If it wasn't for Pludder, I have no doubt that we would not be walking weeping today behind the hearse of one of the noblest men to ever grace the green land of Ireland.'

'He was a character all right,' said one of the aldermen. 'There's no doubt about that. The town will seem empty now without the rattle of his oul tin can.'

'He was a power,' said Gaeglers. 'Dovetail was a power, because no man ever saw him that he wasn't happy. He was a true philosopher, because he had no use for money. He just wanted to spread happiness.'

'He had no use for his own money,' said the other alderman, 'because he never had it, but he made powerful use of O.P.s.'

'Unkind! Unkind!' said Gaeglers with reproof.

'He'll be missed anyhow,' said the man hurriedly.

He will be, too. Anybody who knew the town will know that the town without Dovetail would be like beef without mustard, or porter without froth. And all because of the turkey.

Pludder had a lorry. It was an old lorry. Sometimes it worked and sometimes it wouldn't work. It wouldn't work this Christmas Eve, and Pludder stood there in the wide yard before his pub and kicked it and cursed it until he ran out of curses and hurt his foot, but it wouldn't go. So he went back into his pub and he poured himself a stiff tumbler of whiskey and wiped the sweat off his big bald head. There were a few people there and they sympathised with him. Pludder was a very big man. If he had been a pig he would have sold at any bacon factory in the country for a record price. Huge limbs and a huge stomach and a small odd little voice for the size of him.

'It's the turkey,' he told the customers. 'I have to have it in in town be tonight. If I don't, me reputation is mud and I'll never be able to hold me head up in the community again. And of all the days in the year. Any other day there'd be cars and lorries and vans passin' that road in a stream, but today not a one. You'd think that all the combustion engines in the country were on strike.' He groaned and drank more whiskey. He had hardly downed it when in the distance they heard a great commotion that was closing on them, rattles and bangs and large obscene noises that brought their heads up. They looked at one another, and then hope dawned in a great beam on the face of Pludder Finnegan.

'I'm saved!' he shouted at them. 'Be the heart a God, it's Dovetail and he hittin' for home!' and he ran out into the yard and waved his hand in case Dovetail would pass him by. Dovetail had no intention of passing by. Dovetail could no more pass a pub by in cold blood than he could drink a drink of water unadorned. He turned his van into the yard. Once it had been a Ford car. The back had been cut away and a sort of receptacle for odds and ends added, made from bits of wooden boxes. The whole ensemble was held together with bits of wire and canvas and ingenuity and the grace of God, and in a way it was a giant tribute to the original maker.

Dovetail dismounted when it had stopped coughing.

Pludder enfolded him in his arms.

He had to bend to do so, because Dovetail's head wasn't five feet off the ground. A small ill-clad man with clothes too big for

103

him, a green bowler hat and a red face with a large moustache, that was Dovetail.

'You are as welcome, Dovetail, as if you were St Paul coming to the Corinthians,' said Pludder, after raising him up and putting him down. 'It was the God of Israel sent you to me today, Dovetail.'

'This is great,' said Dovetail. 'This is what I call the Christmas spirit, Pludder Finnegan, and let us go into the house and celebrate this meetin', because I'm after comin' all the way from Ballinasloe and I'm as dry as a limestone quarry.'

Pludder ushered him into the pub. He was like a great big cock fussing over a day-old chicken.

'Anythin' you want, Dovetail,' he said, going behind the counter. 'Just give it a name and it's yours.'

Dovetail hoisted himself up on a stool and pushed the bowler hat back on his head.

'I'll settle for a pint, Pludder,' said Dovetail, 'and tell me what I can do for you.'

Pludder filled his pint out and then reached under the counter and pulled a great turkey from underneath it.

'Do you see that?' he asked.

'Begod,' said Dovetail, 'I couldn't miss it.'

'That bird,' said Pludder, 'should be in in the canon's pantry in town, plucked and hangin' for tomorrow's dinner, and here I am here with a shaggin' lorry that won't work for me, and I knowin' the canon is dependin' on me, for I told him, and if this bird doesn't get into the canon this very night, what is he goin' to think about Pludder Finnegan?'

'Quare things, man, quare things,' said Dovetail. 'But Lord, man, amn't I here and won't I deliver it before the night falls, and that's a remarkable bird, Pludder, it's nearly as big as a house; and give us another pint.'

'That's not a bird,' said Pludder. 'It's a bloody biological miracle, that's what it is, and when the canon sees this bird, his eyes will be poppin' out of his head and he will forever after regard me with affection. He did a little job for me, and he might do another.'

Dovetail polished off another pint, and Pludder got a large label and hung it about the dead turkey's neck. It was a large label befitting the size of the animal. It was all done up in green and yellow with shamrocks on it and a little snow-covered cottage.

Dovetail took the bird and headed for the door. The few customers nearly died laughing at the sight of Dovetail and the turkey. He held its legs high above his head and yet the beak of the bird was trailing on the ground.

Pludder was regarding it with admiration. It was a magnificent animal and a fitting gift. From tail-feathers to beak, it was over five foot.

They had to help Dovetail to get it aboard his van, and it filled it to perfection. You couldn't have put a box of matches aboard with it.

'God bless you, Dovetail,' said Pludder, 'and when you come back this way again, I will reward you for your good deed.'

'I'll have that turkey on the canon's table,' said Dovetail, 'before the sun sets.'

He pulled a few wires and delivered a few kicks, and the old van started away, blowing great gusts of black smoke and a smell of paraffin oil back at them, and they stood there watching it go until it had rounded a bend in the road.

'God is very good to me,' said Pludder. 'If He can't help me Himself, He sends His instruments.'

Dovetail was happy as he headed for the town. He whistled and sang and waved at the passers-by. There was hardly a sinner on the road home that didn't know him or the sound of him coming or going, and they liked the sight of his red cheeks and his cheerful eyes. He never seemed to have currency or a place to live or anything to sell or money to buy, but he managed. It made you a bit envious to see a person like him, with no assets visible or invisible, or appendages such as wives and children, and yet all knew him and gave him a sign on the road anywhere in the county.

Dovetail fully intended to get that turkey to the canon straight away, but he was tempted by the drought when he drove into the square of the town. He debated with himself and lost out after three seconds, and it was a pity he did or he would never have ended up in the hearse.

'I'll only have one suck,' he told the air as he pulled up before Daly's and went in.

He was greeted on all sides. The place was a fug of smoke and fumes, and everyone in there was half-seas over because it was Christmas Eve and they were all intent on giving up the drink for the New Year and were drinking hard for Christmas to strengthen their resolution.

Dovetail was glad to see them. He rapped on the counter and called, 'Landlord! Landlord!' He called for a pint for himself and a pint for his old pal Gaeglers, who had sidled up to him and clapped him on the back as soon as he came in the door.

Then he got a rude shock.

'No,' said Mister Daly, a spare man going bald and brushing his side hair over the top in a futile camouflaging effort. 'No more credit, Dovetail, until you clear up the four pounds seventeen shillings and fourpence you owe me for ten months. That's that!' He tighted his thin lips and cracked his hand on the counter.

Naturally Dovetail was indignant. He asked if he wasn't to be trusted. Mister Daly said he wasn't. He asked Mister Daly if he wanted to go down in the history of the town as the first man ever to refuse Dovetail. Mister Daly said he would be proud and glad to be down in the annals on that score. Nonplussed, Dovetail appealed to his friends. Would they all now march out of this pub in a body on a porter strike as a mark of their dislike for the way a fellow citizen had been insulted? Dovetail's friends, who were mainly drinking on tick themselves, thought this request laughable, so they laughed, and Dovetail left that pub in high dudgeon, and only one man whose credit was completely exhausted went with him, and that man was expendable. He was Gaeglers.

He showed Gaeglers the turkey.

'Here I am,' said Dovetail indignantly, 'goin' out of me way to do a holy job for the Church, and they spit on me.'

'It was always the fate of martyrs to be scorned, Dovetail,' said Gaeglers, examining the turkey carefully. 'Great God, that's a smashing bird, Dovetail! That bird is near as big as a two-year-old bullock.'

Dovetail was bitter.

'Fifteen miles I bring a giant like that,' said Dovetail, 'usin' about four gallons of petrol and paraffin oil, with a great thirst on me. Doin' a good deed like that and I'm thrun out on me head. They should make them close all the pubs for Christmas anyhow. The holy season, and they in gorgin' themselves on porter.'

'God forgive you,' said Gaeglers, 'but if you are going to deliver the bird, I will go along with you.'

'You're welcome,' said Dovetail, starting the thing and climbing aboard. 'It makes you think,' he went on. 'If you are bitter and sour like oul Daly in there, you make money and friends hand over fist. But let you be a Good Samaritan and they crucify you.'

Gaeglers was looking back at the turkey, licking his lips.

'A thought has struck me, Dovetail,' he said then.

'Speak,' said Dovetail.

'Suppose you were the canon, Dovetail, and you came home and saw such a terrible big turkey like that on a plate, wouldn't you get a pain in your stomach? It's very big, Dovetail. Wouldn't you say to yourself, "How in the name of God am I to eat a great ass of a thing like that on my own?" Wouldn't the very thought give you a pain in the belly?'

'It's not the belly that counts,' Dovetail pointed out. 'It's the thought of the gift from Pludder.'

'I don't know,' said Gaeglers. 'I personally think that that yoke of a thing out there is a big insult. I'd be insulted if a man made me a present of a horse of a thing like that. I'd prefer myself if I was getting a present of a turkey to get one that'd be about ten pounds lighter.'

'What are you trying to suggest?' Dovetail asked. 'I hope and pray, Gaeglers, that you don't mean what I think you do, and if you do, I'm hurtit that a man a your integrity in the town could even be darin' to suggest that we get a smaller bird for the canon in place a that huge oul thing out in the back of the van.'

'Now listen, Dovetail,' said Gaeglers, 'it's immaterial to me. I was only sad at seeing you insulted. It doesn't matter a damn to me. But you carted that bird a long way with no reward, and suppose, let's face it, that you got a nicer smaller bird for the canon in place of that thing, wouldn't you be only doing him a favour? I ask you. I'm not trying to influence you at all, but the more I think of it, the more I think Pludder Finnegan was thoughtless to offer a great oul thing like that to our holy and popular canon, so I do. Wouldn't you want to have diamond teeth to cut your way through a tough bird like that?'

'But . . .' said Dovetail.

'It's merely a suggestion,' said Gaeglers, 'and I must say you are very unreasonable, Dovetail, to be jumping down my throat like that, and if you do exchange the bird for a smaller one and you have a few shillings over, can't you put the money in an envelope and deliver it with the bird. That way all will be above board and you will be doing a double service to the Church, because if you don't want to give the money with the bird, you can give the surplus money to the poor.'

Dovetail looked at him for a long time, but Gaeglers' face was bland and open.

'Maybe you said something there, Gaeglers,' said Dovetail. 'Sure there would be no harm at all in getting the bird weighed anyhow, just so that we would see the size of it.'

They pulled up at a poulterer's, and Gaeglers took the label off the bird, so that people wouldn't be tempted to exercise their curiosity, and the poulterer was amazed at the size of the bird and he practically pleaded with them to let him have it, and although Dovetail held out for some time, he was after all a soft-hearted man, and here now, as Gaeglers pointed out to him, he could be doing another good turn with the two they had thought of already, and he would be making the poulterer happy by making the canon happy and the poor at the same time.

So Dovetail succumbed and took a smaller bird and twenty-five shillings for the poor.

They debated for a while, and Gaeglers persuaded him that in order that they could collect their thoughts, it would be as well just to go in and have two bottles of stout until they decided how they would allocate the money, and that after all two bottles of stout were not even two and a half per cent of the whole, although agents generally took ten per cent of jobs like that. So they went in and drank their bottles of stout, and when they started to think of the poor, they suddenly discovered that about the two poorest men in the town were two individuals called Dovetail and Gaeglers, and what way could they make the canon happier than by accepting his Christmas box and drinking his health.

And there things should have ended and nobody at all would have suffered. They came out of the pub and drove to the home of the canon, and it was a good job that the streets were almost deserted by this time or they might have been run into by something erratic.

Dovetail lifted the bird out of the back. The big label seemed a bit big for it. He was making for the home of the canon, carefully negotiating the curb on the footpath, when he heard Gaeglers talking.

'That's a miserable-looking bird, Dovetail,' said Gaeglers, peering out at it from the cab. 'An exceedingly miserable-looking bird. I hate to say it, but I think that poulterer cheated us. I think that turkey has shrinking disease.'

Dovetail held it up and examined it solemnly.

'It shrunk,' he said finding the word hard to say.

'Personally I hate turkey,' said Gaeglers. 'I wouldn't eat turkey if I got it on a silver platter. Isn't turkeys only a fad anyhow? Isn't it only a few years ago that people started eating turkeys at all?'

'I never et one meself,' said Dovetail.

'Roast goose,' said Gaeglers smacking his lips. 'Roast goose. Mm-mm. I bet the canon never ate a goose since he was a child. I'll bet you he never did. I bet you the canon would follow you ten miles and thank you with tears in his eyes for making him eat roast goose for his Christmas dinner, Dovetail. What'll you bet, Dovetail?'

'You think he'd really be plazed with roast goose?' Dovetail asked. 'I want to plaze the canon. I'd do anything on the mortal earth to plaze the canon and how good he has been to us.'

'Well, climb aboard,' said Gaeglers, 'and we'll soon have the holy canon eating roast goose.'

Sometime later the canon's housekeeper opened her front door and saw a small weenshie man outside swaying and holding in his right hand a small yellow-looking plucked goose with a green and yellow label around its neck. The label was as big as the goose. She was so surprised that she took it into her hand. The little man raised his bowler hat politely and made a speech. 'A happy Christmas and a bright New Year to the blessed canon from Pludder Finnegan,' he says, and then walks slowly and carefully to a shameful-looking van that was outside the door. She read the label: 'To my good and holy friend,' it said, 'so that he can have full and plenty and feed half his parish with the remains. Martin Finnegan.'

Gaeglers had gone home to bed. He thought that Dovetail should not share the final triumph of delivery with anyone else.

Dovetail drove down by the canal and crossed the bridge and turned off the road by the lake where he had often parked before. There are two roads there. One goes out by the lake and one goes into the lake. They are both good roads and at night they look the same. Dovetail took the long white road into the lake.

Somebody heard him singing as he passed by in the van. He was singing, 'I am a little Catholic, I love my native land.' A courting couple down there saw the car going off the pier and into the moonlit water. The young man was very courageous. He dived in and he fumbled about but it was too dark. It was morning before they got Dovetail out, and he was dead.

Pludder Finnegan, following the hearse as it went in through the gates, thought of the things the canon must be thinking about him. If he only knew (but that might make it worse), the canon was telling the story all over the town and chuckling away in his study when he thought of his housekeeper and the goose. In fact, the canon presided at the obsequies for Dovetail, and few can boast that.

'Ah, well,' said Gaeglers, 'even if Pludder Finnegan is bad enough to hold a grudge and to be willing to follow Dovetail to hell in order to get equal, we citizens can think of Dovetail's virtues as well as his failings. It was a sad thing he did to the canon, but he is before a higher judge now, and let this be his epitaph: he died from a drink of water.'

'God rest him,' said the alderman. 'He will be missed.'

Homecoming

W E UNDERSTAND THAT there was a very great and ferocious war fought in Europe and that it started in the
year 1939.

At least we read all about it in the newspapers, but as everybody
now knows, it is not wise to believe all you read in the papers, so
it is extremely doubtful that we would have believed in this war at
all was it not for two things: the first was the ship that came to us
with the survivors of a torpedo attack, and the second was Mike.

Of course, apart from those two things, we were vaguely aware
that there was some sort of disturbance abroad, but since we were
keeping our nose clean it was none of our business at all, so we
just ignored it except to curse and groan when things started to go
up in price, and somebody stopped sending us coal, and we had to
turn around and light fires with our own ground. Everybody admires
bogs in the distance when they are at the foot of a mountain,
tastefully covered with purple heather and the dainty cotton, but
when you have to turn around and try and burn the bloody thing
in a coal range, your affection for it wanes very quickly indeed. So
that way we realised that there was something wrong somewhere.
Also, of course, it was a fact that many thousands of our people
left the railway station above every year to go and work in factories
and things in England, and it was great gas to go up to the station
at train time and see all the old lassies in the shawls bawling away

and keening, and everybody's eyes red-rimmed and what not, but all that left us cold because there was plenty of money coming back into the town from them, and anyhow they were mostly poor people nobody ever heard tell of, so it wasn't much of an impact on us, except when we'd go to the barber and he'd complain about his loss of customers, that were flitting away like swallows.

Maybe we'd have sympathy for the barber, but not much for the shopkeepers, because what they lost in numbers they made up in increased prices, so that we could go around saying, 'The so-and-sos, call themselves Catholics, do they, mass and communion on a Sunday and they goin' around profiteering shamelessly all the rest of the week.'

The shopkeepers of course denied this hotly, and according to them they were the most generous bunch of philanthropists since the chap that built the Morris cars started giving all his money away. Charity burned in their breasts like a cipin in the middle of an iceflow, and even though they all suddenly blossomed forth in new cars and new clothes and cheque books and a fur coat for the wife, that was all a coincidence and had nothing to do with this supposed war that was being fought out in Europe.

So you see why we were inclined to doubt all these things we were reading about millions of men, women and children dying under hammer blows from the skies. We tsk-tsk-tsked about it, but we weren't quite sure. If any of our own people who had gone away died in the war, we didn't know that either, except by bush telegraph, because they weren't supposed to have gone away and died in this war. The government didn't approve of it, so if your son Johnny got a bullet in the breast in a battle, you couldn't put this fact in the paper. All you could say was that Johnny had died, God rest him, and for all we knew he could have died from hydrophobia or a bad dose of flu. No chance to make a hero out of Johnny. He wasn't in a green uniform. He was a traitor to his country, a deserter from the cradle of democracy. No flowers by request. Let Johnny rest in pieces.

But Mike beat them. Mike really got under their skin and ripped their hearts wide open.

It was some time after the ship business.

We had a great time with that ship. There were a couple of thousand of them got blown up somewhere out in the Atlantic, and the ship that rushed to the rescue decided to put into our port for succour. Boy, did we succour them. We nearly killed them with kindness. Admittedly they were a very pitiful sight to see, with their disordered hair and torn clothes and black faces, and the little kids holding on to other people's hands, because their Mammy or Daddy couldn't hold their hands any more. That was really pitiful and would bring the hot tears to the back of your eyelids. And you could cut the tension with a knife when the stretchers were carried down the gangplank with the terribly silent bodies covered with a sheet, or the others waving a weak hand from a mass of bandages. Really pitiful. We almost broke down and called the Germans bastards, even though at this time we weren't quite believing that it was their torpedo which had done the dirty deed. Of course we were told in the papers that it was, but then the Germans were saying that it might have been a cute move to make the Americans mad. So there you were. Who was one to believe?

One thing it did, it gave definite proof that there was a war on somewhere, so that was the first time we really believed in the war. We gathered our blankets and our food and our hot Bovril and our cars and ambulances, and we looked after those people as if they were nearer to us than sisters and brothers. It was grand while it lasted. It gave us something to do that was out of the ordinary. Then, of course, *everybody* wasn't allowed in to help. That might have been confusing. The better-class people are better at those things. Better organisation and all that, so afterwards we had great and sometimes exclusive stories to tell about our personal acts of charity. Modestly we could relate the heroic deeds we performed, privately, so that nobody could tell about them, only

I'm telling you now because I know you are discreet and won't breathe a word to a soul, I hope.

It was really moving, and for some time we were none of us selfish, and each and every citizen would have really given the shirt off his back or a tenth of his wordly goods in order to bring a smile to the pale face of a child or to bring colour to the good side of a horribly burned face. That was true, and let it go down in our history. And whatever the government might have thought about it, there was no doubt that a good many simple people cursed the man with the moustache very fervently and foretold the place he would go to on his death, and passed pleasant moments thinking about the fate in store for him down there.

All the same, although this was all very poignant and sorrow-making, still it wasn't personal, if you know what I mean. It was a detached and transitory sorrow, one you could suffer for a time without its leaving a really deep mark on you.

Mike left his mark.

Everybody knew Mike. You couldn't miss him. It wasn't exactly because he was very big and very bulky, because in our town we rear many men who are big and bulky. It was because he was so happy. He exuded happiness. He was like the sun in the morning after a wet night. His hair was very black and it waved and was always falling down over his face. You'd swear your oath that he oiled it carefully and tended it like a mother would her child, but he didn't. He was privately a little ashamed of it and kept it cut as short as possible, which was a pity in a way, because it was the best part of the top part of him. Even his own mother couldn't claim that he was good-looking. His head was very big and his forehead was short and his nose was definite only because it was big and fitted into his big face. His jaws were big, too, but they would want to be to support his mouth, because Mike had a very big mouth and he used it. When Mike laughed he would disturb the gulls nesting out on Mutton Island, and he laughed often, but it

was a pleasure to hear him laugh. He only laughed when he
wanted to or when he thought something was really funny, and
then he would throw back his head so that his neck was almost
buried in his broad shoulders and his eyes would vanish into a
million wrinkles and his teeth, big and strong and as white as a
laundered sheet, would flash at you. It was a 'Ho-ho-ho' laugh like
the deep notes on a big drum, and then he would double forward and it became a 'Hee-hee-hee' laugh like a violin tremolo.
Looking at him laughing was enough to make you laugh yourself,
so it was our delight to think up a really funny thing, just so that
we could send Mike off and start roaring ourselves and out of the
corner of our eye see the passing people, frowning first and then
grinning broadly and then going off laughing in their bellies and
probably stopping after half a mile to ask themselves what the hell
they were laughing at.

I'm talking about his laugh because it was the most obvious thing
about him, coming as it did from his big ugly face. But a laugh like
that can only really come from good people, and Mike was a good
person. It was almost as easy to make him cry as laugh, because he
was the sort of chap who would take other people's troubles on to
himself and be really hurt by them. In this way, when we were at
school, Mike was always the mug. If there was anything wrong, or
we wanted to have an imagined wrong adjusted, Mike was always
the one who would stand up in class, braving the anger of the brother
to speak our minds. Sometimes he won, and sometimes he lost.
'What does it matter?' Mike would shrug it off. 'Sure he couldn't
hurt me even if he tried.' And indeed it was amusing to see the
brother dwarfed by this clear-eyed schoolboy, and he roaring, 'Out
with your hand, Mike,' and Mike holding out a hand like the sole
of a size twelve boot, and the brother lashing away at it with the
cane, when he knew in his heart and soul he might as well have
been lashing at a lump of mahogany. Exasperated, he would have
to desist and glare furiously at Mike.

But the brothers liked him. It's hard to explain, but Mike was fatal. He was the epitome of everything that was ordinary, but he was extraordinary in the sense that he seemed to be completely lacking the ordinary failings. He was very modest, but I think his charm mainly lay in the fact that he never thought about himself at all. Himself meant very little to himself, and that way meant far more to you. He hadn't a lot of brains. It was something to see the gigantic wrestling that went on when he tried to solve a sum that even our limited brains thought not too difficult. He went into agonies about it, visibly sweating with the intense effort to understand, and ended up by having every one of us sweating, too, trying to explain it to him, and the brother going out occasionally for a drink of water to cool his brain before he went mad. And all this time you were liking him, liking the stupidity of him at the sum, and the concentrated look of stupidity on his face, and he wrinkling his forehead at you apologetically for being so stupid. You see what I mean? What chance had you against that?

At games he excelled, and became really well known in the town.

When we played rugby he always hooked in the scrum. He was at least as strong as two horses and he had a pair of legs on him like the hindquarters of a Hereford bull. He played the game with great fervour, so that when he got down and gathered the scrum into his arms and pushed, there could be only one result. Then in a loose scrum when he would get the ball under his hand and start running for the line, you should hear them roar. He always wore a scrum cap and a ferocious countenance of concentration, with bits of his hair emerging wildly. He wasn't very fast running, but then neither is a thirty-ton tank and it gets places. It was a terrible thing to see Mike coming for you head down, and you can imagine how your heart would sink when you realised that you would have to tackle him. If a hand like a steel sledge in the iron foundry didn't come out to push you in the face in what is euphemistically termed the 'hand-off', if you managed to evade this destructive lump of meat and dived to catch him about the legs, it would be the same as diving at the trunk of a moveable tree. It was not unusual to see Mike headed for the enemies' line with members of the opposing team swarming all over him, tugging and pulling and hauling on his back and his head and his legs and his arms (you would think of a bullock with a lot of flies clinging to him), and on he would go. More often than not, he would get across, unless the whole fifteen of the other side grounded him from sheer weight of numbers.

So you can imagine the hero Mike was at school, with all the kids roaring, and their parents roaring, too, and flags flying, and afterwards, 'Hurrah, hurrah, we won the Junior Cup. Hurrah, hurrah, we won the Junior Cup. For the forwards did their duty and the backs they backed them up, And we brought back to Galway the Connacht Junior Cup.' Oh he was a hero all right at school, and far more of a hero because he was genuinely modest and met everything with the grin and the big laugh, and nobody could even think of Mike and a 'swelled head' in one breath, so what more can you say? The cups and the cheers and the lemonade spoke for themselves.

He left school then, but he didn't stop playing games. He went into one of the town's senior teams and just took up where he had left off, so that in the end there was hardly a citizen in the whole town that didn't know Mike to say 'hello' to, and 'Are ye goin' to win today?' and Mike saying, 'Well, we stand a good chance, I think.' The opposing team would be up all night working out plans of campaigns to muzzle Mike, knowing in their hearts that it would take so many men to do that that the rest of Mike's team would be left with their hands free.

Mike's last game will be remembered for ever, for it was a Cup Final, the year before his life was changed for him.

There was a very big crowd in the field, the stands were packed, and there was a constant stream of people coming from the graveyard side of the field where they were climbing over the tombstones in order to get in to see the game free. This was regarded as a good sign, because if the game was going to be a bad one, nobody would bother their barney going to the trouble of climbing walls to get in to see the game. The opposing team were a bunch of outsiders from one of the minor counties in our province, and it would have been a very poor do if they were allowed to take the cup out of the town. As it happened they didn't, but that has nothing much to do with it, since in our opinion the result was a foregone conclusion. Mike playing ordinary games was tough enough, but when he had the cup fever he would go through anything short of seven-inch armour plating.

About half-way through the game Mike got the ball, and whatever miracle happened, he wasn't cluttered up with the opposing forwards, so he started to run in a clear field. One of the other side's backs ran for him, stretched a hand and missed him, but his fingers managed to catch in the band of his togs. Mike ran, the hand pulled, there was a ripping noise, Mike's ruptured togs floated gently to the ground, and here was Mike beating it for the line, presenting what must have been the largest bare backside in Ireland to a dumbfounded and then delighted audience. For a few seconds you could have heard a pin drop. The way was clear, Mike had the ball and only about ten yards to travel to the line when he realised his predicament.

We all waited.

Would he run or what?

He threw away the ball and sat down there on the grass.

Well, look, you could have heard the roar of delight from that crowd of people if you were a hermit living on the top of Croagh Patrick. They clapped and cheered and dug one another in the ribs and shouted and bent in two and howled to the bright sun until there was a roof of sound on top of the town. You could see Mike's red face through a fog, shining like the light on the Margarita Buoy, and many afterwards swore that the blush wasn't on his face alone, but had spread downwards before he hid his behind in the green grass.

So you see what I mean about Mike and how we all felt about him; by the time the change came there was none of us in the town who didn't feel an affection for him, so that when you met and chatted and laughed with him, you felt nice that he was such a good citizen and that he belonged to the town, that he was something to boast about.

Then we went to play football up the north, the pick of Connacht against the pick of Ulster. This served to make us realise that there was a war on somewhere, because, as you know, some-body took away the six counties up there and gave them to a bunch of bastards who were camp followers of Queen Elizabeth, and their descendants decided that we down the south were lewd fellows and not worth associating with, so they go to war while we keep our noses clean, and there you are.

We were beaten in that game. It wasn't Mike's fault. He worked like ten men, but they were fleeter of foot than us and all Mike's struggles were in vain. We lost the game.

We also lost Mike.

We were all getting ready to depart for the train when Mike came up to me, clutching this letter in his hand.

'Look,' he said, holding it out, 'would you ever go to me mother and give her this? It'll explain all.'

'Why the hell do you want to be writing to your mother?' I asked, naturally enough. 'Can't you whisper it into her ear when you go back.'

'That's just it,' said Mike, pulling his eyebrows over his eyes worriedly, in the way he had. 'I'm not going back.'

I laughed.

He let me finish the laugh until it tapered into nothing from the look in his eyes, serious.

'What's up with you, Mike?' I asked.

'I'm going to the war,' said Mike. 'I want to fly.'

That was it, just like that.

I'm a very gabby fellow, as you can see, but I had no words left just then. I was shocked into silence. Apart from anything else, I just couldn't fit Mike's bulk into an aeroplane. But there you were. Mike was serious. Mike meant it. Looking at him then I didn't have to be told all the thought that had gone to the decision. Mike was a slow man, rarely working on impulse unless it was to do something to help somebody else, so there was nothing I could say. I still haven't made up my mind if he was an eejit, but that's the way. It's the difference between the ways that men think for themselves, and it would be a sad old world and a worse one if men couldn't think for themselves and decide their own destiny.

So I parted from Mike on the big railway station there.

The others didn't know. They thought he was just staying over to visit some relatives.

So I watched him leaning on the grimy ledge of the train window until I could see him no longer except in the retina of my eye. A huge man standing with his legs apart and his big arm raised. I remember well, he was wearing a tweed sports coat that made him look even bulkier than he was, and I can still see the creases in it where his arm was raised, and I can see the ends of his trousers raised up from his shoes with the action of his arm, and I can see his eyes, not smiling now, just looking at me with the lonely message in them, that big strong man with the great heart who was afraid to face his own mother, because he didn't want to hurt her directly, I knew. 'Goodbye, Mike, goodbye.' A wave of my hand and cinders in my eyes.

I spent a long time in the gents' toilet working it out.

I couldn't go into the others yet, singing away and clowning and carrying on like all football teams do when they are coming home. I couldn't face that yet. So I thought it out, and I asked myself where did all this leave me, and I realised that it left me holding a very big baby. I was resentful in there for a while. Why, I wondered, should I have been chosen to be the harbinger of such glad tidings? What the hell had it got to do with me? Even, I considered posting the letter when we got to Dublin, so that it would be there before me. But then could I live with myself afterwards, I wondered? I looked at my face in the cracked mirror. 'It must be my face,' I thought, 'that makes people confide in me and think that if kicks in the belly can be delivered with the minimum of pain, that I am the one to do it.' I brushed the picture of Mike's mother from my brain and put the letter in my pocket. 'I'll decide later,' I thought, knowing well that there was nothing else for it but to knock on her door and enter on her invitation and give her the letter.

I went back to the others then and added my quota of dirty stories.

Railway stations are lonely places, but I thought I had never been in a lonelier place than our station when we entered it that time, and all the familiar places down the town seemed lonely, too, as if they were all looking at me with raised eyebrows and saying in a surprised, hurt way, 'What! No Mike?' Like that.

I went directly to Mike's mother. You know how fast rumour works in any town, and I wanted to beat it. It would be sad if she was taken by surprise.

They lived, Mike and his mother, in a small house set back from the bank of the river, a very lovely little place with a small garden in front and the broad river before you rushing to the sea over the weir. Shades of rising fish in the evening time, and the rippled water and the overhanging trees shedding their leaves in the autumn time, thousands of brown and yellow barks launched in the soft and gentle bosom of the streams.

I knocked on the door.

She answered it.

She was a very small woman. It was the stock joke with her, how a weenshie bit of a thing like her could give birth to a giant like Mike, and then she would say with a wistful look in her eye,

'His father was a very big man, too.' The father was dead, for a long time. With Mike he was only the memory of a pair of arms raising him up to the ceiling. There was a photograph of him over the mantelpiece in the parlour, head and shoulders, a man with a moustache, his hair clipped tight to his head and a big grin. You took away the moustache and you had Mike. Mike's mother was a teacher once, and now she was living on her pension and the money Mike had made from the job he got when he left school. Do you know, I don't know what job exactly he had. It formed such a short part of his life, anyhow, that it doesn't really matter. It's only Mike that matters, Mike and this little woman with the kindly eyes, sitting there in the parlour, bending down to poke the fire, and I looking at her and feeling as if I was a very bad piece of news in the papers.

Her hair was as white as a country cottage in the sun, and she wore a dark brown dress and a sort of salmon pink cardigan over it. She was so small, like a little bird. I'm very ordinary in size, and yet she made me feel that I was colossal, and that my hand was like a pliable shovel when I took her hand in my own.

'What delayed Mike?' she asked then. 'I have the tea ready for him.'

She knew immediately that there was something wrong. I'm a very poor actor. You could have heard my nerves screaming a mile away, and I was flushed and awkward and sweating even though it was January and very cold.

I handed her the letter and covered my face with my hands.

I didn't look at her at all, but every bit of me went over every line of that letter with her.

She took it very well.

That's a grand easy thing to say, so it is, 'She took it very well.' How do I know whether she did or not? She couldn't possibly have taken it very well, but she was calm, apart from the quiver in her hand as she put it up to her chest.

'Poor Mike,' she said. 'I knew he was getting restless.'

She put the letter on the mantelpiece under the picture of Mike's father.

'You'll stay and have the cup of tea with us,' she said, as she had said so many times before when I was calling for Mike to come to the pictures or to come to a dance or to come out for a date with a couple of lassies.

'I'd love to,' I said, lying like a hero.

So we had tea. She didn't tell me what Mike said. It was a long letter for Mike, who covered a lot of space with extraordinary big writing. But I'm sure whatever he said was the right thing, because we all knew that there was a funny bond between Mike and his mother. They understood one another. God, there I go again! Such a silly thing to say. They loved one another. All you had to do was to look at them when they were smiling at one another and when Mike in an exuberant mood would reach out his arms and gather her into them and raise her to the ceiling like his father did to him, and Mike laughing and she laughing, too, and you knowing that the 'Hee-hee-hee' part of Mike's laugh came from her.

I left her.

She only talked about his going away once.

'It will be no different in a way,' she said. 'Every time Mike went to play football, or went boxing, my heart was always in my mouth expecting him to be brought home to me on a stretcher, with some part of him broken.'

'There was little fear of that,' I said. 'To break any part of Mike you would have to use a sledge-hammer on him.'

This made her laugh, and I was glad.

'Well,' she said, 'he was never a huge big man to me, but only a baby with soft bones.'

'He'll come back,' I ventured, 'like he always did. Mike is indestructible.'

'Yes,' she said, 'he will come back, with the help of God.'

Mike came back all right – on a December evening two years later.

I had known practically all about him. So had everybody else in town. Every time you'd walk up town for a stroll or to have a pint with the chaps, it would be, 'Here, tell us about Mike. What's the latest about Mike?' Because he wrote to me, and as soon as I'd get his letter, I'd hop down to his Ma and she'd read bits out of hers for me; she'd skip a bit here and there, saying, 'This bit wouldn't interest you.' So we all knew about Mike in England and later about Mike in Florida. You'd think he was doing nothing at all out there except doodling around on beaches in front of the rippling sea, burnt brown by the sun, and most sophisticated looking lassies in bathing togs lolling around him with most beautiful smiles and chemist's shop complexions. It rains a hell of a lot in our town, and we'd be there somewhere huddling out of the rain, and somebody would say, 'Think of that bastard Mike now, getting his chest browned by the sun and we here.' And, 'Do you remember the day Mike lost his togs?' We'd laugh then and the rain wouldn't seem so depressing.

I know nothing about aeroplanes. I only know enough to keep out of them. I like aeroplanes on picture postcards and advertisements of them flying in the sky and all that, but I'd as soon take a ride on the back of a seagull as go near one of them. Many aeroplanes dropped over our land, English and German and American, that got lost in fogs and bad weather and things, and we were always hearing yarns about them and what happened, all very hush-hush because we were neutral and nobody wanted it to be known that we were sending the crashed planes back across the border, and the pilots, because we weren't supposed to be doing that, but we should have interned them like the Germans. But all that was all talk anyhow and we didn't believe half of it.

And then Mike came home.

It was the coldest December of my life, and even the old fishermen with the whiskers at the docks were shaking their heads over it. You knew the minute you went out the front door that it was bad because your ears would begin to pain you with the cold, and no matter how many coats or scarves you'd put on, you would still be shivering, and we knew it was very cold when we'd have to be clambering up on the roof, cursing, to knock the thick ice off the water tank so that it would flow again.

I heard the plane all right, because I couldn't sleep. I was so cold in bed that I was even thinking seriously of getting married in order to acquire a hot water bottle that would be permanent for nights like this. There was a north-west wind. You know, the blizzard type, the one that goes 'whee-ooo, whee-ooo', like an owl on a top register. A rattle of the windows, and out there you knew that there would be narrow vicious waves licking at the bosom of the sea, and you would think, 'Imagine being in a boat at sea on a night like this,' and you would shiver at the thought and snuggle more closely into the blankets, reaching an arm behind you to pull the damn things closer to your spine.

It was hard to distinguish the noise of the plane above the persistent wind, but it came closer and it seemed to be low, and you knew it was a powerful bit of work from the way the noise rattled the foundations of the house. It made me sit up in bed. I heard it pass and it seemed to make its way towards the sea, and then I heard it curving back again and going east and coming back over the house again and then running up east again and coming right up along the line of the bay and then turning out to sea, and soon the sound of the wind had drowned it. I was a little annoyed. Why the hell, I wondered, can't the government do something about keeping those planes away, disturbing honest citizens from their slumber? It was a grand grouse and it sent me to sleep. I didn't wake again until the knocking came on the door below.

Mike was in the plane.

Mike and seven others.

We were never told where they thought they were going or why. All we ever knew was that they were going somewhere and they got lost because there was a blanket over the stars and there was fog on the ground, so that they had to make their way between a sky corridor of ignorance. It was a plane with four engines and a lot of bombs. Big bombs. If they had dropped them on our town, then this would never have been written, and our town would have been just a memory. Engines want a lot of petrol, and they had been so long doodling around trying to find out where they were in order to land that they were left with very little fuel, so they decided that they would have to land in the first break in the fog.

They spotted it over our town and they swooped joyfully out of the fog.

They called Mike up front.

'Can you make out where we are?' they asked him. 'It must be Éire on account of the lights. It's the only country this side of America where they have lights. Think quick, Mike,' they urged him, 'or our number is up.'

Mike looked and thought and roared.

'This is it,' he shouted to them, 'This is definitely it! I'd have recognised it long ago only this is the very first time I have seen it from above.' And he loosed a loud bellow of joy from him which almost succeeded in combating the powerful roar of four mighty engines.

'Stop howling like a great Irish wolf,' said the pilot to him, 'and come down here to me. We have about ten minutes left.' Mike left the blister and wormed and shoved his way towards the pilot's lair. 'Talk fast now,' said the pilot.

'How long have we left in the tanks?' asked Mike.

'We are lucky if we have ten minutes,' said the pilot. The pilot was very worried. The lives of seven men in your hands would be a severe strain even if you did not have to think of colossal bombs in the belly of a plane costing thousands and thousands of pounds. Then you can't just drop your bombs anywhere over neutral country. He looked hopefully into the bronzed face of the Irishman now peering through the perspex.

'There's only one place,' said Mike, 'and it's in a straight line about twenty miles away. That is if they haven't got it spiked.'

'Twenty miles?' The pilot could almost feel the tension of the others as they waited for his decision. There was only one decision he could take. 'We'll have to jump for it,' he said, 'and ditch the ship. We'd never make it. A straight line from here is heading directly into a forty headwind. Only God knows where we would come down. If we landed on a village with the load we have aboard. . . .' He left the rest unfinished.

'Listen now,' he went on. 'You can just see the line of the bay, on the fringe of the town. I'll take her well up into the wind and run back. As soon as I turn her start jumping and jump quickly. There will be very little time left to get rid of this baby.'

The pilot ran up east before he was finished speaking and then turned whilst the rest of them were tightening their stuff and taking this and discarding that, and very soon that neutral sky was amazed to see the rounded canopies like large umbrellas floating gently towards the white earth.

Mike was sixth.

He felt the tug of the straps at his crotch and then settled and saw the plane going towards the sea, getting behind him. He heard its engines and that was all, because he was soon taken up with his own thoughts.

What were they?

I bet he laughed at first, thinking over it all. I bet he thought, 'Wait'll I get down and go along the road and walk up to Mother's house by the river and knock on the door and bring her down in her dressing gown and her white hair all tied up in little bits of cloth, and when she sees her son Mike standing there, a present from Heaven.' I'll bet he laughed out loud at that point when he thought of it, throwing his head back first to 'Ho-ho-ho', and then coming forward to 'Hee-hee-hee'. The surprise that the lads would get as well. I bet that made him laugh again.

He wouldn't have laughed for long.

First he would have realised that it was very cold. Even though he was all wrapped up in leather jackets and trousers and fur boots and helmets and what not, after the raised temperature of the plane, I bet he felt cold. I bet he got a shock as that north-west wind went in and out through him like a sword through a turnip. He would have been shocked first with the cold that would make him draw in his breath sharply, and then he would have looked and he would have seen that after all he wasn't going to float gently to the earth. He would have realised that a north-west wind was not wafting him gently over the land, but with persisting and jeering cruelty was taking him over the sea. Over the sea, where the waves were small and white-topped and very vicious, and seemed to be lashing their tails like lions waiting to receive him. Did he become afraid then? I don't think so. I don't think Mike was ever afraid of anything. I think he would have looked around, peering into the whiteness to find out where exactly he was going and to get ready for it. When he saw where he was going, in the few minutes left to him before he hit the water, did he reach down in his harness and unzip his fur boots, knowing what a drag they would be to him in the water? Did his thick gloves go the same way? And if so, did he then realise how cold it really was as the night stretched for his hands and feet to caress them with icy fingers.

He fell far out.

He must have fallen far out, because Mike was a great swimmer. Mike could stay in the water longer and swim farther into the bay than anyone in town. He seemed to be insulated from the cold always with the size of him. So Mike fell into the water far out, out there, on his own. But he had often been far out there, on his own, long ago. Of course, then it was summer or autumn, and you weren't really alone since you could see all the figures in there at the place, watching your bobbing head far out in the water. Then you had to swim to get home. Now he had to swim to save his life.

It must have been shocking in the water. It must have been a terrible thing to feel the awful cold of it, reaching into his clothes, finding the openings in order to get near to his flesh. How horrible that would be, the first feel of that water on your skin. If he hadn't been wearing that thing like a woman's bust that they named after a film person, he would have gone under the water at that first shock, but he stayed afloat and he started to swim. He couldn't have missed the place. The sight of those fairly tall cliffs of white stone must have been visible in the moon. And he would have recognised the beach, and that would have given him some courage, that he knew where he was going.

But it must have been a long way.

It must have been a long weary way, with those white-capped waves lashing him in the face, with him powerless to retaliate. What did the wild waves say to Mike that night? 'We have you in our power now.' Lash. 'You trumpery human being.' Lash. 'Why don't you scorn us now, you who brushed us aside contemptuously so many times in the past?' Lash. 'Raise your arm now in cheerful greeting to your weaker comrades on the shore.' Lash, lash, lash.

They must have opened his powerful jaws and forced their way into his stomach, so that the last warm place in him became frozen with the terrible cold, and the cold must have begun to take the power from his big legs and the strength from his huge frame.

No man knows how far he swam. I can guess because I knew Mike so well, and I can tell you that Mike must have swam many miles that night, with his jaws clenched and his heart strong. I don't think that Mike ever gave way to despair. If it was only that he was coming home to his mother, I think Mike swam very far and I think that any other man in the whole world would never have swum as far on such a night, in such water. But Mike swam, and Mike reached the shore.

For the love of God, let that always be recorded about him, that on that night Mike did something that no man living could have done. He reached the shore, alive.

What then?

It was three-quarters-way to the dawn when I was dragged out of my warm bed and sent jumping into my Local Defence Force uniform to go out and join in the search for the airmen. One of them had landed safely and reported to the barracks, so they sent out the tocsin for us all to struggle into our green uniforms and grab our rifles and blow the dust off them and sent us scouring hither and thither on bicycles.

I didn't know about Mike at all. If only I had known.

We separated and I was sent to the west. We had heard all about them being dropped on the line of the land. We scoured the roads and we scoured the beaches and the fields well back from the shoreline, and after several hours we were very frozen and very fed-up, and we were inclined to regard the whole thing as an elaborate joke. We cursed fervently at the so-and-sos that had dragged us out when there was nothing at all, probably just for the dirt of it, while they were warming their fannies in front of roaring fires in the barracks and probably drinking hot tea or toddies. All the same, it was such a bitter night that we knew if men had fallen and been hurt that it was no night to have them out in it. That's what kept us going.

Even the sergeant got fed up at last.

'Let ye go along be the coast road for a bit,' he said at last, 'and have a look around be the cliffs, and if ye see nothing there, ye can go home to hell out 'f it.'

Stamping of feet and clapping of green-gloved hands on arms, and off we went again, not enthusiastically. We said a few prayers for the sergeant, and two of us went on, on the bicycles, on the lonely unlighted road with the frosted trees on either side moaning mournfully in the filthy wind. We came to a crossroads, where I took the road to the sea and he went to the bog. The lane I went down was rutted with the cutting of the iron-shod cart wheels, and these ruts had been frozen as hard as the devil's heart, so I had to abandon the bicycle and make my way cursing and sliding and slithering towards the sea. I could hear it, lashing away with the cut of the wind behind it, but it was getting light. Away over in the east the sky was coloured the green of an early apple low down and flushed a little on top of that, as if it was ashamed of its powerlessness against the north wind.

I emerged on to the white strand.

It was very bleak and sad-looking in the gloaming, the sands ruffled and waves making their way in on the shore despite the wind that was trying to blow them off it. It would make you cold just to look at the sea. I searched the sand with my eyes. It was virgin. Away at its other end were clusters of black rocks, covered with brown seaweed. No movement there. No movement at all on the whole expanse. I took a few tentative steps on to the sand, realised the awful loneliness of it all, thought how unnerving it was to be standing alone in the dawn on this immense cliff-backed strand, with no stir at all, no movement to give you cheer, just the whining wind and the sea, so cold, and the rustle of the coarse edging grass.

I turned away and made for the mouth of the lane.

Nothing there.

I stopped then.

Nothing? Except the gulls. Those gulls. Funny how I didn't notice them at all with the wind and my own fears. But there were gulls. I threw a look back over my shoulder. There was a flock of them, wheeling low and crying shrilly. You would think it would have been too cold for even them to be abroad. You would think that the cries should have been frozen in their throats before they were emitted at all. So what? Gulls crying and wheeling. Weren't they always doing that. I walked another step, and then of course

I had to turn back again and walk on to the strand. I found the gulls with my eyes. They were wheeling and crying over the black rocks. I hitched the strap of the rifle higher on my shoulder and started across the strand, feeling the sands giving under my heavy boots. Sometimes I wake at night now, and in the corner of a dream I have seen myself, a green figure in a green dawn, trudging across those sands, because there was something in me that was crying out against my going there at all. My feet were reluctant and my heart had commenced to throb dully, so that I noticed it in my ears. I had to swallow. It seemed to me that I would never get to those rocks at all. 'Why should I fear?' I asked. Me, a grown man that gave up believing in the fairies a few years ago at least.

I reached the rocks, rested my hand on the tallest of them, and looked. A sigh, nothing there. Nothing but the brown-covered rocks. Brown-covered rocks. One in the middle. Very dark brown, almost like the black rocks. I stepped across and went closer, and there saw the barely distinguishable bulk of a man hugging the small stones. It was the colour of his clothes, you see, that had me fooled. It would have fooled any man, a brown-covered body in the middle of brown seaweed. I dropped the rifle and went close to him.

As sure as God is my judge, I knew before I dropped on my knee beside him that it was Mike. As sure as if a voice had cried it to me from the vault of the sky. Something about the way he was lying, maybe, and the build of him even in a shapeless leather jacket, and the black hair. I don't know what it was, but I knew, and I dropped to my knees behind him and pulled him over on to them.

I was looking at Mike, and Mike was dead. I didn't have to see the awful white of his face and the blue lips, to see the hand that was flaccid on the small stones – it was white as his mother's hair – and the freckles that were on the back of it standing out now for all to see. His hair was beginning to curl again as it dried under the freezing wind, and it was falling down on his forehead, and his lips were drawn back from his clenched teeth. And if it wasn't for the awful waxy white of him, you would expect any minute to see him break in to the 'Ho-ho-ho'.

'Oh, Jaysus, Mike,' I said, feeling the awful pain starting in the pit of my stomach, and I pulled his face up to mine, to try and warm it. So cold it was, poor Mike's face. So awful cold that I could see him swimming in that sea and clenching his teeth to come home, and I could see him drawing himself up on the rocks out of the grip of the water, and just lying there in the shelter of the rocks. No move out of him because he had left all of himself behind in the cruel waves. No move. Maybe a helpless lift of his head and a straining of his misting eyes to look back to where from here you could see one or two lights shining in the faraway town. Even those powerful lungs had no cry in them, no cry that could even reach to God, so that he might have given us some hint that Mike was back there on the lonely beach and if we hurried up with our search we might find him before his life ebbed away from him with the tide. We doodling and cursing and shagging around here and there, when we might have come quicker, quicker so that Mike wouldn't die from exposure on a lonely, lonely beach.

'Oh, Mike,' I said to his cold, cold face, 'I didn't know, on me oath, I didn't know or I would have come, honest to God, I would have come.'

The tears poured from me then, hot and warm and stinging on to his cold cheek. So useless, Mike, to weep for you now, although it tears my guts to think of you, Mike the strong, the invulnerable, the indestructible, with the life sucked clean out of you by weak water and wistful wind.

And so I left him.

I turned him on his side again so that his face was towards the town and his cheek was caressing the round pebbles, and I pulled his arms close to him and then I took off my heavy green topcoat and I put it over him, not over his head, just over his cold body and I walked away from him, backwards, so that I could keep seeing him until I came to the lane, the green standing out against the brown, and I could distinguish the shape of him.

I could see the side bay then stretching before me in the cold light. Mike had conquered the sea. It could never claim him. Mike was mightier than the sea. There. I could hear his laugh booming above it. On this beach where he now lay so cold and still, I could see him in the summertime with his big chest brown and he holding the polo ball in his hands. Not a lonely beach like now, but one that was filled with the laugh of Mike and the screaming of children and the smell of oranges and bright colours under a scorching sun, and brown limbs flashing in the water. So different to now. Oh my God, so different to now.

And then over all that I saw a small woman with white hair and a salmon-pink cardigan, and there over the loneliness of the beach and the cry of the gulls, I heard her voice. 'He will come back,' she said, 'with the help of God.'

Mike had come back all right, with the help of God.

I went stumbling blindly up the lane, and above the awful whine of the wind I could hear a cry that was my own.

Homing Salmon

S HE CAME FROM the sea like a silver bullet, glinting, before the great body curved and dived again, the powerful tail and fins catching the mass of the green water, holding it and levering her body forward through its depths at incredible speed.

Behind her there was great commotion as the black bulk of the porpoise scattered the shoal of her companions. The hot sun from above lightened the calm water, reflecting deeply into the fathoms, so that the darting silver salmon looked like many sixpences dropped in a shallow pond.

She was afraid but exultant.

Afraid, because in that leap above into the air she had glimpsed the bulk of the islands ahead and behind them the waters of the enclosed bay, at the end of which she knew the river lay, the river and beyond that home, from which she had been exiled for many years. So fear entered her, lest after her journey of thousands of miles, she should be so near, and that death and oblivion should be so near, too, in the black shape of her enemies.

But she exulted in her strength.

She knew her power as the water opened before her face and she felt the fast flow of it traversing the length of her body. She swerved her tail and darted off to the left, with the instinct of fear sent from behind, where one or two wounded fish were turning gleaming bellies to the sky, their mouths opening and closing spasmodically before the gleaming teeth found and gulped them into the red oblivion of a colossal belly.

She swam faster and faster.

She was fat and full. She knew the way her chest rounded out below her chin and the way it curved powerfully above her head, so that she had width and depth and length, and glorious power. She knew that her flesh was pink and healthy, that her skin was thick and tough and that she was streamlined for speed, the most beautifully streamlined thing that swam under the sea. Her only irritant now was her fear, that and the few lice from the sea that moved over her skin, travelling in their formulated jellies, taking blood from her that she could afford, but making her long for the clear fresh water where they would die. She had a picture of herself, already there, leaping from below into the clear air, halting in the middle of the leap, so that her big body would flop down on the water of the lake and smash the remaining lice into memory.

She went faster still.

She was conscious of the others near her. They swam in ranks, closing together now after the depredations of the porpoises, sending out to each other waves of messages, but all the time watchful. They knew that they were coming home, and many things would try to prevent them from reaching home.

Out there in the great fastnesses of the ocean, they had been safe from all their enemies. A mysterious disease might lay them low, but in the main they had peace. And then the homing instinct reached out to them from the continents of the world, the great longing to go back, to a broad river in a great plain, or a small tumbling pool-strewn river near a great mountain, or a great lake spread like a blanket on a green field. They had each got a picture of home, a sandy bed in a river where their small eyes had first opened to translucency, where they had grown and played with their brothers and sisters until the time had come for them to make their mysterious journey into the great salt, where they had gone and grazed on luscious pink food until they had swelled and grown strong and frolicked where gigantic waving trees send their shoots from the bed of the ocean. A beautiful place to be, where they could play and eat and be safe until their instinct to return beat at them, and they set forth to run the gauntlet, conscious of their strength, or their speed, knowing that to be alert was to be happy, and to relax was to die.

They slowed their speed now, as they felt the undulations from the island on their right.

They scattered again as the sun reflected from the shining coat of the darting seal, as the gleaming white teeth below the kind little eyes sank into the tortured body of a salmon.

Fear leaped in her again as she dodged and twisted, terribly conscious of the sleek black thing behind her, following every dodge and twist of her body with the ease of a practised hunter. Once she felt the touch of a flipper on her skin like the touch of a red-hot poker, and it rocketed her into faster action. Every muscle in her stretched itself and urged her on, so that she went through the green water like an almost invisible flash, and the slower seal turned and darted back and followed a slower and less powerful form.

To relax is to die.

The shoal reformed and broke again into two streams, the one on the left sending farewell messages to the rest of them as they turned in towards the land and the grey Spiddal river for the fight up the narrow and waterfall-blocked river leading up into the hidden lakes and rivers near the mountains.

She went on with the town salmon. No narrow rivers for her, but wide ones and broad ones and a great lake with broader, faster-flowing rivers leading out from it. She was conscious of a faster beating of her blood, and she was conscious, too, for the first time, of the big body that sidled beside her, almost nudging her, his powerful tail sending him along effortlessly beside her, and from the eye near him, she could see the gigantic build of his body and the dour look of the lower cock-snout. She felt warmer. She had a protector, the milt to her baby eggs, a great body to ward off danger. She sent him a message of pleasure from the twitch of a fin.

He warned her then just in time, and his head turned up, and instinctively she followed him, left the water with him in a twin leap, and both of them sought the depths again on the far side of the bobbing corks of the net.

Almost too late, he had seen the helpless body of a salmon with its head caught in one of the holes of the net, its body drooping like a hanged man, the whole net standing in the green water like a living wall of struggling fish.

Not salmon.

Just one salmon who had served as a warning sacrifice to the shoal who, warned by his approaching death, went over and under and around, to form up again on the other side and swim desperately and triumphantly on. She was frightened. In her leap she had seen the black boat with the brown sail, standing motionless on the calm sea, and the men in the dark jerseys, standing high on it, one of them stretching an arm to point as they leaped from the water.

'Holy God, did you see that?' the man asked, and then they were down again in the silent deep, away from the menacing look of him.

And caution descended on them again as they sought the narrow channel between that island with the peculiar flashing light on it and the land on their left. They swam fast and true. To pause here meant danger, where the clusters of weed-covered rocks lay calmly waiting, rocks that sheltered the fierce eels, the lampreys, small and hungry with their gaping round suckers of mouths panting to fasten their mouths to the side of your body and suck the blood from your flesh and your bones and your very heart until, weakened and thin and ill, you would turn over and die, and they, bloated and fat and fulsome, would slip away to seek another victim. She shivered as she thought of it. Coming out she had got one. It had taken a long time to be rid of him, to swim against rocks, trying to pull the deadly sucker off her. She had been lucky. Others had not been so lucky. She could look around her now, at her companions, and from one or two of them she could see the trailing body of the clamped eel riding them, waving its body grotesquely to their movements, and on others she could see the round white wound in their silver flesh.

They cleared the channel, and she breathed freely.

They got the river then into their mouths, a soupçon of river where it had entered the sea and had come to the end of its flow. But it was distinctive. She wriggled her body ecstatically as she felt the softness of it, as she felt in her mouth the taste of many things so different to what she had been used to.

The taste of bogwater, that made you see the river to where you were going flowing quietly between the banks of purple heather and the thorn bushes on the banks and the alder trees and the slender mountain ash rising delicately to the sky with its red berries. All that from the taste of the bogwater. All that and the thought of shallow streams with the bed of yellow gravel where you would burrow your body when the time came and give birth to the eggs that were swelling in you now.

She left the shoal as the thought came to her, cleared the water and leaped high into the air.

When she returned again the big cock was waiting just below, where he had watched her leap, his eyes turned to the sky. So she swam sedately beside him again, answering his anxious queries with waves from her body.

And then they came at last to the river.

No salt remained, just the fresh water of the river tumbling into the bay, holding back with a strong hand now the ebbing sea tide.

They leaped when they got into its freshness.

Every one of them leaped, except the old warriors who had come out before and had gone back again, so few of them there were, but hardened sneering veterans, who despised this exuberance of youth. She leaped again and the cock leaped with her. They saw the big wall of the docks with the masts of the ships and the town behind, the black bulk of the fertiliser factory reared into the sky and the church tower with the clock, which had been there since ever salmon memory went.

They paused here then and rested, milled around or lay facing the stream of the river, allowing the fresh water to wash over them and in to them, weaving to its flow, joyful as the irritating itch of the sea-lice lessened. 'God is good,' they said, as they rested. 'He saw us home again.'

They lay there for some time, becoming familiar again with the familiar, crouching lower and lower to the bed of the river, ever careful to keep away from the rocks that might hide a watching lamprey. When they felt the drag of the river become less strong as it met the approaching tide, they became a little restless again. When the tide had given them another foot or two of water, then it would be time to move on again, so they jostled around and twitched their tails and opened their mouths to the clear water already becoming tainted with the salt, and then, slowly and stately and almost imperceptibly, they made their way up the river.

The black shadow of the shallow-bottomed boat on the top of the water sent her scurrying quickly to seek the shelter of the tall green-mouldy wall on the left. Fear sent her there and brought the cock fish protectively to her side. She lay there hugging the wall, twitching nervously.

Some of her companions had not moved. They were out of the radius cast by the shadow of the black boat, so they did not know that brawny jersey-covered arms were dragging, behind their boat, the net prepared for their destruction. They did not see the men pulling furiously to the anchored black raft at the side of the river, leaping from their boat and hauling with arms first and then with the capstan and the taut ropes of the net. Three of the salmon wondered at the change in the appearance of the water in front of them, and then they felt the hard cord touching their sensitive sides and they went wild, threshing and lashing with their bodies, straining at the net to find a weakness in its strands. They turned over and over and around and about, struggling, sending their fear and despair to the other salmon outside, so that they turned their noses to the stream and swam madly on the racing tide at their tails, helping them with its flow.

Behind them they were conscious of the net being hauled, and the rise and fall of the heavy black stick in a strong arm, and shuddered at the sound of the dull blows travelling over the water.

She was terrified again as she swam. The awful thought that to come home meant not peace but more danger, that even from the peaceful places, death could stretch a long arm with a black stick at the end of it.

But memory is short, and so she swam on again, soon forgetful. She was conscious of the shadow of the bridge above her head, and she could hear the rumble of wheels and hooves and walking feet, thundering in the space between the bridge and the water, a roof of sound that they shortly left behind, to meet it again more loudly still at the other bridge, which cast a wider and deeper shadow. Then they swam into the clear and nosed their way through. Just one more bridge now and they could rest before their very last journey to the wide spaces.

They cleared that bridge and then they lay in the clear shallow water, thankfully, almost lazily luxurious, feeling its shallow warmth that was heated by the beating sun reflecting back from the limestone and granite bed of the river.

They sought a place there in the throng and rested.

Such a beautiful place to be.

She did not feel alone, since the water was clear and on every side of you the salmon lay, side to side and head to tail, almost like the miles of swimming sardines met on her travels in the great salt. She was conscious of the people, too, leaning over the bridge above her head, their fingers pointing. She leaped from the water in a great splurge of power, turning to fall on her side and disturb the lice.

She could almost hear the two children leaning precariously over the parapet and saying, 'Oh, look at that one! Isn't she a beauty?' And as she leaped she smelled the flowers, the banks of them lining the sides of the river, and on the other side the very tall green trees rising, and at their feet, wooden seats where old men sat and rested, their walking sticks between their legs, their old heads nodding in the heat of the afternoon sun.

A good job for her she wasn't hungry. Else how could she have resisted the tempting bait of the full-bodied fly that floated above her head, tied to invisible gut, attached to a strong silk line, a thin miserable line that was nevertheless more powerful than she, because it had been made by the hands of man, and she had been made by God.

No salmon was hungry that day. They ignored the flies and the lures and the beautiful pink prawns tied to hidden hooks, baited skilfully and dangled almost in their open mouths. It was too hot, no breeze to fan the haze from the water, and besides they were just coming home, so the men and women on the banks with the long poles in their hands were exasperated and red-faced and sweating.

And night fell and the moon came up, and the salmon weaved.

Terror entered her life again, like flitting lightning on a tree in a plain. There was a splash beside her as something entered the water, and she could feel the drag, and then she heard a groan from the cock as three barbed snatch-hooks bit into his side. A terrible flurry and agonised wriggle of his powerful body, and then he was gone from her.

She turned away in panic and went down the river, her eyes raised to the star-studded sky. She saw him clear against it, struggling fiercely at the cruel hooks, and above she could see the cap on the man, who was a dark silhouette, and she could see his big arms hauling at the line. She lay there watching, a great anguish biting into her, and then she saw the powerful body above her head wriggle and struggle again, and her heart leaped and she sent herself forward as she saw him freed from the hooks, reaching out towards the water again with little grace, and the man with the cap fading away.

She was beside him then, to nuzzle at him as the blood ebbed from his slashed side.

He moved then through the thronged ranks in front of them, which made way for his impetuosity and his weight, and they reached the weir, and he didn't hesitate, but took a great flying leap at it, curved and green silver as his body left the water and flashed into the gaze of the admiring moon. One great leap and he was over and nosing into the deep water beyond. She followed him exulting, and soon she was beside him and they were swimming steadily and powerfully against the deep flow of the river. When morning dawned they would be more than half-way home and heading towards the great narrows leading into the wide lake.

Behind them lay the winding river and the rushes and the trout who had welcomed them, and the menace of the huge ugly pike dug into the mud of the pools, their cruel eyes watching, afraid to tackle them because they were too big for even those cruel curved teeth and gaunt bellies. Friendly things, like the coloured perch with the frightened eyes, darting incessantly, and the pitiful shapes of the spent salmon, like swimming corpses, their great frames barely covered with the white bleached flesh, making those who had succeeded in getting to the sea feel big and strong and very healthy.

And so at last they reached the lake and leaped again.

It was early morning and a swirling mist covered the ruffled waters of the lake.

At the same time as the two salmon turned north-east to traverse the twenty miles separating them from their own river with the yellow gravel, a boat with three people put out from one of the summer bungalows on the lakeside: a man and a woman and a boatman.

The woman's laugh was loud on the morning air. Drunk still from the previous night, she was big and blowsey and her hair was dyed; her overflowing body was poured into navy blue slacks and her big chests barely confined in a red pullover. Her eyes were bloodshot, her lipstick smeared, and her face was hard. The boatman was a tall man with big sloping shoulders, wearing a cap on his head. His face was burned black from the sun and his hands were big and capable. His eyes were clear and blue, the whites of them as clean as newly washed linen. He felt sick to his stomach at the thought of taking this woman on to his lake, for the sake of a drunken whim.

He didn't like the man either. He was a short man, dressed in a crumpled sports jacket with a high-necked pullover that was stained. His flannel trousers were crumpled, too, and untidy. He had red hair on his wrists; his voice was high, and he was constantly putting his hand on the woman. They laughed a lot: about the night they had had, the whiskey they had consumed, and about George, her husband, lying back senseless now on the bunk. They weren't sorry, the boatman could see that, from the way they were playing about with one another.

If he had dared he would have refused to go at all, but no matter how a man might feel about destroying the cleanliness of his lake and the distaste he felt in his stomach at the sight of them, at home he had a neat wife with greying hair and five children, and this was his profession.

They pulled away from the land, his casual pulling at the oars being deceptively strong. The woman knew he didn't approve of her. 'Imagine that, a country gob like him.' Her mouth tightened and her laugh was loud, and the man with the red hair at his wrists used bad language and double-talk and laughed and broke into a fit of coughing induced by the clean air on a whiskey throat and lungs clogged with incessant smoking.

About two miles the boatman went before he paused and silently reached for the rods. They were rods he didn't like either, colossal big bamboo rods that would kill a fish like you would kill a mackerel at the sea on a lead-loaded line. But he controlled his distaste as he baited their hooks with the fluttering mayfly. The woman screamed. Was she doing this right and was she doing that right? She had never had a rod in her hands before. And the red-wristed man laughed coarsely and said her hands were practised enough at handling other things to be able to handle a bamboo rod. Their laughter rang out over the water.

The boatman bending over the bait had to clench the muscles at the sides of his jaws to prevent himself from crying out curses at them, they ruining the morning, with the sun breaking through the mist, its light radiating from the millions of dew-drops clinging to the bushes and grasses on the islands, so that you seemed to be blinded with the glare of winking diamonds. And the heat inducing the mists from the water. All that, and he had to be here with these vandals.

Below, the two salmon went through the water faster and faster as they found the channels that would lead them to their river. They were impatient now, she feeling the birth tugging at her stomach. They hadn't so long to go really. This was the reason she had come home, the reason for the many miles of danger and wear, just to reach a certain spot and feel the gravel under her.

They went along blinded in their dreams of birth.

She saw the mayflies dancing above her head on the top of the water.

She didn't stop to think. She just answered a call of her stomach and rose sharply towards them.

If the cock fish had possessed hands he would have prevented her, for he was not that blinded that he hadn't noticed the grey shape above and behind the flies, which wasn't rocks or river weeds or floating birds. It was an alien shape that spelled danger.

He rose quickly behind her.

He was too late to stop her rising, to prevent her mouth opening and sucking into her the dancing water nymphs. His heart pounded and he paused terrified, but then he relaxed as she turned and came down to join him.

She broke away then as she felt the gut against her jaw, as she tried to eject the iron from her stomach. Even there, below in the water, he heard the human scream that came from above as the woman pulled at the rod with her fat hands.

The salmon felt the steel biting into the side of her jaw, the barb probing into the bone and catching it, and she went frantic. She sped away and left the water in a great leap. High, high into the air, wriggling her head, curving her body to free the foreign painful thing at the side of her mouth. Pain drove her up, and terror drove her down.

The cock fish couldn't keep up with her pain-filled movements. Away to the left and back to the right and turn again and up and out of the water again, all the time following her, his eyes wide, his mind dying with fear. He could feel the waves of pain coming from her and then he could feel the weariness that descended on her as her strength ebbed against the pull of the fearful rod. Her movements became slower and slower. He got near to her once before the end. He could see her eyes on his, and in them he saw the death of a dream, her awful farewell to a river with yellow gravel. He went frantic himself then, and he sped away and back again, and he too left the water in a leap. He came down again and circled the boat as the lax body of his lady was dragged towards the top of the water.

The boatman was disgusted to see the terrible death they were giving the salmon. The red man was beside the woman. There was no playing of the fish at all. Just to keelhaul her into the boat. He winced as the red man got the gaff and dug it into the back of the salmon. Just dug it into the back, the fool. He could almost hear the salmon screaming before it broke away from the gaff and made one last dive for freedom. But it was no use. It was hauled back again by force to lie panting there, its wounded back visibly bleeding, and then the boatman leaned forward and forcibly removed the gaff from the hands of the man, bent and with a quick movement pierced the belly of the salmon, hauled her in as quick as a thought, reached for the priest and with two blows on her head gave her merciful oblivion.

She started to die then, painlessly.

Just a picture she had of herself in the river and the eggs falling from her belly, small soft rounded eggs, sort of grey in colour, and over her head she saw the milt falling from her cock fish, and miraculously she saw her eggs turning to a ripe yellow colour like oats in the autumn. All that she saw, and she smelled the heather on the bank of the river.

In the boat the woman and the man were standing up, rocking it, with his arms around her, and they were screaming laughter at the sky.

The boatman was bending over the salmon looking at her.

Below, the cock fish circled, circled, circled, hoping that it was not the end.

The sun was rising higher and the ruffled water was dying away to a gleaming glassiness.

Spanish Joe

IT WAS A certain night in March that saw the beginning of the change in Joseph McGee, a very respectable citizen of the city. On account of all that happened afterwards, it is necessary to point out who exactly Mr McGee was, and his status, because looking at him now, people are inclined to forget his beginnings, thinking that he could never have grown from that. It is even necessary for the many good friends of his who drank frequently and equably at his public house.

It was in the heart of the city, and yet not of the city, because lying as it did where the respectable part of the city met the docks, it was a sort of half-way house where businessmen in good broadcloth and shined shoes could meet and rub shoulders for a time with the hairy men of the sea and the men with the dirty faces who unloaded the coal boats at the docks. Where seedy solicitor's clerks could for a few seconds forget the dreary, dusty burden of their lives as they sniffed the spices of the East from the absorbing jerseys of sailors and could listen unapprovingly to oaths that had been coined in far-off places at the ends of the earth. Where men of money could stand shaven cheek by bristled jowl with men who went to sea dangerously to catch their Friday's dinner and dinner on fast days and ember days and quarter days and Lenten days, in the beautifully arranged famines of their church which were a boon to gastric ulcers.

This was Joseph's place. A quiet place. Never rowdy. Never very noisy, because even if Joseph was the possessor of a big stomach, most of it was muscle and he had a very powerful arm. Not that he ever had much cause to use either, because he had made his place peaceful and quiet from the strength of his own quiet personality. He was the quietest man in the city and the most affable, and even the ladies who were the wives of the men who frequented the place were not too unhappy if they knew their spouses were there, because it was well known that if you were inclined to get too much under the weather, Joseph's big hand would come out and quietly put the cork back in the bottle and look at you, and that was that. No persistent drunks ever got a foothold in Joseph's, so you went there because you knew it was safe and quiet and you wouldn't be allowed to get roaring drunk. The company would be good and Joseph would be good.

Apart from which, he never sold anything but good whiskey.

It was an old place, with the walls three-quarter panelled with dark timber and whitewashed above that, prints of sailing ships hanging on the walls and one or two of Joseph's ancestors, gloomy gents with mutton chop whiskers, but respectable, so that you felt it would be a sin to offend them with rowdy roaring. There was a big double door where you came in and another door in the far corner, and Joseph had his pub here, a small one with a counter around the door taking little room, so that the sawdusted floor was spacious for spits or crowds. A few forms to sit on under one window where the phoney bottles of this and that were on display with the cigarette and tobacco advertisements. Very simply appointed.

You were expected here, too, to have a strong control over your functions, because Joseph's place had no convenience. You either whispered to him and he'd raise the flap of the counter and let you in through to climb the steep linoleum-covered stairs to the place on the top of the landing – a tiresome journey – or you went outside and looked around to see if anybody was there to be offended and, if not, performed against the wall of the place next door, which was a warehouse anyhow and didn't matter. It was nice to go out there occasionally with your head muzzy and breathe in the air that came from the sea or the river and look at the stars before going back to take up a conversation or your unemptied pint glass.

So you see, a pleasant place, one to suit the ambitions of serious drinkers, as opposed to your modern cocktail loungers.

Joseph himself leant against the counter on his bare arms when he wasn't pulling or pushing or pouring. He had a big face. He was bald in the forehead, so he let the hair grow long at the back and pulled it over his bald forehead in streaks. His head was big and his ears sat close to it, and his jaws were big, and he had two chins, a small nose, deep-set eyes, grey in colour and set honestly apart from each other.

His voice was a very soft one, and he spoke correctly and almost precisely, so that if you were a stranger and went in to him you would be momentarily startled to hear that gentle voice coming from a big rough-looking man, with no trace of the Galway accent, so that you would say, 'Well here's a man of education and what is he doing in a pub?'

Actually Joseph hadn't a good education, not much better really than some who spoke with ferocious Galway accents. He was just made that way, so that it had become a fetish with him to speak correctly, to pronounce all his -*ings* and to put the tip of his tongue between his teeth to get the correct -*th* sound, unlike the rest of us who say *wather* for *water* and *dere* for *there* and a lot of other things – sheer carelessness or else we don't want to speak English like the English.

That was one fad of Joseph's.

The other was history.

It was a pity about the history. Nothing might have happened to him at all if it wasn't for the history, the history of Galway mainly, but if he was put to it he could tell you a lot about the

County Galway, too, or even a smattering of Connacht. But he was a dab on Galway. He knew the whole of Hardiman's *History of Galway* off by heart: when it was built and where the walls went around it and who built them and the charters of the corporations, the number of times it was besieged from within and without, the names of the thirteen tribes and all their coats of arms. Everything. If you said to Joseph, 'Hey, Joseph, what happened in 1692?' Joseph would think for a time and begin, 'Well, in 1692, we were at war with such a one, but our trade with Spain had sadly declined owing to the depredations of pirates from the Cornish coast.' He could trot it all out. He had associated himself so closely with it that with anything that happened from the year of Our Lord or the coming of St Patrick, Joseph always spoke of it as 'our' time and 'we' did such a thing. Whereas if we were speaking about everyday matters of the present, giving out steam and giving off stink about the corporation or the government, Joseph would say, 'The dunderheads, why don't they. . . ? Now in 1843, when we were faced with a somewhat similar situation, . . .'

So you see. Joseph had come to associate himself with the history of the place, and it's true that if any notability came to the city and they wanted to impress him, they collected Joseph and walked the celebrity around the place with him so that he must have gone away again bursting with knowledge and very impressed with our past. One thing is sure, he would never forget Galway once Joseph had walked him around the miles where the walls had been and pointed out a piece here and there to him and shown him the tombs in the churches and the stones here and there where coats of arms still lay imbedded in modern buildings. Anyway he would remember when his feet ached, and he would say, 'The curse a hell on these corns; I got them walking ninety miles in the City of the Tribes, may they roast in hell.'

So here is the night in March in Joseph's place.

Outside the sky is clear, and the stars are bright, and it's very frosty.

Inside it is cosy and warm with the oil lamp hanging from the ceiling, which isn't an oil lamp with oil but one with an electric light bulb camouflaged into it, and there are not many men in the pub because it is Lent and for their sins many citizens give up alcohol altogether during this time and stay at home like bears with sore heads, longing with all their souls for twelve o'clock on Easter Saturday and the end of their penance. There that night were only four men: Jack Calder, who travelled selling something that nobody was very sure of, a bulky man with a red face and a camel-hair coat, with a soft brown hat always worn at the back of his head; and there was Mike Tarpin, the skipper of a fishing trawler, a huge man with a moustache and a peaked cap, with his enormous thumb stuck into the band of his trousers as was his custom; and Matty, the small wee lad with a blue suit that was too big for him because it was ready-made and the multiple tailors hadn't got around to making his exact size, a yellow-skinned little man with twinkling eyes who was something to do with horses; and then there was Peter Michael, who was something to do with the trade union, another big man in a blue suit and a cloth cap, with a voice that could boom like the foghorn out in the bay there.

Joseph was behind the counter as usual, but not so usual, he was more than a little drunk.

It was his weakness.

He was a bachelor. Nobody knew why exactly, even himself. If you asked him, he would lift a great fat arm to scratch his head and then thumb his stomach with the other one, and say, 'What's the point, friend, what's the point?' So he lived alone in the big house behind the shop except for a gaunt old lady with tight lips who did for him, a most depressing woman, very holy in an unctuous sort of way. But apart from her and the customers, Joseph had no company, so sometimes he became very depressed. He never knew why, just that he got depressed, a black pit yawning deeply inside him so that he went to the bottle and drank, and things seemed to be a little better for the few days until sanity and his good humour came back to him.

He was drunk tonight.

The others knew that from his silence. Glooming there at the counter with his eyes fixed far away, silent. He didn't know what he was thinking about or if he was thinking of anything at all. Just a great grey vacuum he felt inside himself that would become red for the little time that the whiskey soaked into him. But out of this greyness gradually there came to him words that the four were saying. And the word 'Spain' was the one that called at his attention. 'How dare,' he thought, 'anyone talk about Spain and me the authority here!' So he shook his great head and rubbed his eyes with his hand, and the look of the place came on his retina, and his ears opened to sound.

'Franco,' Peter Michael was saying, 'is a . . . !' and he used an alliterative word, that left no room for doubt. 'And double distilled at that,' he went on, raising his glass to his mouth to emphasise it.

'Now, Peter,' Jack Calder was saying, his free nicotine-stained hand waving in front of his face. 'I don't know. Where would the country be if Franco hadn't come along? Wasn't it sunken in anarchy, wasn't it?'

'What's this, what's this?' asked the voice of Joseph.

They gave him their attention then, with surprised looks. 'Joseph is coming out of it,' they thought. They were used to his silences when he was that way and they left him alone.

'It's Peter here, Joseph,' said Mike Tarpin, waving a hand as big as a foot in the direction of Peter. 'He has a proper down on poor oul Franco, so he has.'

'Aye, the bastard!' said Peter.

'Franco,' said Joseph slowly, 'is a gentleman. Spain was always a land of aristocrats, and Franco is an aristocrat.'

'They was never any good at turnin' out nags,' said Matty, adding his piece. 'Oney bulls, that's all. Bloody bulls. Imagine that!'

'The Spaniards,' said Joseph, leaning over the counter and fixing Matty with a glassy eye, 'were rearing thoroughbred horses when your ancestors were scraping the dung out of the hides of their asses, you donkey.'

'That's tellin' 'm, Joseph,' said Jack, and he laughed.

'I was oney sayin',' said Matty aggrieved.

'It'd take Joseph,' said Peter, 'to stand up for the aristocrats. Them's the boyos. Aristocrats, me ah! It's all right to be an aristocrat when you're livin' on the backs a the people. Yeah, abolish trade unions. Let every man get what the bosses decide to give him when they have their whack, and if yeh don't like it, into jail with yeh! D'ye know how many million men that fella still has in jail, honest workin' men like me and you! D'ye know how many?'

'No, how many?' Mike asked.

'Millions,' said Peter, waving his arms, 'shaggin' millions.'

'Too good for them,' said Joseph. 'Lucky men they are to be in jail. Up against the wall he should have put them, for trying to pull down the glory of Spain. Spain was always glorious. Spain needs aristocracy. How could they have been the great people they were if they hadn't been aristocrats?'

'And who med them aristocrats, answer me that?' Peter asked indignantly.

'God,' said Joseph, succinctly.

'Sweet hour,' said Peter, raising his eyes to heaven. 'Thim fellas never kem out a heaven. They kem outa hell and crawled to power over the backs a common people. That's what happened.'

'What about the Inquisition?' Matty asked vaguely.

'Aha!' said Peter expressively.

'That's it,' said Jack. 'What did they do to our holy religion?'

'Yeh,' said Mike, 'what did the Reds do that for, Peter? What did they knock off eighteen thousand priests for? Imagine that, eighteen thousand priests!'

'Aha!' said Jack.

157

'Didn't they have it comin' to them?' Peter asked furiously. 'Didn't they spend their whole lives livin' in luxury while the people were poverty stricken? They oney stirred outa their bloody mansions to preach to the poor suckers to put up with their lot. That's what God had all laid out for them, and any man that thought a betterin' himself was goin' to hell.'

'Ah, that's a shockin' thing to be sayin', Peter,' said Jack.

'It's not the kind of conversation I like in here,' said Joseph ominously.

'Aye,' said Peter, properly worked up now, 'and there's many more like you. Why the hell shouldn't ye leave everythin' just as it is? But mebbe the day is comin', too, when this country'll have a bloodbath, and it'd be the best thing that could happen to it.'

'The Lord save 's,' said Mike.

'They killed eighteen thousand, did they?' Peter went on. 'Well what did that do? Didn't it purify the Church for them. Cut off the rotten branches, didn't it, and med another few saints for them. So what?'

'So,' said Joseph, reaching behind him slowly and bringing out the cork, 'so it's time you left here, Peter Michael. The shop is shut.'

'Now look here, Joseph,' said Peter, the red going out of his face, 'this was oney a friendly argument. Mebbe we were carried away.'

'You can be carried out now,' said Joseph, looking at him sternly.

'Ah, I have to be goin' anyhow,' said Mike, draining his glass.

'I'll be off meself, too,' said Jack.

'Me, too,' said Matty. 'But I don't believe that about the Spaniards and the horses, Joseph. Thim fellas could never train anythin' but a gennet.'

'They had horses from the Moors, Matty,' said Joseph, leaning towards him, 'that'd make any of the nags that run in the Galway Races look like cows with the dropsy. They had them here. They brought them over in the fifteenth century and had races with them out there where the fish market is now. The most beautiful animals in the whole world.'

'I didn't mean that about the priests, Joseph, really,' said Peter. 'It's just that so many a ye can't look on the side of freedom at all because yeer blinded with all the trappins, that's all.'

'Goodnight, Peter Michael,' said Joseph sternly.

'Ah, to hell with you so!' said Peter, hitching his trousers and heading for the door.

'Goodnight, Joseph,' said Jack and Mike and Matty then as they wiped their hands across their mouths and followed him out.

'Goodnight, gentlemen,' said Joseph, lifting the lid of the counter and following them out, closing the heavy doors behind them. He came back to the counter again, closed it, opened the till and scooped the light takings into a canvas sack, went out switching the lamp off and climbed the stairs. He was very angry with Peter Michael, he thought. Joseph had always a soft spot for the Spaniards. Sometimes he felt like that Mayor Lynch of Galway who had hanged his own son Walter because in a fit of jealousy he had murdered a young man called Don Gonsalvo Gomez for flirting with his girl. That's how the mayor had felt about the Spaniards. That they were worth cultivating, that their friendship was worth the life of his son. Even yet Joseph liked nothing better than the visits the Spanish fishermen paid to his pub when they put into the docks below with their trawlers. It required little imagination for him to strip them of their fish-smelling clothes and clothe them in the clothes of the early times, and look at their modern steam trawlers and see them as tall looming galleons.

All this talk about Spain!

It was odd it should have come up tonight, Joseph thought, as he donned his coat and took his walking stick and went into the cold frosty air, walking down the narrow street between the high buildings where it emerged at the fish market and the river. On his right there was still a bit of the old wall preserved. 'There was a great gate here,' Joseph thought, and he never passed this spot without imagining himself pausing whilst it creaked open for him. That was the way it had been in the past, as the citizens strolled down to the riverside to bargain for their fish with the despised Claddagh men who lived in their little disgusting village on the far side.

He crossed the bridge, pausing for a second to look down at the rushing water of the river. 'No bridge here then,' he thought. The river was a natural moat for protection. Then he crossed on and came to the wooden bridge, a swing one that went over the branch of the canal. The moon was out now and Joseph was staggering a little. 'I'm quite drunk,' he thought, 'but what harm? I will be drunker before the night is out.' He sighed loudly and hesitated to cross the wooden bridge. He was superstitious. Even horses were superstitious crossing a wooden bridge. They disliked the hollow sound of their hooves hitting the timber. 'It was said, too,' Joseph thought, 'that sometimes the devil might be waiting here, and before you saw him, he would paralyse you with fright, so that you couldn't move.' He shivered, and crossed. 'Such nonsense,' he thought.

He walked another half a mile before coming to his destination.

It was another public house, with blinded windows.

He gave a peculiar rap on the door and was admitted. Another man, like himself in appearance, opened it cautiously and said, 'Ah, it's you, Joseph,' and Joseph entered and was soon sitting in front of the fire in the sitting room with a large glass of rum in his hand. He thought idly of the incongruity of a pub keeper going to another pub in order to get drunk, but it seemed natural to him.

It was well after midnight when he left. Little talk. That's why he went there. Just to sit in front of the fire, with the other man in a chair opposite him, sympathetic to his depression.

He had to pull himself together when he got into the air. Had to walk very carefully indeed. Right leg down and dig it into the hard ground to get purchase before bringing the other one from behind. An extraordinary lightness in his head, as if his skull had been lifted and a current of air was being sprayed on his brain. That's the way he liked to be. It effectively excluded thought, and when you couldn't think, you had ceased to be depressed. It lasted until once again he reached the wooden bridge where he had to pause. To pause is to think. He didn't really like crossing this bridge on his own. It always made the hair on the back of his neck rise a little. It stood there as a challenge in the moonlight, with the water in the Claddagh Basin on his right, grinning at him. He looked about. There was no man abroad. Strange that there shouldn't be. If there was even the sound of a footfall in the distance, it would have been something. Then for some reason Joseph thought of Peter Michael. He saw him standing there in the pub with the glass and his chin stuck out and he tearing at the Spaniards.

He felt mad of a sudden.

''S not right for him!' he said aloud, and having said it, walked across the bridge, his muddled thoughts deafening the hollow sound of his crossing. 'Peter Michael is no good,' he thought. Ever since Peter Michael had come to the city, there had been strikes and murmurings against things. 'What for? Why can't he let be? Men should be forcibly restrained,' Joseph thought, 'from stirring the filthy mud of today. Let things rest. Let our minds caress yesterday, when all men knew their places and stuck in them. The graceful living of acceptance. That's what made men live graciously. Not struggling against their lot. Peace of mind and quiet contentment. That was the way. Stir things up and you have wars and blood being shed and business put out of joint and passions loosened.'

He was across the bridge that went over the river before his eyes focused themselves in amazement on the sight before him.

He rubbed his hand across his eyes, closed them tightly and then opened them again, expecting to see what he had always seen, but it was blotted out. What he saw now rooted him to the ground and sent cold shivers feeling at his back.

It was no longer the big empty fish market he was looking at, with the two streets leading out of it. What he saw now was a forty-foot wall confronting him, set away back with a tower on his left and a great yawning portcullised gate. Right around the wall went until it swung right towards what Joseph had known as the decayed Spanish Arch. It was no longer decayed. It was built tall, and on the top of it the moon was glinting from helmets of pacing sentinels. He peered closely, hoping for the sake of his reason that it was the soldiers from Renmore Barracks on manoeuvres. It wasn't. He could see the moon glinting, too, from glittering weapons they carried on their shoulders. If that wasn't enough to convince him, what about the people who were forming in front of his eyes? And the carts? Yes, carts with horses, but not the carts he knew. These were big heavy things with solid wheels, as if they had been cut round from the trunks of wide trees. All the fish market was covered with upended carts and with stalls gaily covered with silks and bunting and the smell of spices and fish. People there roaring, 'Plaice, plaice, fresh plaice!' Not the Claddagh fishermen he knew, but funny-looking men with tangled beards and hair cut level across their foreheads like young girls in convent schools. Dressed queer, too, with trousers that stopped short at the knee and rough tunics of coarse undyed stuff tied to them with leather belts from which hung all sorts of things. On some, daggers. And around strolled men with curling whiskers under helmets, broad legs covered in different coloured stockings that left the shape of their legs to be seen all the way up the thigh. Short rounded britches caught there, and bulging out and slashed to show different colours. Over that, covering their chests, great things made of silver or tin or some damn thing and on their heads curved helmets. Swords at their waists.

Joseph felt like collapsing.

He heard talk then coming out of it and laughing, and the dark coloured men in the funny clothes were laughing the most, showing their teeth and gabbling. Foreign gabbling which Joseph had heard before. Where? 'Why,' he thought, 'from the Spanish sailors off the trawlers.' So these must be Spaniards, too. The place was thronged with people. Only the moon shone on them and lighted braziers on the top of the walls that cast a yellow light over them, and flaring torches stuck into containers on the stalls. Dazed, Joseph moved into the throng, towards the arch. People didn't get out of his way. He just seemed to be able to pass by them or through them, he didn't know. There were girls there in long dresses and gay silken shawls thrown over their shoulders. Girls at the stalls and girls leaning on the arms of the Spanish soldiers, laughing up at them saying, 'Yes, yes, is it?'

And then above the talk and the screams there came a clatter of horses' hooves on the cobbled ground. Joseph looked around him startled. He saw four horses almost on top of him, coal-black horses with froth on their lips and they pulling a great four-wheeled coach. A chap up on the front standing and roaring, 'Clear the way, clear the way!' And the carriage rocked by, barely avoiding killing half of the crowds. Angry men waving their fists at it and cursing. And as it flashed past, Joseph saw the arms painted on the sides, and from his knowledge he said, 'Why, these are the Blake arms.' And inside he saw a man sitting back with a pretty girl beside him, her eyes dancing, an oldish-looking man with a sort of black velvet cap and his sleeves of black velvet puffed out with red satin lining, and the buttons in front were glistening.

The carriage rattled on over the cobbles and went under the arch.

Joseph followed through the arch. Different. There were recesses in it. It was gloomy and there were figures here and there of men and women holding one another in a close embrace, unmoving. 'That hasn't changed anyhow,' Joseph thought, passing into what he knew as the Long Walk. Instead of the rotting hulks tied to the bollards, now he saw three towering ships with their backsides high in the air, and three masts on them with the sails furled around them. 'These are they,' he thought. 'These are Spanish ships, but what are they doing here?' There were lights on them and shouts coming from them, and the moon again glittered on the accoutrements of sentinels who walked their decks and shouted something in an unintelligible tongue. Then Joseph looked left.

Before this the Long Walk had been the narrow homes of people who were not very well off. Something had happened. All of them were moved farther back and they were taller and made of stone, and every second one of them had great noises coming from them, roaring and singing. The doors were wide, and from the street you had to go down into them by steps. He looked around fast again, as if somebody was playing a trick on him. He went to the river. It wasn't the same. The far bank was green grass. The Basin had disappeared and was covered with a collection of hovels, from which dull lights glowed.

Joseph moved with the current of people who were pressing all around him. He walked half-way along the Walk, and then turned down the steps of one of the houses. He went down cautiously, feeling the worn steps with his feet. It was a place with a low ceiling, with barrels and seats and men sitting at them, other men standing up all around, all sorts of men, and girls on their knees. A great clamour. The place was lighted by unevenly shaped candles guttering on thin iron brackets plugged into the whitewashed walls.

A big fat man like himself with a sort of a bag for an apron was shoving his way through the throng with his stomach and three tankards held in each hand, shouting, 'Make way there, make way there!' In the corner two Spanish soldiers were sitting at a box holding two girls on their knees. They were pretty girls. Young. You could see the tops of their breasts peeping above their low-cut blouses. One of them particularly took Joseph's eye. She was small and her face was round and her hair was black and curled around her face. She seemed to be struggling a little with the man who held her. They all seemed the same to Joseph, black men with whiskers curling up to meet their noses and their faces as black as their hair. He was saying something in his own tongue to her. She was turning her face away from him, saying, 'No, no, no.' Trying to get away she was, Joseph saw, but the man's arms were around her waist fastening her to his knees.

Then something was pressed into Joseph's hand. He looked at it. It was a tankard, a half pint one – not unlike what he had at home with a handle on it – of beaten metal. He raised it to his lips and tasted. It was wine. There was a sort of table in front of him and he left it down on that. On the table there was a round uneven coin of some sort. Joseph took it up to look. It was kind of black gold.

He pulled back hurriedly then as the place seemed to be invaded by a few young men with coarse tunics and unshaven faces and their eyes glittering. One of them brushed past Joseph and went towards the four in the corner. There was a silence in the place. The young man went to the young dark girl and reached for her with one hand and pulled her from the Spaniard, and then reached out with something else, and the next moment there was blood flowing from the Spaniard's face like water from a tap. There was silence for a short time and then pandemonium. The next moment the place was a seething mass of swaying figures with shouts and cursing, not much different to the cursing Joseph knew. Then there was steel flashing in the light and a great splurge of people being pushed up the stairs. Joseph went along with it, feeling his ribs caving in from the pushing. He smelled men around him, and the piercing shrieks of women rose over the din. He felt the cold night air on his face as they got into the street outside. It was just as bad there. There were sticks raised in the air and the sound of steel rubbing against steel. All as far as he could see, the whole Walk was a mass of swaying men, clearing circles with their swords, and the sight of cudgels rising and falling, and words roared in Irish and in English and Spanish. A clattering of hooves from the end of the arch and the sight of men on horseback laying about them indiscriminately with the flat of their swords, and then Joseph was brushed back further towards the river as the carriage of the Blake crest came back the way it had gone before.

The man on the inside was leaning out of the window, his face convulsed, urging the driver of the four horses to go on, go on, and the young girl with the dancing eyes was crouching in the back. The horses went through, knocking people left and right, and the last thing Joseph saw was the horsemen meeting the carriage, and then, overcome by a terrible pressure from the panic-stricken mob, he felt himself falling and the waters of the river closing over his head.

When he opened his eyes he was lying flat on the ground. Hard concrete was pressing into his chest and his face. He raised his head and looked around him.

It was coming bright, the bright that Joseph associated with the dawn. Slowly he raised himself to his feet. He saw that he had left a puddle where he had risen, and he felt his clothes. They were wet. He looked behind him. There was the river all right, just the same as he had always remembered it, and the steps up which he had dragged himself. He looked around. He was in the Long Walk all right, but it was the Long Walk he had always known. There was no sinner abroad, and behind him were hulks rotting by the side of the river.

'I must have been very drunk,' Joseph thought, 'and I fell into the river. How did I get out of the river?' he wondered. 'It was the luck of God that I came out. The luck of God who watches over drunken men. What's all this business I was dreaming?' he wondered. 'What does it all mean?' He shook his head then and sloppily made for home. 'My God,' he thought as he went, 'this is the worst thing that ever happened to me. It's better to be depressed than to be that drunk.'

Joseph would have disregarded the whole thing and would probably have become a total abstainer if something hadn't happened when he got home.

Taking off his clothes, a strange black coin fell out of his pocket, a worn black coin that could have been black gold, not with regular edges, with inscriptions impossible to read.

Joseph looked at that coin in his palm, and said, 'Holy Christ, it really happened to me, all that really happened to me!' He felt exhilarated. He changed into dry clothes after rubbing himself down. He boiled water in an electric kettle and made himself tea, and he sat there and thought and thought. Then he went down and he opened up the pub. He was impatient for them to come. Every morning, regularly at nine thirty in the morning, he could be sure of Jack Calder and Mike Tarpin and Peter Michael coming in for their pint. He waited in a fever of impatience for their coming. He paced backwards and forwards across the floor and left the counter and looked out the door and went back and looked out the window.

Eventually they came.

He drew their pints for them and his eyes were glittering. He placed the glasses on the counter and he said, 'For Christ's sake, listen will you, until I tell you what happened to me last night!'

They looked at his gleaming eyes and his pale face, and one after another they said, 'What in the name a God is up with yeh, Joseph?'

He told them, exactly as it happened. He described it for them in detail, and as a clashing finale he pulled the black coin out of his pocket and placed it before their eyes on the counter.

They looked at him and then at one another, and Mike expressed their feelings for them.

'Jaysus, Joseph,' he said, 'the rum must a been very strong last night.'

Joseph looked at them incredulously for a moment.

'Do you mean to say?' he asked then, 'that you don't believe me?'

'Ah, now look here, Joseph,' said Jack Calder.

'But wait, but wait until I show you,' said Joseph, and he left them and went upstairs and grabbed his wet clothes and brought them down and placed them on the counter himself under their noses. 'Look,' he shouted at them, 'feel, can't you. It's wet, isn't it? Can't you feel it?'

They felt it.

'You were in the river all right,' said Peter Michael.

'We'll take the water, Joseph,' said Mike laughing, 'but not the wine.'

Joseph glared at them. He could hardly get his breath. His big fists were clenched on the counter.

'Get out of here!' he said then, biting out the words.

They looked at him.

'Look, Joseph,' said Jack then, laying down his glass carefully, 'maybe you ought to go to bed. You might have got the fever.'

'We'll get the doctor for you, Joseph,' said Peter.

'Get out of here,' said Joseph, his voice a shrill screech. 'Get out of here, you dirty disbelieving sons of bitches! Get out of here! I don't want to see you any more! Any of you!' And to their great dismay, he reached behind him and grabbed a bottle and sent it flying past Peter Michael's head so that it smashed to smithereens on the other wall.

They went out like scalded cats.

They heard the crash of glass behind them and they saw him tearing at the counter with his hands and coming out and running for the door, so they scattered again and paused a little bit away as the big doors banged shut and they heard the bolt ramming home.

They looked at one another.

'We better get the doctor for him,' said Peter Michael.

'We better get the Guards, too,' said Mike, with a significant pursing of his lips. They turned up the street then, silent, with their foreheads frowning.

From the closed doors behind them came the noise of breaking glass, breaking and breaking. It went on for a long time.

Now, you can believe any of this, or you needn't, but if ever you go to the city, walk the length of its main street, and half-way down, some time or another, you will meet a man. He will be called Spanish Joe, and if he sees you looking at him with lifted eyebrows, he will come over to you and he will address you. He will say, 'Friend, I would like to tell you a story.' You will go with him into the nearest pub and you will order for him a pint of stout and another one and still another one after that, because the story is long and dry in the telling, but he will tell it to you just the way it's put down here. You will look closely at Spanish Joe, and you will try to see in that wasted figure with the red pockmarked nose the big man who was Joseph. He will be hard to see, apart from the clothes hanging loosely on what was once obviously a big frame. That is the evidence you have to go on. That, and the black coin he will show you and the evidently cultured way he speaks.

If you enquire abroad people will raise their eyebrows significantly and smile and so on, and you will see kids following him sometimes to shout 'Sí, sí, Señor,' until he turns and chases them away with colourful language. On closer investigation you will discover that he was undoubtedly at one time the owner of a public house and that he spent a short time in Ballinasloe Asylum. All that is true.

All towns have 'characters'. Spanish Joe is a 'character'. He tells his story well. He tells it very well and very fervently. He is not exactly a bum. After all, he gives value for money spent.

So there is only one thing left to decide. Is his story true?

Colm Comes to the City

COLM'S MOTHER DIED in the spring.

'The Lord have mercy on her,' the neighbours said, 'but she is small loss, the oul bitch, God forgive me!'

It was a small community that lived on the shores of the great Lough Corrib, compact, hidden in the folds of a valley, and they were all and all to each other on that account. The land was lush, and nearly every man had enough of it, so no man envied his neighbour – not much anyhow – and life was very pleasant and free if it wasn't for Colm's mother. A tall, big-boned woman she was, with a voice that would knock the rust off a three-legged pot, it was so coarse. It was impossible to ameliorate her. Her poor oul husband (a small frightened man with brown eyes) knocked one child out of her, Colm, and died shortly afterwards with hardly a word out of him, and everybody was very sad and said what a grand man he was and what a great ease it must be to him to be dead.

She was a hard-working woman, there's no doubt about that, but there wasn't a single soul in the village she hadn't blistered with her tongue. No living thing, a hen or a goat or an ass or a man, dared venture inside the walls of her domain, garden or pasture, for fear of the disgraceful things she could call down to the listening ears of the village about your ancestors' sins and your own sins. She would cast doubt on the certificates of birth of yourself and your children and your unborn grandchildren, and you daren't attack her physically since she was so tall and as strong as a four-year-old bullock.

Oh, a fearful woman indeed. Poor Colm. A nice lad indeed, with brown eyes like his father and the great strong build of his mother. But cowed. Saving your presence, he couldn't hardly pee without her knowing it. He daren't look the side of the road a girl was on in case she'd catch him, and the things she'd say out loud to and about that young girl! So here was Colm at the age of thirty-four, and he'd never even seen the sight of a girl's leg above the knee.

There was one girl, Delia Maloney, and we all knew he had an eye for her. A fine big girl that could give back chat with the best, and if Colm had only backed her, Delia would have bucked the oul wan. But devil a fear of him. A sight of his mother and he was off like a rabbit.

Then the mother died, in the spring.

Lookit . . .! Ah well, she's dead now, so let her rest. Amen to her and long may it be before her like grows again in the valley.

'Now,' said we all, 'Colm will up and marry Delia.'

He didn't.

He changed all right: whistling in the morning coming off the lake in his grey boat; singing out there, too, trolling his bait for the trout. A coarse voice it was, like a corncrake with the common cold, but it made your heart lift a bit to hear it. He came into the pub below of an evening now and sat on the half barrel and smoked his pipe, and there was a light in his eye. It was the light you may have sometime seen in the eyes of a yellow chaffinch that's freed from a cage.

So then the next thing we know is a morning in late July we see Colm heading out of the village dressed in a new blue suit and a pair of black new boots that you'd hear creaking over in Cong. That and a brand new bicycle. So we stop to chat about the weather and that, and then casually lead up to the enquiry, and he tells us.

'I'm off to the Galway Races,' says Colm. 'I have never been away from home, so I'm off to the races now for a solid week, so goodbye to ye and let ye throw a forkful of hay to the animals and a grain of meal to the hens.'

And the last we see of him then is the tail of his coat laid out on the breeze as himself and the bicycle went over the hill.

When he cleared the hill, Colm felt free. He was doing this queer thing now that he had wanted to do since he was a small lad and had heard men talking about the Galway Races. 'Maybe now,' he was thinking, 'this will free me from my mother at last and make me my own man.' He was uncomfortable when he thought of Delia, with the brown hair and the blue eyes. One night after his mother died he woke up and thought this: 'Suppose Delia turns out to be like my mother when I marry her?' That made him sweat. 'Is it nice Delia is? Well, me mother was nice one time, too. Long ago before she soured when she considered that God was turning his blind eye on her because she had been forced by matchmakers to marry a quiet man much older than her.' Colm knew that. But he thought, 'Just suppose Delia was to dominate me like me mother did. Wouldn't the colour go out of me life again? Wouldn't I be afraid? Wouldn't I lose the manhood that flowed back into me when I heard the soft sand raining on her coffin? God forgive me,' he thought then, and blessed himself.

It was a bright day. There was a blue sky with white clouds decorating the fringes of it. The bushes and trees were heavy with leaves and blossoms, and the birds were abroad in great strength.

He was free now like the birds. He was his own man. His suit was new and his heart was new, too, and he had twenty-five new pound notes in his pocket. 'What would me mother say if she knew I was after spending that much money in one slap?' He whistled and cycled and looked around him.

Forty miles to reach the city.

Dust on his blue suit.

He didn't care. The miles were so far shorter than the years, the futile years he had left behind him. He was looking forward to the city. He had never been any nearer to it than the red reflection of it that he saw sometimes when he was fishing on the lake at night and the air was clear.

He didn't go into the city unaccompanied. He cycled the long straight road leading to the city under the span of a railway bridge, and in front of him and behind him, cars and buses and lorries and side-cars and traps stretched away and slithered and honked and whinneyed, the jammed people in them dressed in gay clothes and cheering and laughing and calling and making his heart beat fast. It seemed to him that Ireland was vomiting vehicles and people into the maw of the city.

It took his breath away to be caught up in the great crowds in the crooked streets, crowds stretching from wall to wall, pedestrians oblivious to cursing, blaspheming drivers and sweating Guards trying to get impossible tangles of traffic moving. People with queer accents roaring, 'Race ca-a-rd, racing ca-a-rd!' waving coloured books under your nose. People buying them and arguing with red faces over their contents, their fingers pointing at names in them – of horses presumably.

It took him over half an hour to shoulder his way through to the great square where he had been directed by a Guard to look for a place to sleep. It was a weary pilgrimage, door to door on a long line of houses of the main streets, met by laughs or pity or hot-faced impatience by red-faced housewives, bulging with visitors. Colm shy and embarrassed but doggedly persevering under their taunts or sneers or hurried sympathy or directions to try Mrs So-and-So of such a street. On and on, until the feet of him were being burned by the hot pavements. And then in his thirtieth effort, he met with success.

Yes, she had a room, a small room at the back of the house. A window looking out to the lake. A smell of garbage from the back lanes. So unfamiliar to Colm. A small bed with a white quilt. Two other beds in the room and you washed in the backyard and had to answer a call of nature there, too. 'The bloody Urban Council. Easy known they don't have to trot out to their own backyard gettin' pneumonia. Two pounds for the night with dinner after the races and breakfast in the morning, roast lamb and parsley sauce and an egg and rasher and two sausages, and if you don't like it there's oney hundreds'll be glad to take it, and you can come in whatever time you like, the front door is never locked, just put your hand through the letter-box and pull out the key that's tied to a string and thanks for the money in advance because you never know, do you?'

So Colm paid and then went to the races.

It was too much for his mind to assimilate all at once. The four or five miles to Ballybrit, every inch of the way taken up with cars and carts and cyclists and pedestrians, all sweating under the hot sun. Colm went in a sort of a dray jammed like sardines with people, old people and young girls and middle-aged men with the smell of porter off them, all talking hotly about what would win the Plate, whatever that was. Into the course with the democrats. The stands were different, ten bob a skull. Dress in your best so that you might have a chance of appearing in a picture in the *Irish Press* or the *Independent*: 'Miss Loughatalia at the Races Yesterday.' This side, the long green fields with the common people. Most cheerful, pausing on the way in to be taken in by the shabby men with the three-card tricks; to give money to the singing beggars with dirty children held out in supplication, or a man with no legs on a small trolley and a notice, 'Shot Off In The War'. And the man standing up with his hand behind his ear, singing very tunefully: 'Like sunshine on the Wicklow Hills, You set my heart aglow. My bosom with sweet rapture thrills, Because I love you so.'

The milling multitudes lined the rails watching the parade of the horses. The lovely silk jackets of the jockeys in all sort of colours. The grand looking yoke of horses with the sheen on their coats, the proud tilt of their heads. Picking a horse by the look of him and timorously putting a shilling on him to win. Watching them going over the jumps, exhorted by the people. Your heart thumping to see your own horse up there in front. Then to see him falling, the bastard, but still excited as they came up the hill and headed for the stand. Oh great! You didn't know who won, but it didn't matter. Down then to the cool tents to drink a pint of porter and eat a ham sandwich, fresh ham between thick slices of bread and butter. Just smiling at people shyly and wandering down to the big jump, where countrymen sat in the shade of the bushes and talked in Irish. Soft lilting voices like the village at home in the evening when the sun was dying on the lake.

He came away into the mess of the end, tired and weary and surfeited with unaccustomed sights. Thinking as he went, 'Well, God now, wasn't it grand that I came! Haven't I enough thoughts now to keep me thinking for twenty years?'

Home to the house then and sitting at a kitchen table with seven others. All men. Horsey sort of men, who left him alone to his shyness. The language of them about this horse and that horse. The woman of the house visibly shrinking from their language. Saying nothing with her tight mouth, but with her eyes, 'Well, two pounds is two pounds, but won't I be grateful to God when it's all over.'

Into the streets after dinner. Getting late. The streets alive with carnival. All the public houses wide open and alive with people like flies around the decayed body of a dog. The hotels with windows wide and men and women sitting and hanging out of the windows, waving to friends below with their glasses. Side-cars with the horses pounding out to Salthill with 'Hurrooing' drinkers going out to the pubs there for a change of air. The bells on the horses' collars tinkling madly and musically. The places jammed with people as the night came down. The place in the square. All sorts of things. A big dancing tent with the soft music coming from it and the shadows of dancers big on the walls. The sight of grand girls with dresses sweeping the dust of the road and chaps in black coats and white scarves.

Behind that. What were they? Chair-o-plane things and swinging boats and wee cars that ran around with sparks coming out of them, bumping into one another. Tents where you saw a chap spinning a wheel and you bet money on the colours that would come up. Throwing rings over packets of cigarettes and half-crowns. And music blaring out of big mouths of things. Loud, awful loud and tinny music. And the lights everywhere and voices of people trying to talk above the din and the screaming of girls as they came down a long slide on a mat trying to hold their skirts over their thighs. Boy and girl, boy and girl, man and woman, young boy and young girl. That way all over. He felt lonely. Soft looks were flashed at him, but he was too shy to make anything of them. He just felt himself getting red to his shame and turning away. Feeling himself a big thick ignorant countryman.

He went over and forced his way into a pub, and he drank four pints in a row, one after another, just like that. It was terrible in the pub, the press of bodies, red faces and singing faces and cursing faces and the fug of porter and smoke all mixed. He came out, and the clothes were sticking to him with the sweat, but he felt better. He wasn't feeling as solid. He went into the square again. He tried his luck at this and that awkwardly. He stood at the bottom of the slide and he watched a girl coming down screaming. A girl with brown hair and a blue jersey, and her breasts were pushing against it jauntily, and she had a grey sort of skirt, and it was short, and she came down the slide and didn't try to keep it down. He saw her legs and the flash of what she was wearing underneath the skirt. Her mouth was open, screaming, and her teeth were shining.

He stood there grinning inanely.

She got off the slide and shrugged her way into a light coat with a belt. She went to walk past him, saw him grinning and his eyes on her. She passed him by, taking him in with her eyes, and then he heard her turn, and there she was standing in front of him.

'Hello,' she said, her hands in her pockets, her legs spread.

He swallowed, but the porter was strong in him.

'Hello,' he said right back at her, feeling himself getting red.

She was small and well built. Older now that she was near him than he had thought. Colour on her lips. Her eyebrows were black, different to her hair. It made her eyes gleam. She saw a big young man with clear sunburnt skin and light blue eyes, his muscles bulging his coat.

'I saw you up there,' he said, gesturing with his big hand.

She laughed.

'Great fun, isn't it?' she asked. 'Where are you from?'

He told her.

'I love the lake,' she said. 'I do go up the river sometimes in a boat, when I can get somebody to bring me. Did you oney come for the races?'

'That's all,' he said.

Then, a miracle, he found her walking around the show with him, her small hand resting on his arm.

'What's your name?' she asked him.

'Colm,' said he, 'me name is Colm.'

'Mine's Delia,' she said.

'Delia!' he wondered. 'Isn't that very quare now, that her name should be Delia, too?'

He went into the flying chairs with her and laughed as he kicked her seat ahead of him. He went into the bumping cars with her and was warm when he felt her little hand on his arm. He bought her tickets for sets of china. She didn't win them. He bought her tickets for other things. He fired pellets at targets and hit the bull every time. He told her about the wild duck in the lake, how you waited in the fields in the autumn evening when the corn was stacked. How they flew in to get the heads left in the stubble and how you met them with the shotgun. He told her about the frosty days in winter, how you waited in a camouflaged hideout to meet the wild geese. How they fell out of the sky.

She praised him with her eyes.

He fought his way into a pub for her, and held her by the hand and pulled her after him.

'What will you have?'

'I will have a gin and tonic,' said she.

Colm went for it.

'What's a gin?' he wondered. The pub in the village at home. Half barrels and bottled ale, and a few bottles of whiskey for a few who could afford it. That was all. 'So then,' thought Colm, 'I suppose this gin is what young ladies drink instead of lemonade when they have pioneer pledges.'

He went and sat beside her on a seat. He could feel the leg of her beside his own. She linked his arm and felt the muscles of him with her small hand. 'Oh, you're strong,' she said, and Colm laughed and had never felt better in all his life before. He felt her breath on his cheek. It was soft, like the breath you get on the cheek when you disturb a bird and he whirrs beside your ear.

'I should have come to the city long before this,' Colm thought. 'See all I have been missing, living out there in the great silence.' He looked into the pale blue eyes of Delia now, and if he had had the courage, he would have said to her, 'I love you, honest to God I do. Will you marry me and come to live with me in my cottage beside the lake?'

She talked about herself. She worked in a factory. Not just an ordinary factory girl, of course. She had a responsible position in charge of a department. The boss was in love with her, but she wasn't having any. Laugh. 'Tell me more about you. It must be wonderful to just have to fish on the lake for a living?'

'And don't forget there are fields, too,' Colm told her, 'and bogs and things like that. It's not easy.'

179

'What's the use then?' he thought after that. He tried to place this slim sophisticated girl in the bog, leading the ass loaded with turf, and it wouldn't come.

They drank some more and went back to the carnival again.

There was a church clock striking twelve midnight when they left. Imagine that?

Twelve. Never been up that late before even.

She brought him down the long winding street. She was holding his hand in her own, had it tucked under her own arm so that he could feel the warmth coming from her side.

Bathed in a rosy glow he was. His head as light as bog-cotton in a breeze. The streets gradually emptying themselves. Just here and there men standing up with their arms around one another singing, 'I'll take you home again, Kathleen, Across the ocean wild and wide.' Pausing in the middle of the song to clap a back and stagger. Doors opening and men being gently ejected, pausing lost outside to gather their wits about them. Doors here and there holding people clasped in an embrace, and all the time the side-cars with the jaded horses being whipped into a final spurt carrying the drunken revellers. Behind them the blaring music of the loud-speakers made pleasant with distance.

She took him to a turn off the main street and into a winding lane and across another main street and then into a street of tall warehouses where there were few lights and down a bit there was a large gate, and she pulled him in there into the gate and put his back against it and pressed herself into him and pulled his head down and glued her lips fiercely to her own. He could feel her breasts hard against the shirt of his chest, and he felt the palms of her hands shifting and moving over his chest, seeking the buttons of his shirt, opening them and exploring the hollows of his body.

Colm was lost, like a river that has been dammed for twenty years and finally breaks free. His lifetime of repressed fears and lonely silences wanted to express themselves all at once. Her lips were wet under his own. 'Strange,' the thought flashed across his mind. 'To look at her, her mouth seems so small. Like a perch,' he thought. You see the mouth of a perch. If you press a fingernail on his lower snout, the mouth opens wide, large enough to swallow a fish of its own size. He felt lost in her. He felt the hard roundness of her breast in his palm, the softness of her thighs against his own. The fulfilment for him of thirty-four years of living. A dream that wasn't a dream now, but a miraculously beautiful reality.

She gently but firmly pushed him away from her then.

His eyes were closed tight, even when she took her mouth away from his. His arms fell limply by his sides.

She reached back to look up at him, and then she went in to hug him, her hands on his chest.

Speaking into his chest.

Hoarsely, but how calmly, when Colm couldn't talk at all.

'It's the first time,' she was saying, 'I ever met someone like that that I could love in a second. You have soft clear skin like a woman. Your eyes around are white and clear. I never saw a man yet whose eyes hadn't the bloodshot in them. Your arms are as thick and strong as the trunk of a tree. I will see you tomorrow, maybe?'

It was a question.

Colm had to answer it.

'You will, please God,' he said, looking at her. The words barely came from his tightened throat. He wanted to tell her things. So many things. But how could he, he a man who had barely used the tongue God gave him except to grunt replies to his mother's ill humour or to make noises at animals? He hadn't the words to say it all. What this meant to him, a man who had been chained to solitude and dreams for thirty-four years, that here he was on a Galway street with his eyes open for the first time, and terrible deep emotions inside him struggling with one another for expression. So all he could say was to repeat, 'You will indeed, please God.'

'I will go home now,' said she then. 'Me father is very severe with me if I am out late at night.'

'It's the right thing, too,' said Colm, feeling that if he had charge of her he would lock himself away with her forever like a miser with a golden guinea.

He walked home with her to a house in the middle of a row of houses, poorly lighted houses, that didn't look poor houses to Colm at all. Could anything be poor that was housing an angel!

She said good night softly and leaned up on her toes (the gesture of an innocent child) and pecked him on the cheek. She stood there with her hand on the latch of the door and her eyes misty.

'Let you walk off down the street now,' she said. 'I want to take the image of you to bed with me, until tomorrow.'

Until tomorrow.

Colm turned silently and walked away, conscious of her eyes on his back. She waited until he became small with distance and until a turn of the street took him from her sight, and then she removed her hand from the latch, turned away, went farther up the street, cut off through an intersection and down another street, and taking a key from the pocket of her coat went in a door. Met by the growling of a drunken man, bending over the fire.

'Ah, go to hell, you,' she said. 'If you can be out, I can too.'

Colm walked up the streets of the city and he felt as if he was walking on clouds. 'It's all Fate,' he was saying to himself. 'All this. That my mother should have died and I should have come to the Galway Races. Up there in His heaven, God had it all fixed up in a little book.'

It took him into his own digs and upstairs to his room, and it sat beside him while he took off his boots and then his coat, and then while he reached into the inside pocket of his coat so that he could take his money and put it under the pillow, because there would be other men sleeping in the room later, and for all that he had the caution of a countryman.

The money wasn't there at all. The money was gone.

It took a long time before it dawned on Colm what had happened to his money. It took a long and bitter time while the fumes of the love and drink waned and died and left his head as clear as it would ever be.

Something inside Colm crumbled then and decayed and died, never to suffer rebirth. He sat on the edge of that bed for a long time, deliberately allowing the hurt to eat into every single bit of him, and then, big man and all as he was, and thirty-four years old and all, he sank his face into the pillow of the bed and let himself be overcome.

It lasted a long time, all that.

A long time. Thirty-four more years, say.

Then he put on his boots again, and he put on his coat again, and he gathered his few belongings and went down the stairs and opened the back door into the yard, and he got out his bicycle, and he got into the lane at the back smelling sour with garbage, and he went out of the lane and got into the main street, and he cycled along it blindly, deaf to the music that was there and the loud yahoos of people in his ears, and he went down the street and headed for the railway arch where he had come in that morning. Only that morning?

Of many things he thought, but not clearly.

When the morning was chasing the dawn, he came to the hill over the village, and he looked down and he saw the lake spreading palely and eternally at his feet, and he saw the white of his own house rising over the hedge of the blackthorn bushes.

The bicycle brought him down of its own accord, almost to his own door, and he bent and got the key from under the stone, and he opened the door and went in. The kitchen was still warm from the raked turf coals. He left the front door open and saw the light growing outside, and he went to the window at the back and saw the sun rising redly out of the lake. He surveyed his kitchen, and it seemed to him a very friendly place indeed, so he got on his knees in front of the open hearth and started to separate the ashes from the still-live coals.

'Oh God, it's good to be home,' Colm thought. 'Oh God, it's good to be alone, at home!'

The City

ALMOST INVISIBLY AGAINST the background of the white-cloud-studded sky, the young gull rose from his rocky home in the centre of the great expanse of Corrib water, rose jerkily and breezily, a little ungraceful yet as his immature wings caught and held the air, propelling him ever upwards.

He screamed shrilly as his wings found the feel of the air and used it, and then he ran his body along the river of a current, zooming out of it triumphantly and turning his head downwards again to skim the gentle waves of the water, casually stirred by the summer breeze of an early morning.

He rose again then, high up in the air, where he hovered, as if he was suspended from heaven by invisible wires, and paused there to regard the world below him.

He could see his own small home, a few jumbled rocks holding pebbles in their hollows and a rib or two of grass stoutly defying all their enemies, the black rocks whitened like the outside of a cottage by the droppings of the nesting gulls; this bleak home so different to the hundreds of islands below him, with the grass very green, and most of them tree-clad like maiden ladies with long skirts. All these islands he could see from his great height, and the big lake glinting in the hidden sunshine, a lake that stretched away behind him until it met the black bulk of the shadowed mountains of Connemara, standing at the head of the lake as if to say, 'Thus

185

far you come and no further.' And along one side, the foothills of the mountains ringed the lake, and on the other side there was a great plain with evenly divided fields and crops ripening in them, and on the other side still there were woods and long fields sloping to the water and townships camouflaged by woods and the ruins of monasteries and churches, very old and crumbling beneath the weight of time.

And then there was the river.

He could see away where the lake poured itself into the river, its bottled bulk tumbling through the narrows into another wide barren stretch of water, and then the river again, and away at the end of the river this time there was a hint of another gigantic stretch of water that couldn't be a lake because it glinted green, and a lot of dusky smoke like brown clouds was rising from somewhere in the valley.

Probably because he was young and adventuresome and had just left the tender care of his mother, the young gull suddenly swung away and swept widely over the lake towards the place where the mouth of the river lay. Fast he went and joyously and sprightly because he was young and there was little need to conserve his strength.

His bright little far-seeing eyes were fixed before him, at the rib-boned river and the green water that lay miles at the end of it. As he came near the mouth of the narrows, if he had looked he would have seen a village hidden in the folds of the hills. Clustered cottages with the white walls glittering and the yellow thatch of their roofs golden in the brightness. He might have swooped down over this village had he wished and seen the tall young man that was Colm, pushing his grey boat on to the waters of the lake for his morning fishing, and farther on past the narrows, he might have come down a little to investigate the one island where the brown dots that were goats darted from rock to rock and cropped the green shoots and looked warily over their shoulders in case there might have been a sign of John Willie chasing them.

But the eyes of the seagull were fixed on the sea, and his slim white body followed his eyes.

He sheered away, frightened, as he saw the sprawling city below him swallowing the river. Such an unfamiliar jumble was beyond his comprehension, so he swung north and approached the sea over the grey roads leading into the countryside.

He cleared the land and came over the sea in wonder. The sight of it was unfamiliar and the colour and the taste and smell of it that came up to meet his beak. It was a boxed-in bay he saw, its mouth stopped up by the Aran Islands that stretched themselves protectingly across it, their western ends heaped up into tall cliffs to take the batterings of the Atlantic waves. And on the other side of the bay a long range of hills was stretched, barren hills of granite rocks where even the grass refused to grow. So unlike the lake, the sea. No bottom to be seen, except down the middle where the earth shelved up and a few rocks came forth and floating brown weeds swung away from them. And near the end of the bay there was a white house that looked like a ship, and black boats with brown sails that floated along. So unfamiliar to the eyes of the lake gull who was used to small short grey boats with the things sticking out of the sides of them and bending bodies jerking the things at the water to make the boat go.

He came down from his heights now, ready to swing over the black boat to give it a closer look, but as he dived, circling gulls, enormous ones with red beaks and black backs, rose up to meet him, crying shrilly at this impudent invasion of their domain, so the gull rose sharply again and passed the boat without another look.

He might have looked at the boat. It could have been *The Black Swan*, and he might have seen the old man with the white hair and his gnarled hands tight on the tiller.

But he passed on and headed where this time the sea was pouring itself into the city, and chose the city as the lesser of two evils.

The size of it surprised him.

Cranes rising into the sky and big black gates holding water above its natural level and big ugly red and black boats with smoke pouring from their bellies. And buildings that were sheds and men walking and horses and carts being loaded. These things were familiar enough. He had seen men before and horses and carts. He swung away from the docks and went over the river where it went tumbling into the sea. He looked the length of it and he could see that it divided the city nearly in two and that bridges ran across it three times to join up the roads on either side. If he had paused to look to his right, he might have noticed the small houses beyond the arch where Spanish Joe had been created from a respectable citizen. But he flew ahead, and rose high at the sight of the tall church spires. He chose the one on his right and flew towards a squat one with a round white face on the front of it, bisected by two black hands. He landed on the tip-top of this and rested.

He was near now and he could see the winding street of the city below him, a narrow street, with thin footpaths on either side of it, and it nearly jammed with the cars that went and the cars that came, simple traffic that looked complicated in the narrow street. He took off and followed the street, over the heads of the people and the horses and the carts and the asses, and the funny smell of petrol came up to him and rubber and the sun striking on stone and slate. Up the street he flew until shortly it opened out into a wide square, a plot of green grass surrounded by railings, and all around that again, tall houses and short houses and hotels in most disorderly array. If it had been the proper time he might have seen the carnival in the square or he might have seen the fair of the horses and he might have seen the policeman Sean Martin and Big Peadar the tinker face to furious face, with the big sergeant hovering behind them.

But it was the wrong time, so he swung widely again and came back along the main street. On either side of the street, he could see side streets stretching out in an order that was more apparent from his position. He could see the red brick building that was the police barracks and the docks down on his left and the several churches, four on this side of the river, where the people got rid of their sins when they sinned, which was often, because they were only poor, weak mortals like any other people. But he crossed the river and followed the main street. It wound into more side streets and past more churches and rows of houses with their doors opening on to the footpaths, a warren of streets built up around the church with the slender spire. If he had paused here for a time and come down to investigate the small figures playing there, or leaning against the walls, or pelting one another with cabbage stalks, he might have met Jimjoe or seen Bill slouching along and looking curiously at the Boogie Man.

If he could have seen into the church of the slender spire, he might have had a glimpse of Pugnug, assing in the sacristy, but he couldn't, and by this time he was a little sick of this city. It meant nothing to him. That it was nearly as old as his ancestors didn't mean anything to him. That it was known as the City of the Tribes, on account of the thirteen tribes that had more or less owned it, meant nothing to him. That it had been stormed and blood-bathed by Irish and Norsemen, Danes, Normans and Cromwellians meant nothing to him.

So he rose up and turned his back on Galway, like many more before him. It didn't matter to him if it was teeming with life and drama and suffering and poverty and wealth.

He preferred fish.

It didn't matter to him if the citizens were born or died, robbed or worked, sang or jeered, whored, swore or prayed.

He preferred the aroma of the bog myrtle to the stench of man.

It didn't matter to him if the air was warm and the sands of the sea-shore were silver, that the buildings were old and ugly and that twenty thousand people worked out their span there, beggars or boys, priests or policemen, tinkers or toilers, pub-keepers or pariahs, deputies or dunces, good, bad or indifferent. Pagans, papists or peddlers, it was all one to him.

He preferred to sweep low over the waters of the lake and scoop the delicate mayfly into his mouth.

It didn't matter to him if it was a sleepy town, good-living or bad-living, nor that it took nineteen thousand citizens to keep the other thousand living luxuriously, because they were too indolent for revolutions.

He preferred to get back to the freedom of the lake and the clear air.

So he rose from his spire and winged towards the river, passing over another church on his way, where he might have paused to see the long funeral procession that was the last tribute to Dad or the sparse one that was a credit to Bridey Corcoran. He might have turned left a little and seen the shallow basin of stagnant water and the green grass that cradled the bare feet of Mary Ann. But he just flew on, pausing at the Salmon Weir Bridge for a moment to look hungrily at the jammed salmon swaying in the river, and then seeing the lake in the far distance, he headed for it joyously with a cry.

Behind him the city rested, heavy with its tales.

An Act of Charity

I AM AN HONEST man.

I am also a just man who is seeking justice – if it is to be found. I am setting it all out here for you so that you can come to a decision, and I have no doubt that you will be outraged at the injustice perpetrated on me.

I own a four-storey premises near the bridge, a good solid house. On the first floor I have my licensed premises which I conduct with absolute honesty. Malicious people claim that the back of the premises leads to so many crooked lanes and turns that the police can never catch people drinking in my premises after hours. Facts speak for themselves. I have never been convicted for selling drink after hours, but I'm telling you what they say to show the lengths people will go to blacken the fair name of a decent man.

We keep lodgers, generally four or five, but I admit we pack them in fairly closely at festival seasons. My wife conducts this part of the operation. We don't keep a maid. You couldn't trust one of them; their wages are too high, and they'd steal the milk out of your tea. No, my wife is an active, hard-working woman, and since she never had any children anyhow, she can easily cope with a few lodgers. I have never chided my wife on our lack of children. This is another lie! Like most men, I get drunk once or twice a year and I say things in my cups – like most men – but it is only the evil-minded who pay attention to what a man says when he is not himself.

I think that clears the air, takes care of the lies, and gives you my background.

The trouble arose when I decided to get the outside of my premises painted.

I didn't see the need for this, but everybody in the town seems to be gone paint-mad. Good weathered stone or grey cement was good enough for our fathers, but it's not good enough for us. No! You look at the town now. It's painted like a rainbow.

You have to move with the times. People were complaining a bit about the look of my place. They can't see that, with a pub, it is *atmosphere* that counts. I had to tidy up inside. They were even complaining about sitting on barrels! You see? The place was dark and gloomy, but that made it cosy and charming, I thought. When I lost a few customers to the bright places (they were no good anyhow, came from bad stock, and I was better off without them), I had to do something. If you can't educate people you have to go along with them, even if it's going down you are. So I smartened up inside with a new counter, shelves and stools. It looked brighter, if that's what they want, and God knows it should with what the robbers charged to put in a few pieces of timber, a lick of paint, etc.

One thing leads to another. With the inside bright, the outside drew comments, so it would have to be done, and I asked for an estimate from the painter. Well, look, if they were going to do the whole place over in gold leaf and use raw diamonds for window-panes, it couldn't have been dearer.

I went to him, of course.

'Roger,' I said, 'I don't want my place gold-plated. I just want it painted in good oil paint. Is it so much to ask? You seem to have made a four hundred per cent mistake in this estimate.'

This seemed to annoy him.

'Mr Manton,' he said, 'we all know you are a man who looks four times on each side of a halfpenny before parting with it, so I pared that estimate so low that all the profit I will get out of it is the empty paint tins if I can sell them afterwards to a tinker.'

'If that's paring,' I said, 'your toenails must be long. If I bought the paint and brushes myself, I could get the job done for one-tenth the price.'

'Do that!' he said. 'Do that!' He was red in the face; he was always a fiery man, easily roused. 'Do it yourself, if you can borrow a ladder in the country that will hold you.' This wasn't a kind remark as I am a man of robust build. In my youth I was good on the sports field throwing the weight, etc., and in later life good athletes are inclined to get a little weighty.

'Just for that remark,' I said, 'you have lost yourself a contract.'

'Thank God!' he said. 'Thank God!'

'In fact,' I said, 'I will get the job done myself and let you see the bill of costs afterwards – just to show you.'

'Do that,' he said; 'please do that, and tell me the date so that I can come and watch the work. I need a laugh.'

I left him, of course, because you cannot argue reasonably with men like that. I wonder he is successful in business. It won't last.

Now you see the dilemma I was in, and this was where the act of charity came in.

I could easily have gone to another painting contractor and got a more reasonable estimate, but I decided that charity came before self, and I knew that Mike Ireland and Gosling could do with a few shillings and a few free drinks. They were frequently in my place. Mike had a pension which he got from the British for being in their army in an early war and getting gassed. He regarded pints of stout as the only real cure for his lungs, and who can say that he wasn't right. Doctors don't know everything, and you'd want gold dust just to pay them for a single visit. Gosling is a strong, able-bodied boy, a bit weak in the head, but an amiable youth who doesn't talk back to his betters like some we all know nowadays.

So I surprised them this night by laying two free pints on the counter. Their credit was exhausted. I believe in being decent to people by not letting them owe me money. Owing money is the curse of modern life. Early on there were a few men who owed me money and died. I never recovered the debt, and I often thought with pity of their agony in the next world, swept out of life unable to pay their just debts. Their horrible sufferings on the other side of the grave – a terrible thought – hardened me in my resolve to save further souls' suffering, etc.

'Are you going weak in the head, Jonjo?' Mike asked, staring. He has a sort of a sense of humour.

Gosling just said, 'Jay!' and swallowed the porter very fast.

'Mike,' I said, 'I have heard that you did some painting in your time.'

'That's true,' said Mike. 'In early times I was noted for my landscapes. I'd have been hung in the Academy if it wasn't for the mustard.' He swallowed half the fluid.

'I don't mean genteel stuff,' I said. 'I have been thinking. Here you are with two weeks to wait before your pension day, and here I want a bit of painting done on the outside of the premises, and I thought, why shouldn't I give you and Gosling a little money for the work?'

'You mean real painting with brushes and ladders?' he asked. He was a bit dismayed.

'You could send Gosling up with the tin and the brush,' I said, 'and you hold on to the ladder.'

'You begin to interest me,' said Mike. 'Gosling, you have done some painting in your time?'

'I ha',' said Gosling. Gosling wore very tattered old hand-me-downs. 'I done whitewash. Do' know where. Burned me hand.'

'You see,' I said. 'There's nothing to it. First an undercoat, after brushing the wall. Then good oil paint. Take a few days. I'll look after you well. I'll show that Roger how easy it is.'

'You will provide meals and refreshment at difficult times, Jonjo?' Mike asked.

'Certainly,' I said. 'You won't go hungry and you won't go thirsty. You will find me generous.' I would, of course, deduct the price of the food from whatever sum I gave them in remuneration. It wouldn't be charitable to give these boozers too much actual money. We all knew where it would go – down the red lane.

'We will take the contract,' said Mike, holding up the empty glass, 'and we will seal it with another fill.'

'I will have everything ready for next week,' I said, pleased.

I tried to rent a tall ladder, but found the price they asked was outrageous, and was inspired with the thought that the priest had a good expanding ladder in the church, so I went along and borrowed it from him. After all, I support the church. I bang a shilling on that plate every Sunday morning, which is more than a lot of wealthy men in this town do, I can tell you, so he should have been pleased to loan it to me. 'I hope you make better use of it to get to Heaven, Jonjo,' he said. Not understanding this obscure remark, I laughed heartily, as it must be a joke. I got five or six schoolboys to bring the ladder to my place. These kids would do anything for a threepenny bit.

I bought the tins of paint and the brushes. The man here was unmannerly. He didn't like the colour I chose, if you please! It was a kind of red-pink. I thought it would look well; make the premises stand out. It was the colour of my dear dead mother's geraniums. When you do these things, it is better to do them well, etc.

Things went well with us, at first.

It was April and the weather was nice and dry. Gosling was active on the ladder, I must say – a bit like a monkey. He brushed down the wall with the wire brush we had for cleaning the range, and he got the undercoat on very nicely. This took nearly a week. Mike held and shifted the ladder very well, but he had a terrible thirst. I went across the road frequently to view the work in progress. It gives a good impression to the citizens to see a man looking at his premises being painted, chatting to one and all, etc. Of course there were a few complaints that our ladder was taking up a lot of the main road, creating a bit of a bottle-neck near the bridge, so that sometimes there were long lines of cars and lorries held up, honking impatiently. I felt it my duty to address a few words of reproof to these people about their manners, but in the main all were favourable to the project.

Until this day, which was a Saturday and, being market day in the town, very busy. Gosling was applying the final coat of paint right at the top of the building, so the ladder was well out on the road and there was a bit of a traffic jam. Mike held the bottom of the ladder well and had three tins of paint ready for Gosling to use when the one he had was exhausted. It was a busy scene I viewed from across the road. I thought they shouldn't let lorries or horses-and-carts or asses-and-carts on the main streets of towns in this day and age. I said this to some of the cart drivers: why wouldn't they go by the back streets and not hold up the business of a city? Their replies were obscene, I'm afraid, and if I could have got near to them, I would have taught them manners, but didn't like to lose my dignity.

Then some of these lounging, lazy-wall fellows who wouldn't work in convulsions were passing by, and they started to jeer at Mike, pretending to faint, etc., at the sight of him working, and they called up rude things to Gosling on top of the ladder, causing him to look down and sway a bit with anger. I admit it was only the friendly baiting of a couple of morons, but this was hardly the hour or the place for it, and besides it was on my time. I was about to cross the street through all the stalled traffic when Mike reacted unfavourably to their funning. He swung a full tin of paint at them, cursing indecently, I thought. There was only a wire handle on the tin, which parted, and the can flew through the air and sprayed the geranium paint on a few cars.

Immediately there was uproar. You'd think the cars were sprayed with acid. Mike's antagonist became indignant, clouted him and knocked him down. Mike rose with another tin of paint and threw it at him. This went over his head as he ducked, and indignant drivers who had emerged to examine the paint on their cars now got a few drops of paint on their clothes as well.

This led to terrible scuffling and yelling. For myself I saw that the ladder with Gosling on top of it was beginning to fall. Gosling let go his tin as he grabbed for the ladder. It was not my fault that it fell on the policeman who was coming up to try and sort out the tangle. I was engaged on a humanitarian act – *I was trying to save Gosling's life!* I forced my way across. Maybe I had to hit a few people, but I was only brushing by. I reached the opposite side, and as the ladder fell I kind of deflected it. This changed its direction and it went out over the street. It did land on top of a car and crushed it a little, but I had managed to save Gosling from death. He only broke a leg.

This is what infuriated me. After this heroic action, Willie Healy gets out of the car, red-faced. I admit it had a bit of paint on it and the roof was crushed a little, but what are insurance companies for?

'Jonjo Etcetera!' he shouted at me in an ill-bred manner. 'You lousy . . .' (You will have to imagine the dreadful language!) 'Look what you have done to my car, you overgrown beetle! You water-in-the-whiskey fornicant! You bloated hypocrite!'

You will agree I had to react to language like that, but I was polite. I merely said it was far from motors that he was dragged up, since his mother was a tinker and only God knew his father. I insist that my language all through was temperate. I had to hit him. Will any man of honour listen peacefully to the things he said to me? Not only that but he hit me back. There in the court I had a black eye and a swollen nose to prove it.

The whole place was in confusion by this anyhow. How could anybody know clearly what was happening? It took them hours to sort out the terrible mix-up.

But why was I made the villain?

Is there any way that magistrates can be indicted for maligning honest men in a court of law? My language was *not* vile! My own wife testified in open court, on oath, that she didn't notice any difference in my language to normal. Why shouldn't the evidence of a decent woman convince him?

I was put down for everything. It was the most disgraceful miscarriage of justice in the history of the world! Motorists are billing me for oil paint on their cars and clothes. Gosling is claiming money for injury under the Workmen's Compensation Act, whatever that is. And here is my premises, one third geranium coloured paint and the rest the colour of a dog with the mange. Who will compensate me for this? Now none of the painters will come and finish the job for me at any price. They are all too busy, they say. Too busy! I know that Roger is avoiding me. I know he is laughing at me. If I wasn't bound to the peace, I'd seek him out and teach him a lesson.

You, sir, are a barrister-at-law, a senior counsel. I know you are the best high lawyer in the country. That is why I want you to come and defend me against all those people, all those lies. You will see for yourself that I am completely innocent, and I know you will be burning with indignation, because as you see the whole business arose from an *act of charity*. I want you to go into open court and reverse the decisions of that magistrate, who is a cretin and appointed through politics. You will now know that I am a poor man after all the claims laid against me, so I am sure you will keep your fees temperate.

I know you will get justice for me, and I tell you now, as long as I live, I'll never commit another act of charity.

Pugnug

P UGNUG AT THE tender age of ten.
In the sacristy of the church after last mass. The most disgraceful day in the annals of the altar boys. To be held up as a
horrific example for evermore to the generations who followed
him. A long cool room with windows looking out on flowers and
green playing fields. Tall presses holding the soutanes and surplices
of the boys, black for every day, red for Sunday, and the other small
cupboard for the sand shoes so that you walked silently on the
polished tiles of the altar. Some days if you hadn't the sand shoes,
just your own ordinary hobnail boots, you sounded like the advance
of an infantry regiment, disturbing people from their prayers,
causing the frown to come on the concentrated face of the priest
saying mass.

A nice place the sacristy, where you could relax after being so
good, with your hands joined and your hair brushed and remem-
bering not to be daydreaming or picking your nose and to strike
the gong decorously at the right time, instead of hammering it like
a blacksmith's anvil at the elevation. Here, when the priests had
departed and the sacristan, you could have a little run about,
special little games that could be played all around the beautifully
polished table with the carved legs. Here, in the smell of flowers
and the smell of incense and all that, a sort of cowed playing, since

you were so near the holy altar you kept your shouts down to hoarse whispers and your laughs down to croaks.

Like now.

Pugnug was saying mass.

It was funny and it was horrifying at the same time. He had dressed himself carefully in the holy vestments of the priests where they were laid out there, every one of them, and he looked funny. There was no doubt about that, because Pugnug wasn't tall. He was fairly tall for his age, but on the thin side and his shoulders sloped a bit, and the green chasuble he was wearing came down behind him resting on the floor. And sticking out of that at the top was Pugnug's head, a red carrotty-coloured head with the hair standing up on it. Pugnug's hair was like that, like the stubble on an oat field after the oats are cut.

His eyes were green in colour then, and he had a narrow chin and high cheek-bones, and his nose was definitely pug, just as if somebody had put a palm against it and pushed the day he was born and it had never recovered.

He was going through all the motions after the elevation part. Not even Pugnug, with all his nerve, went that far. He started off under the presumption that that part was over. And although the chalice was there in front of him, he refrained from putting his hand on it. He didn't go that far. Just on the dare, he had proceeded to garb himself in the priest's vestments. All starting from that. Tom Martin and Jay Finnegan and Whopper Maloney had started it, talking about the fellow seven years ago who had been sacked for just the same thing. Neck and crop, out in disgrace, but preening himself; it proved him a bit of a devil. And afterwards, if he had never done anything else of note in his whole life, he would be remembered as the boy who had dared and had been sacked.

It was Pugnug's air of devotion that was getting them.

The funny part had been to see him putting on the big white alb and tying it with the cincture, a white tassellated cord, and then

the stole and over that the chasuble. It was very funny, each one at
a time, although it had been a work up, and behind in the backs of
their minds they had never thought Pugnug would dare, and when
he did dare they had expected him at least to be struck down by a
bolt from heaven at his audacity. It was as funny as seeing a fellow
dress in his sister's clothes or his father's trousers, that kind of mirth,
only this was tinged with a touch of fear, and there was more than
a hint of hysteria in the laugh. That he should have dressed up and
given them the laugh was enough. He should have discarded the
clothes then in a hurry for fear anyone would come, or to placate
an angry God who would take a poor view of this sort of thing.

But Pugnug went on.

'My God, Pugnug,' said Whopper in a wheeze now, his ears
sticking out from his head listening for noises in the corridor.
'That'll do now!'

'Lay off, Pugnug,' said Jay. 'You'll be caught, so you will!'

'And we'll be caught with 'm,' said Tom Martin, 'and that's the
trouble.'

'Dominus vobiscum,' said Pugnug, turning and opening his
joined hands.

They looked at one another and their eyes were frightened. Tom
Martin was the biggest, on the point of getting out of short trousers.
Jay was small and seemed to be all eyes under a mop of black hair,
and Whopper was fat. His knees were big and red and his wrists
were big where they grew out of his coat.

'Lookit, Pugnug,' said Tom. 'We're not goin' to stay here. We're
goin'. D'yeh hear, we're goin'?'

'Jay,' said Jay, 'if anyone comes we'll be crucified, so we will!'

'I'm not waitin' any longer,' said Whopper, sidling to the door.

'Benedicat vos Dominus, omnipotens Deus, Pater, et Filius et
Spiritus Sanctus,' said Pugnug turning and blessing them with a
thin hand and the voluminous sleeves slipping over his jerseyed
arms, 'ye pack a cowards ye!' Then he turned and moved over to

the other edge of the vesting table, signing his lips with the cross and saying, 'Initiu in Sancti Evangelii Secundum Joannem.'

Tom Martin, moving towards the door, felt his stomach turning to water and at the same time thought that it was the fervent way that Pugnug was doing it that frightened you. You had to admit that Pugnug was a good actor. That made it worse in a way, because it seemed as if Pugnug was really saying mass. He didn't wait to think anymore. He skirted the table and headed for the door with little Jay after him. Whopper was there before them, with his hand reaching for the knob, when it turned and the three of them fell back and the priest came in.

First he was smiling.

'Well, boys,' he said, 'not gone home to breakfast yet?'

Then he studied their petrified faces and the smile went away. The three pairs of eyes were glued on his own with patent terror. He looked and then heard a mumble to the side of him and turned his head. The three boys saw him stiffening, and then all you could hear was the sort of whimper that Jay emitted.

Pugnug sensed the silence then and turned.

'What's . . .' he began, before he saw the priest.

The three boys looking at his face saw it first flame as red as the colour of his hair and then saw the red ebbing out of it to leave it as pale as the whites of his eyes. The priest moved towards him and stood in front of him and looked at him awfully. He was a tall priest and up to that they had all liked him because he was quiet and didn't shout at you after mass if you had forgotten some of the responses or were late with a gong, or were sunk in a day-dream and had to be hissed at to go up and bring the last wines.

Pugnug saw the muscles at the side of his cheeks working, and he saw the skin tightening across the bridge of his nose, and he saw terrible things in his eyes, and he felt a tremble in his own legs. The priest didn't say anything for some time and when he managed to speak, his voice was low and very controlled.

'Take them off,' was what he said.

Pugnug proceeded to do so, under the gaze of those eyes, a very hard business because his thin hands were shaking and his stomach seemed to be caving in and suddenly his fingers seemed to be all thumbs, but he worked hard and he got them off and folded them neatly and put them back exactly as they had been before he had touched them. Then he stood up there, in his dark blue jersey and his small pants that were short for him and showed a lot of his thin leg above the bony and scarred knees, with his hands by his side and the priest still watching him.

'Do you know what you have done?' the priest asked in a low tight voice. 'Do these boys . . .' turning back to the others, but they weren't there anymore. There was just a blank space at the door. Pugnug had a vision of them scuttling down the long linoleum-covered passage as if the devil was after them. The priest turned back to him again.

'I,' said Pugnug, finding he had to clear his throat. 'I . . .'

'You little vandal!' said the priest, and he brought up a narrow hand and hit Pugnug on the right cheek. Pugnug staggered. 'You will leave this sacristy now, and you will never come back here again. Go, before I lose my temper with you!'

Pugnug walked slowly to the door, but he paused there and turned back.

'I didn't mean any harm, Father,' he said from there in a hoarse voice. 'I like being a server.'

The priest looked at the green eyes firmly fixed on him, and he saw the marks of his fingers on the pale face.

'You have forfeited the right to be a server,' he said. 'No boy could do what you have done unless he were a sacrilegious lout. Get out now, boy, and don't come back!'

Pugnug closed the door and walked down the long corridor with his head low. 'I didn't mean it,' he thought. 'Even though it was a joke, it wasn't just for fun. It just shows you how I learned how to say mass. I nearly know it off by heart.' Then, he thought, 'Never again to be on the privileged side of the altar, to hit the gong with the paddle stick or swing the thurifer with the pungent and exotic smell of the burning charcoal covered with incense. To dress yourself in the long soutane and cover that with the lace-frilled surplice. And to be inside the rails, feeling superior to all the other chaps who weren't servers.'

It brought him into the air outside the door, and he felt very despondent.

Then he thought about Tom Martin and Whopper and Jay. 'The way they stuck by me,' he thought bitterly. 'The way the dirty cowards ran out on me!'

Then he started to run to the gate of the church. 'I'll murder the dirty bees when I catch them,' he promised through clenched teeth. 'I'll murder them.' He ran and ran, and then he slowed his gait considerably as he thought, 'What in the name a God will I tell me mother?'

Pugnug sighed.

'It's a hard life,' he said aloud as he turned up the lane to home kicking at a stone.

Pugnug at the less tender age of twelve.

Nightime in the streets. These ones shaped like a hollow T. A row of houses along and a row facing them broken in the middle by another double row of houses leading off, the whole lighted by a tall electric standard in the centre of the complex. Pugnug and the boys at one gable end, conducting their games in a suspiciously loud tone of voice.

'The priest of the parish lost his considerin' cap,' chants Pugnug. 'Some say this and some say that and some say that it was Blue Cap took it.'

'Was it me, sir?' asks Tom Martin, having to come in quickly, since everyone had a different coloured cap name for recognition, and if you didn't answer quickly you were slapped hard on the head by a stick wielded vigorously by the 'parish priest'.

'Yes, you, sir,' says Pugnug.

'You're a liar, sir.'

'Who then, sir?'

'Red Cap, himself, sir.'

'Was it me, sir?' asks little Jay, two years scarcely seeming to have made any difference to the smallness of him and the bigness of his eyes and the blackness of his hair.

'Yes, you, sir,'

'You're a liar, sir.'

'Who then, sir?'

'Green Cap, himself, sir.'

'Was it me, sir?' asks Whopper taking it up, a big Whopper who seemed to be going out every year as well as up. Even now his face seemed to be growing outside his ears, and as ever the front button of his coat had a hard stretch to get across. Whopper, too, a little bit slow on the uptake, looking into Pugnug's green eyes that were alive and laughing with mischief.

'Yes, you, sir.'

'You're a liar, sir.'

'Who then, sir?'

'The priest of the parish himself, sir,' handing the ball back to Pugnug, who was the priest of the parish.

At this point they broke out laughing, because even above their own voices they could hear the sound of the knocker banging the door across the street. A most mysterious knocking, because there was neither soul nor sinner within knocking distance of the door, and it was funny out of the corner of your eye to see the heavy iron knocker rising and falling, seemingly of its own accord. All the houses abutted on to the footpath and they all had those heavy knockers above the heavy iron knobs.

'He's out now,' whispered Whopper. 'Here he's out now.'

They proceeded again with their talkative game.

Grinder opened his door and looked out expectantly and grumpily, because he was a very sour little man. Compactly built, he was like a miniature of what a real man should be. He had the two lines of woe down each side of his nose and his eyebrows were also taking a downward slant, so that he had a very mournful looking face. A drooping moustache, outsize as if to make up for his lack of height, grew on his upper lip, and that, with a red nose peeping tenderly out of it, made up a visage that would never have won a prize for cheerfulness.

His eyes narrowed when he saw nobody confronting him. Amazed, he stepped outside on to the footpath. In his shirt sleeves he was, and the greasy riding britches were very dirty over the skinny legging-less legs and an open neck showed up surprisingly muscular. He looked left and then he looked right and he scratched his head, and then he looked over at the only souls to be seen, the boys across at the gable-end.

'Here!' he roared, putting an end to their chanting.

They looked over at him innocently, all except Whopper, whose cheeks were bulging with the force of his suppressed giggles.

'Did ye see anyone knockin' at me door?' Grinder asked.

'Oh no, sir,' answered Pugnug very politely, and as it happened, truthfully. 'We saw nobody knocking at your door.'

Grinder surveyed them sourly and suspiciously. He knew that none of them could have knocked and run away and been back over there at the gable-end in that space of time. All the same! He would put nothing past that Pugnug. He had, on many occasions before, gone over to Pugnug's mother loud with complaint about him. As Pugnug's mother said to him with a sigh, he was only one in a queue. She would really have to do something about Pugnug, but that he was a good boy under it all.

'Well, if you don't do somethin' to him,' said Grinder, 'I will. That boy a yours, Ma'am, wants the livin' bejasus kicked out o 'm, and you won't find wan neighbour in the whole street that wouldn't be glad to do it for you.'

So the innocent look of the green eyes meant nothing to Grinder. It was only the physical impossibility of the feat that assured him of Pugnug's innocence. So he scratched his head again and came out on to the path and looked left and right again in case the figure of the knocker might be hidden in the shadows of the shallow doorways. No sign. So he looked over at the boys once more, warningly, and then retired.

He was no sooner in with the door closed than Pugnug pulled again at the black thread in his hand, the thread that was tied on to the knocker and hooked around the electric light pole and held in his long fingers.

The boys nearly died laughing when the door opened again as soon as it was closed and Grinder came out like a tornado, as if to say, 'Hah, I've got yeh this time!'

A most stupid look of puzzlement came over his face then, so stupid that the peeping boys couldn't keep in their laughter any longer, so they laughed out, loud and long. Pugnug, holding his sides. Grinder glaring at them. Pausing, shouting across, 'Here, what's all the laffin' for?'

Pugnug turning to him and stifling his mirth.

'I beg your pardon, sir?'

'Oh, the politeness of the little bastard,' Grinder thought, clenching his teeth.

'What's all the laffin' for, hah? What's all the laffin' about?' Coming half way across the street so that little Jay got frightened and prepared to bolt, giving the game away, but Pugnug stretched his free hand and took the slack of his trousers into it and held on.

'Oh, something else altogether we were laughing at,' said Pugnug. 'Weren't we, fellas?'

'Oh, yes, that's right,' said the fellas dutifully, spluttering, all except Jay who was looking over his shoulder with widened eyes.

'I see,' said Grinder, looking at them once more and going back quickly and closing the door.

They gave him longer this time before Pugnug pulled on the thread. It would knock a laugh out of a Sybarite to see that knocker rising and falling of its own accord. A mysterious thing of beauty it was, and they looked and laughed and waited, looked and laughed and waited. But this time the door didn't open. Knock again and a pause, and still the door didn't open.

'Is he gettin' wise, I wonder?' Tom Martin asked.

'He's canny,' said Whopper. 'He's waitin' like an oul fox. Give 'm another rap, Pugnug.'

'Mebbe he'll ketch on, fellas,' said Jay. 'He'll have a proper grind on then, so he will. He'll murder us, so he will.'

'He'll have to catch us first, so he will,' said Pugnug, pulling once more at the thread.

All their heads were turned watching when the avalanche descended on them from the unexpected quarter. From their backs.

'Ye hoors, ye!' roared Grinder, breathing heavily, standing within feet of them, his arms held out from his sides and his moustache laying out on the breeze of his breath from his quick run out his own back and his circle around the block. 'D'ye think I'm an eejit, do ye?'

He jumped.

There was a scatter like would come on goldfish in a bowl from the paw of a fishing cat.

Left, right and centre, and in the middle. But Grinder knew his own mind where the others didn't. He went for the big fish. Pugnug felt the hand descend on his collar and grasp the band of his shift and the top of his jersey. 'Ow!' roared Pugnug, as a hand thumped him on the back.

'Ow!' roared Pugnug, as a heavy boot bit into his behind.

'Yeh sly little bastard yeh,' Grinder was roaring, 'I'll give yeh what yer father never gev yeh, yeh trickster, yeh good-for-nothing, yeh!'

Hollow thumps on the back that could be heard up in the slaughter house, Pugnug's thin arms up protecting his neck, and then his long leg curled out and came into satisfactory contact with Grinder's shin. Grinder howled and raised his leg and rubbed at it, but didn't release his hold. Pugnug twisted wildly like a fish at the end of a line, but he remained caught.

'Yeh bloody little criminal yeh!' A smack on the unprotected head and then he felt himself being hauled along.

'Down home with yeh,' Grinder roaring. 'I'll tell yer mother what kind o a bee of a son she has.'

Pugnug went along towards his home willy-nilly.

He thought of his mother: her calm eyes, the grey hair and the way her kindly mouth turned up at the corners. But it could turn down too, he knew. The sigh. 'Pugnug, why oh why!' No sixpence this week for sweets. No pictures for the next fortnight. No new suit for Christmas. She had her ways of punishing that were efficacious enough. She could hurt you more materially even than could oul Grinder with all his kicking.

'If you hit me again,' said Pugnug to him with his eyes blazing, 'you'll regret it, so you will. Let me go now, and I'll go home with you all right.'

Grinder released his hold of him. Pugnug shrugged himself free and walked along beside the other.

'At the end of a rope, ye'll be, yeh wait and see,' said Grinder. 'As sure as yeer walkin' along this street, yeh'll end up at the end of a rope.'

Behind them the three boys were tentatively joining the procession, keeping at a safe distance, cupping their hands around their mouths roaring, 'Hey, Grinder, Grinder, randy oul ram! Grinder, Grinder,' and then shouting derisively the rhyme from which he got his nickname,

> Seamus Partridge had a wife,
> He didn't know how to mind 'er.
> He put 'er on a window-stool,
> And gev 'er a ha'penny grinder.

Grinder turning back, waving his fist at them so that they paused, prepared to run away again.

'Wait'll I catch ye! I'll crucify ye, ye bees ye! I'll tell yer mothers!'

Answered with hoots and catcalls. Rude lip noises until Grinder was ready to burst.

Then they came to Pugnug's door, and he waited patiently like a saint waiting for torture. He felt mad with the fellas. 'How is it,' he wondered, 'that I seem to be always the one to be caught?' And then he felt sorry for his poor mother. 'This has happened so often,' he thought, as Grinder rapped on the door. Pugnug broke a winda. Pugnug hit my Tomeen. Pugnug this, Pugnug that. Pugnug sighed and looked shamefully into the apprehensive eyes of his mother. Then dropped his head resignedly.

Pugnug at sweet sixteen.

They still talk about it as Pugnug's Raid. It's as famous as Kitty the Hare or the Croppy Boy. It was planned out like a general would plan out a battle.

Saturday night, when all the male citizens would have a half day and would shave and dress themselves in their navy-blue suits and go for a few pints and then hop down to the church and get confession, and after that come back up the street and gather together and then adjourn around the back of one of the rows of houses where there was a light, and there they would play pitch-and-toss until midnight sometimes, or until winner had won all, and they went home to be exacerbated by their weary wives. A good night this particular Saturday was, and there was a very great school. Nobody ever bothered about the pitch part. It was all toss.

Two ha'pennies placed side by side on a small wooden tosser, spit upon and then sent curling into the air to come down either heads or harps. All the neighbours were there, the young married men as well as the young bachelors. Mico was there and Mungo and Gaeglers and Snitch's brother Mosso, and Packey and Terror and Panther Bones. Oh, a great gathering of the famous men of the street.

Pugnug was there at the side, very grown up now. Wearing long pants that were getting too tight for him as it was, skimpy around the leg and pinching in the ah, and his wrists were growing out of his coat sleeves. His red hair as bristly as ever and his green eyes as dancy as ever. And he had all the jargon! 'Up she goes. Look out now. Down they come. Roly-poly. Heads.' Or Harps. Or head and a harp. Big bets in the middle covered by the man tossing. And side bets on your fancy. Pugnug winked over the other side where Whopper was, a very big Whopper, as tall as a man nearly and as wide as two and a half men, his small mouth lost in the fat face and his eyes disappearing every time he showed his teeth in a smile.

'A tanner on the heads,' says Pugnug, throwing down sixpence and casting a quick eye on the ground. There was nearly two pounds there in silver and coppers. 'It's a shame for them,' he was thinking. 'Some of their kids'll have to go without something this week now, because their oul fellas has lost money playing this racket.' Then he grinned and wondered if Jay and Tom Martin were doing as they were ordered. This pitch-and-toss was against the law, but like many other things of that nature, such as drinking after hours and making *poitín* in the hills, people just ignored it. Periodically the Guards would carry out a raid, like they would on the poor public-house keepers, but they'd want to have eyes like hawks and divide their bodies into thousands of portions to be able to stop it all. So apart from an odd raid with plenty of warning beforehand, everybody knew that the wife's tongue, if they lost, was more to be feared than the heavy hand of the law.

Jay and Martin came up to scratch, like at rehearsals.

Down below, away past the street that debouched on the main road, they stood at the corner, two ordinary looking boys, poorish boys in long trousers that had once belonged to their daddies, with the legs too big and the waists too small and large patches where bigger behinds had won them well. Tom Martin, a big fellow with a fine chest, and Jay, growing up like a leek with a black wig on. They leaned at the pub wall on the corner there and waited patiently. When they saw the two Guards ambling towards them with their hands behind their backs, they moved.

'Now,' said Tom Martin, 'I'll be waitin' back up,' and he vanished from Jay, running and turning his head until he got into position a good fifty yards away.

The Guards came along, and Jay stepped in front of them.

'Hey, Mister, Mister,' pulling at the sleeves of the nearest and making his voice as boylike and as pleading as possible.

'What is it, son?' the Guard asks.

'It's me oul fella,' says Jay. 'He's up there behind, well oiled, and they're at pitch-and-toss and they're robbin' 'm, and me oul wan says, "Go for the Guard, you", she says, "or we won't have a pinny in the jug for the price of a crubeen."'

'H'm,' said the Guard, stopping and looking at him closely. 'Up where?'

'Up here, Mister,' said Jay, walking back a little and pointing.

They looked at one another.

'Oh, well,' said the other Guard then, shrugging his shoulders, and they set off with long strides.

Tom Martin watched and kept backing away in front, dodging. He scuttled off like a rabbit when they came out of the lane and headed for the back where the school was in full swing. He got around the corner then and waited in the shadow until the Guards came into view, with Jay hanging back now, well behind in case he would be seen. As soon as the light from the lamp shone on the peaks of the Guards' caps and reflected from the silver buttons on their jackets, Tom Martin moved towards the school, roaring like a bull.

'The Guards!' he roared. 'Hey, the bloody Guards, fellas! Hey, 's the Guards!'

The men at the school took one startled look over their shoulders, saw the Guards, cursed and then scrambled for their money.

Pugnug and Whopper, of course, didn't have to look over their shoulders. They stopped first to the ground and scooped into their palms whatever was nearest to hand, and then as the other scores of hands scrabbed at the ground, they rose and ran. The school disintegrated as if it had been hit by a bomb. The Guards ran shouting towards them, but men disappeared as if the ground had swallowed them, up the back lane and down the side lane, and muscular and agile leaps over the high walls that enclosed the yards of the houses.

Pugnug got away laughing.

He saw no sign of the others, but he kept running until he had put two streets between him and the by now disgruntled 'scholars'.

Then he slowed down and looked at his catch. Three and ninepence, it amounted to. Not bad. It was nearly all that he had lost in the venture so far. Then he put it back in his pocket and set off whistling towards the rendezvous. After a while he stopped whistling. The venture, he thought, was successful, and for once he hadn't been caught, although he'd have to keep out of Mungo's way and Pather Bones' for a few weeks, because they were very cute citizens and were very quick at smelling a rat. 'Naw,' Pugnug thought, 'I must be getting old or something. There isn't the kick in it all now as there would have been a few weeks ago even. What's wrong with me?' Maybe it was because he was coming to the end of his schooling and he would have to find out what he intended to do with his life. 'Strange,' Pugnug thought, 'this sort of depression that has come over me.'

It went with him all the way to the camp, a ruined house by the canal with only three walls standing. Inside this they had toiled and moiled and had dug down a good six feet by five into the ground, making a nice hole with steps going into it, and over the hole they had put old baulks of timber and over these old rags and bags and bits of tin to keep out the rain. It was a great place. It had been fun building it and coming up here at night after tea to light a bit of a candle and to boil spuds in a black can over a wood fire. Like camping out. Like having somewhere in the world private where you could go.

Pugnug saw he was first there, so he went down and groped for the candle and lit it where it was stuck to a soap box up-ended on the hard mud floor, and then he sat on another box with his chin cupped in his hands and a crease in his forehead. Sat there and thought, 'Is even this going from me now? I don't feel so comfortable in it any more. It doesn't seem to mean so much to me somehow. Why, I wonder?' He thought of his mother's remedy for everything, treacle and sulphur, and he said out loud, 'Maybe that's what's wrong with me; maybe I want treacle and sulphur?' So he routed up a wry grin and gathered a few sticks and paper and proceeded to light a fire in the old chimney-place of the ruined house.

Jay and Tom Martin came first.

He heard them laughing, then they came down.

'Ah, Jay!' said Jay. 'Did yeh see them, Pugnug? Did yeh see the scatter that kem on them when Tom shouted "Guards!" Jay, it'd make anyone laugh, so it would.'

'Honest to God,' said Tom Martin, sinking on a box, 'when I saw Mungo and Panther tearing over the walls like two goats, I thought me heart 'd break with the laughing.'

'You'll laugh the other side of your face,' said Pugnug, 'if Mungo ever finds out what we did.'

'Oh, Jay,' said Jay sobering, 'he'd never find out, would he?'

'I hope not' said Pugnug fervently, thinking of Mungo's hard hand that was tempered in an iron foundry.

'Did yeh get much, Pugnug?' Tom Martin asked eagerly. 'What did yeh get?'

'Three and ninepence,' said Pugnug, holding it on his palm.

'Is that all?' Tom asked disappointed.

'Jay, it wasn't hardly worth it,' said Jay.

'Ah to hell with ye!' said Pugnug rising and throwing it on the ground, 'what do ye want? It was fun, wasn't it? It was only the fun we were after, wasn't it?'

His eyes were angry. They looked at him wonderingly.

A silence there. Pugnug feeling himself boiling inside.

Then a voice from outside to break it up.

'Hey, fellas, fellas!' Whopper's voice. And then his fat legs, the trousers stretched tightly around them, appeared down the steps. Then his face, one hand held behind him holding something. 'What did yeh get, Pugnug? What did yeh get?'

'Oney three and ninepence he got,' said Tom Martin, looking at Pugnug like a disappointed disciple.

'Is that all?' Whopper asked. 'I got twelve and a tanner. Imagine that? Twelve and a tanner!'

'Wait'll Mungo hears about it,' said Pugnug.

'Ah, to hell with Mungo,' said Whopper. 'Hey, something else I picked up on the way. Worth more than twelve and a tanner. Eh, Liz?' pulling the girl down into the light of the candle and slapping her on the thigh with a fat hand. The other boys rose and watched her. A small girl enough with a light dress clinging tightly to her. Brown curly hair and thick lips and a short nose. Lipstick on her and her eyebrows plucked like a chicken at a wake. But a nice girl, Lizzie.

'Look here, Whopper,' said Pugnug.

'Ah, lay off, Pugnug,' said Whopper, following her down. 'It's oney this time. Sure ye don't mind fellas, do ye?'

'No,' said the fellas, their eyes glued to Lizzie's prominent and uplifted breasts pushing against the thin stuff of her dress, 'we don't mind!'

'Well I . . .' Pugnug began, when Lizzie sat on the box he had vacated.

'I think yeer great,' said Lizzie, 'to be havin' a grand place like this. Whopper was always tellin' me about it. What do ye be doin' in it?'

'Oh,' said Pugnug reluctantly, 'things.'

'Not quare things, I hope,' said Lizzie. Pugnug felt himself getting red. Jay sniggered and Tom Martin laughed.

'Isn't she a howl?' Whopper asked laughing, sitting on his box, specially built up to take his weight. 'Here, Lizzie, come on over here to me and don't be sittin' on Pugnug's box.'

'It's all right,' said Pugnug.

'A grand cushion you make, Whopper,' said Lizzie, rising and going over to his outstretched arms and sitting on his knees.

'More than that,' said Whopper taking her in his arms. One hand, Pugnug saw, was around her waist and pressing into her right breast. The other arm was resting on her leg and his hand was on her thigh near the place where her legs met.

'God, Lizzie,' said Whopper, 'I love yeh. Give 's a kiss!' and she bent down and pressed her face against his and his hands practically convulsed themselves on her.

Pugnug felt something stir in his stomach then. Queer things that ran up and down like a centipede on a pane of glass, and he swallowed to take the dryness out of his mouth, and he looked at Jay and Tom. They were regarding the other two with their mouths open and something in their eyes that Pugnug didn't like. A sort of wide-eyed hotness. 'Why,' Pugnug thought, 'these couldn't be Jay and Tom at all, could they?' Then, he thought, 'Is that the look I have in my eyes, too, from the feeling in my stomach? Does it change the appearance of my face like that?' Then he looked at Whopper, who had pulled himself away from the girl.

'Christ, Liz,' he was saying, 'that's hot! Lookit fellas, how about a load a that?'

'Oh, boy!' said Jay and Tom, rising as one man. Lizzie was smiling at them.

The smell of wet bags that have dried in sunshine. The smell of excavated earth. The smell of candle grease and lighted timber and the stale skins of potatoes. And friends he didn't know.

Pugnug left them suddenly and ran away, and behind him in the dark he could hear their calling voices, surprised and disappointed and puzzled. Pugnug kept running.

And now.

A tight valley near the lake, a small one like all Connemara lakes, placid and barely ruffled by a November wind. Off on the left a range of mountains rising from the earth, bleak in the pale sunshine, seeming to be combing the sky with their jagged tops. Small white dots that were sheep picking what they could from the bleakness of faded gorse and rough yellowed grasses. And near the lake here, a winding yellow road coming down from the hills to this one verdant place in the valley where the grass was green and there were whitewashed houses, hiding discreetly from sweeping gigantic winds. A lot of carts, with the animals untackled from them and tied to the shafts with their reins and plucking rather indolently at the grass by the side of the road.

A gathering of the people at this small building, a white-walled building with a slated roof, but apart from that not very distinguished. Just four walls and a roof is the best you can say for it. And a double door opened now, and men pressed into it. Some of them looking in and some of them looking out. Countrymen with *bainín* coats and *ceanneasna* trousers and black hats or caps or nothing at all. The smell of frieze coats as if they had been steeped over a peat fire all the summer and then left out in the rain.

And inside Father Pugnug is saying mass.

A very plain church it is indeed, with a few benches sufficient to seat or kneel the women and girls and the older men up near the altar rails there, and behind the men shuffling on the wooden floor with their heavy boots or kneeling on one knee. A window high up at the far end and under it a very simple wooden altar, just like a solid table with the brass tabernacle and six brass candlesticks and a few flowers. And the priest up there with his robes is a tall priest, broad-shouldered, and his red hair bristles, and there are grey streaks at the side of his head, because there was no easy road to where Pugnug is now.

He is talking to them just before the last Gospel. His eyes are green and his mouth goes up a bit at the corners. There is always a lurking smile behind the eyes of Father Pugnug. Maybe that's why he's so popular. There's nothing high-falutin about Father Pugnug. If a man goes to him on a Friday with a fish for his dinner, you don't get Father Pugnug asking you for the fish's birth certificate or if you had a salmon trout pond in your back garden. Things like that. It was a comfort to have a man like him coming to see your oul granny in the middle of the night. The corpses were known to get up and laugh when he came around, and even if you had to die, it didn't seem so bad. And if there was a wrong that you wanted righted with this authority or that authority, you just went to Father Pugnug and you said so, and a little blaze came into his green eyes as he stretched for his hat and that was that.

'. . . It is from simple things,' he was saying now, 'that things grow. All the most beautiful things are simple. Who knows that better than all of you, who have them all around you? And things grow in cities, too, but there are more weeds in cities, as well as the most beautiful of rough flowers that many people would disdain. There is no harm either in simple things being acquainted with progress. So when you come to the Holy Sacrament, I say that you should come in your best, as if you were coming to a feast or a *ceilidhe* dance at the crossroads. Do yourselves up for God, the same as you'd do yourselves up for a fella, my dear girls. Put on your best dress, or your Sunday suit, and brush your hair and set it if you like, and put on your lipstick. You will be doing yourself up for God. And that is good.'

'The Lord save 's,' the old people were saying, 'what's he puttin' into their heads at all? Paintin' themselves up for Holy Communion is it!'

'Benedicat vos Dominus, omnipotens Deus, Pater et Filius et Spiritus Sanctus,' said Father Pugnug, turning and blessing them, and then turning away to say 'Initium Sancti Evangelii Secundum Joannem,' and for the life of him, he couldn't help thinking of the morning so long ago when he had been saying the same thing with the long robes dusting the ground around him.

'I was a scoundrel,' Father Pugnug thought, 'but it was good practice.'

The New Broom

THE NEW BROOM was a middling-sized man with spiky hair, rimless glasses and cold blue eyes. The closing years of the reign of the Old Broom had left the county in a state of benevolent decay which nobody noticed much until the New Broom started sweeping. He was devoted to the ratepayers. He wanted to save them money. He did this in various ways. If a man was two minutes late in the morning, he had to call and explain it to the cold eyes and listen to a fortunately short, crisp speech about duty and the danger of losing your soft job late in life. If you were in the habit of slipping out at midday for a drink or two or to place a few bets on a horse for the three-thirty, you would have a call from him to explain your sudden absence from your post. If that happened often enough, you could run out of lies.

It was amazing how in such a short time all the departments became very efficient and turned out twice the amount of work in six hours.

This process uncovered a lot of driftwood. There were many political appointees in temporary positions, who had been signing on for years, who suddenly discovered that they were expendable and were sent on the road with a month's temporary salary. Of course, there was a bit of a rumpus at the council meetings, but this capable man had logic and truth on his side, the minister behind him, and the kind regards of the taxpayers when they

221

found out what was being uncovered. So the fixers ran for cover, and public men, even in their speeches, became stiff with rectitude.

The New Broom was a good man; nothing of his past life for which he could be politely blackmailed. He was a good-living man with a wife and family, utterly devoted to his job and utterly incapable of being bribed. It was an awkward situation, so all they could do was grin and bear it. Maybe the fellow might mellow. An honest, upright, God-fearing man is a terrible burden on a community, many thought. He is indestructible, undefeatable and inexorable.

But even the hearts of the righteous sank a bit when he smelled out Doctor Dolmen.

Many mornings, having locked his car, at the entrance of the buildings he would meet this tall, skinny man coming out, almost festooned with papers. He was always dressed in a shiny black suit, a white shirt and a thin black tie. He would have papers under his arm and sticking out of his pockets. He bulged with books. He had a thin aristocratic face. His white hair was long under a well-worn black Homburg hat. He would smile at the New Broom, beam on him and say, 'Nice morning, friend,' even if it was raining, as it often was.

He had so many things on his mind that this meeting with the man went on for weeks before he got around to wondering who he was, and what his business could be, and why he should be leaving the building every morning? Was he a night-watchman? Did he have an apartment in the building?

So he asked, 'Who is he?' pointing out into the rain at the jaunty figure walking towards the main gate.

'Oh, that's the Doc,' said the porter, smiling.

'Oh, a doctor,' said the Broom.

'Not a real doctor, sir,' said the porter. 'The people has given him the title. He's a great scholar. He does be digging up bones and pottering around cairns and old abbeys and old buildings, and finding books that was written hundreds of years ago. That's why they call him Doctor Dolmen. The whole town is proud of him. He could blind any professor living with knowledge, so he could.'

'I see,' said the Broom; 'and why does he come out of here every morning?'

'Oh, he just comes in to sign the book,' said the porter, 'and then off with him to his excavations and explorations.' The porter liked the sound of these words.

'Do you mean that he is supposed to be working here?' the Broom asked.

'Yes, sir,' said the porter, and then saw the cold eyes and his heart sank and he thought, 'Oh, no, not the Doc.'

'At least I think so. At least he signs the book.'

'What department is he attached to?' the Broom asked.

'Oh, I wouldn't know, sir,' said the porter quickly. 'I wouldn't know where half of them work.'

The Broom looked at him. The man's face was bland. The Broom knew that porters knew everything about everybody, but he could also recognise a baby when it was being passed on, so he said 'Hm' and went to his office.

Shortly the bells started to ring. Department heads cursed carefully when they switched off the intercommunications box and answered the call to the office. They examined their consciences on the way, explored avenues, decided where the cat would jump, and how they could keep sitting on the fence.

Rating Department.

'Doctor Dolmen? Oh!' The Broom wondered why they smiled when the name was mentioned. At all times a warm smile. 'Oh, no, nothing to do with me, just it is nice to have him around. He's marvellous on names. He can trace a name back more than a thousand years. He's amazing. Wonderful person. What's his name? Oh. Murphy, I think. Cornelius Murphy, would it be? You forget he had a name. Just Doctor Dolmen. Oh, no, nothing to do with

us. I honestly couldn't tell what department he is attached to.'
Passing the baby.

Motor Taxation.

'Doctor Dolmen? Oh, no, nothing to do with us,' but again the
warm smile. 'You should hear him lecture. Fascinating. He knows
the history of the town from the very beginning. He can draw
plans of it. Fascinating. He knows every mode of conveyance from
the time man give his wife a trip by towing her by the hair. Ha-ha-
ha. Oh, no, nothing to do with Motor.'

Engineering.

'Doctor Dolmen? Fascinating man. Wonderful knowledge of
roads, particularly ancient ones, from the first path kicked out by
boars and Irish elk. Could spend hours with him. Oh, no, nothing
to do with Engineering.'

The Broom was getting angry at this terrible waste of time. He
became curt. The more he heard in praise of the good Doctor, the
sharper became his feelings.

It took him nearly two hours to track him down after going
through Health, Hospitals and various others.

He dug him out of Agriculture.

'I can't say that he is actually attached to us,' said the harrassed
secretary. 'It was a department established some years ago to give
help to farmers. Sort of handing out handbills of advice on things.
Sort of Advice to the Lovelorn column in a ladies magazine, sort
of, ha-ha-ha. A good man. Never heard of any complaints. Must do
his work well.'

'When does he do his work?' the Broom asked. 'As far as I can
see, he just comes in, signs on, and then goes about his business. I
suppose he collects his salary cheque.'

'I suppose so,' said the secretary.

'Is he supposed to work his full hours? Does his job entail being
out of the buildings all day?'

'Oh, no, certainly not. He has a sort of office in our department.'

'Isn't it your job to see that he puts in his hours?'

'Well, not really. It was a sort of special job that was created. Not quite sure that I am his superior really. Never quite thought about the thing, actually.'

'Well, go away and think about it now, and quickly, and come up with an answer,' said the Broom. 'I want to know if the man is productive. I want to know if he is doing the work that he is paid to do. And if he isn't, I want to know why; and if he is an unnecessary cog in this machinery, I want him out of here. This is not a charitable institution.'

So the secretary left, and the Broom rang for his secretary and he said, 'I want all the details on an employee named Cornelius Murphy: when he was appointed, why and by whom. I want all this information by lunch-time.'

Then he got on with his work.

There was quite a wastage in the buildings that morning. The secretary shoved his head in the door of the other departments and said: 'He's after Doctor Dolmen.' It went all over the place. 'The Broom is after the Doc.' Everybody liked him. He was a cheerful person. He had no interest in the present at all. He was optimistic about everything because he wasn't interested in the future. He wasn't a professional optimist, you understand. He was part of the town. They used him to pass the vote of thanks to visiting lecturers.

Often the vote of thanks went like this: 'On behalf of the citizens, I thank the learned doctor for his informative lecture on the Battle of Moyglash. Apart from the fact that the battle took place fifty years earlier than the learned doctor told us and that the Chieftain O'Kane at the time it took place was a suckling infant and could hardly have been chopping off heads with a sword weighing fourteen pounds, we found it extremely interesting.'

He was an asset, you understand. If anyone wanted to hold a pageant, he just had to be consulted about dates, costumes, weapons. He was always digging up kitchen middens and proving that the place was inhabited four thousand years ago and that they ate chicken and knew how to cure a pig and hated their mothers-in-law. He added considerably to the small museum, for which nobody paid him, the citizens not having advanced far enough culturally to support with actual money a decent museum; so they had a cut-price bargain. Everyone knew all those things, but they hadn't thought about them until the Broom took after the Doctor, and then all they felt was dismay, for to the Broom the Doctor was just a person, presumably drawing money that he wasn't earning. The Broom was a stranger. He couldn't possibly be aware of what the Doctor meant to the town.

So the Broom stopped the Doctor.

'Good morning. What a nice morning.'

'Do you know who I am, Mr Murphy?'

The Doctor looked him up and down with bright eyes.

'Why, no,' he said, 'but by the shape of your head and cheekbones, I judge you are of Anglo-Norman stock. What did you say your name is?'

'Please follow me,' said the Broom, tight-lipped.

'I am busy, you know,' said the Doctor gently. 'I have a lot to do this morning.'

'So have I!' said the Broom. 'So have I, and you are unfortunately part of it. I have wasted a lot of precious time on you already, Mr Murphy, and I will waste no more. Now, please follow me.' He turned on his heel. The Doctor looked after him wide-eyed, not used to this sort of behaviour, and then followed amicably after him. Every window in the building had watchers for this scene, and they all shook their heads.

'You were appointed, you are paid, and you do not work,' said the Broom to the gentle eyes watching him. He had a terrible impression that the Doctor wasn't even listening to him, but was examining his face as if it was a skull. It was taking him all his time to hold on to his temper.

'You will report to your department every morning. You will work the hours stated in your contract. This is an order. In the event of your not carrying out this order, I will have no alternative but to give you a month's wages in lieu of notice and let you go.'

'You can't do that,' said the Doctor.

'I beg your pardon?' said the Broom.

'You can't do that,' said the Doctor. 'My appointment was odd. It was under the old statute. I'm afraid you will find, when you look it up, that in order to dismiss me you will have to call a quorum meeting of the council. In this case you haven't the powers of dismissal. Did you know that there were about six hundred people buried in that old yard out there?'

He was at the window now looking down. 'Time of the famine. They died in thousands. Buried them where they fell. Tsk-tsk-tsk. Bad time. Hallowed ground really. You'd find very interesting skulls down there.'

The Broom was silent. He had nothing to say. He watched the Doctor pick up fourteen old battered leather-bound books from the desk where he had left them, stuff manuscripts back into his pockets that had fallen on the floor.

'Nice morning,' said the Doctor. 'It is good to be alive when the sun is shining.'

He went out then. The Broom, seething with anger, rang for his secretary. They looked up books. Doctor Dolmen was perfectly right. He couldn't be dismissed without the permission of the council.

'Then,' said the Broom, terribly still, 'the council will dismiss him. Put it on the agenda for the next month's meeting.'

Soon the whole place knew that the Broom was after the Doctor. People were very indignant, but the Broom had a lot of power: men would want favours in the future. Also, outside the town nobody knew much about Doctor Dolmen except a few influential scholars, and they had gone sour on him when he had corrected dates for them in letters to the newspapers. You couldn't take his case to the minister, because the Doctor had scorched him a bit in a motion of thanks the time the minister had opened a new school and had ventured into past history and had been corrected publicly by the Doctor. You see. Oh, some of the councillors got together over it, sweating over how they could save him. He hadn't much of a case if you didn't know the merits. His father had been a public man, done a lot for the town. That was the reason the job had been made for him. It was necessary, too, at that time. Now agriculture was big-time and handled in a different way, so Doctor Dolmen was a sort of anachronism. He hadn't fought in the War of Freedom, he never killed a policeman, he hadn't taken sides in the Civil War. He had no interest in guns unless they were a few hundred years old.

So they sent old Joe Muldowney to talk sense to him, if such were possible. Joe puffed his weighty way up the narrow stairs where the Doctor lived above a shop in a back street. He was always amazed at how neat the Doctor managed to keep his two rooms. The big room was all books and manuscripts; the small room held a sort of camp bed; there was a small place with a gas cooker. It was all very clean. Even the skulls grinning at you from odd places had their pates polished.

There were human shin-bones around the place and elk jaws and pieces of flint and arrowheads and old daggers. That was why real scholars professed to despise him. He was not a specialist. He was too diversified in his studies.

He welcomed Joe and took a skeleton off a chair so that he could sit down. He insisted on making tea. Joe didn't want tea. He could have done with a whiskey, but the Doctor didn't touch it.

'You'll have to take it seriously, Corney,' he said. 'This fellow means business. In the name of God, can't you put in six hours a day in the damn office? You can do your own work there. Just to put in the hours and you have him powerless, I tell you. We are all worried.'

'You are kind,' said the Doctor, lighting the gas under the kettle. 'This man is like a summer storm. He will blow himself out.'

'No, no, you are wrong,' said Joe. 'Listen to me! He means business. If the worst comes to the worst, there is nothing we can do. You hear that? Nothing. Have you saved anything?'

'Certainly,' said the Doctor. 'I am not profligate. I just spend on books and manuscripts and little rewards for farmers when they turn up things while they are plowing. I have a small barrel of bog butter here that's five hundred years old. Would you believe that? Oh, I have saved all right.' He took a polished helmet from the mantelpiece and upended it on the table. Some notes and coins tumbled out of it. Joe gave it a quick count. There was about seven pounds in notes and say three pounds in silver and coppers.

'Is that all?' he asked.

'It's not bad,' said the Doctor, and went to take off the boiling kettle.

'Holy hour!' said Joe, slapping his forehead.

'I do my work, you know, Joe,' the Doctor was saying. 'I answer all their questions about pigs and calves and bulls and cows and crops. I can do the work in a few hours a week. I do not neglect my work. You must not think so. But more time than is necessary devoted to it would be waste. I am over sixty now. In the normal way I have only another thirty years to live, and I have enough work to occupy sixty.'

'Holy hour!' said Joe, slapping his forehead again.

'I make a good cup of tea,' said the Doctor, giving it to him.

'Look,' said Joe, after gulping it and scalding his mouth, 'just put in six hours a day in the office is all we ask. Just six hours a day. Sign in, sign off, just six hours a day, and he can't touch you. Will you promise this?'

'I'll see what I can do, Joe,' said the Doctor. 'I must say I am stirred at the sympathy you express for me.'

Joe groaned.

The Doctor found a lot of sympathy. Wherever he went, people now stopped to chat with him and hold his thin arm and ask after his health. If he had been married, they would have asked after the wife and kids. Most of them hinted that the town would be happy if only he would be seen more often in the buildings.

Give him his due, the Doctor tried to accommodate them. He went to the buildings oftener and stayed longer, but then he would forget. He would hear from a man who had dug up some bones or stones or bog butter or some damn thing, and people wouldn't see him for days. Not even signing on in the morning!

But the Doctor was genuinely aware of people's sympathy. He knew well that his dismissal would hurt people's feelings. He gave the matter some thought and decided to do something about it. He asked for an interview with the Broom.

'Well,' said he, 'what can I do for you?'

'I have been thinking,' said the Doctor.

'I am very glad,' said the Broom.

'If I change my occupation, I would of course need a reference from you. Would you make such a reference available?'

The Broom couldn't believe his ears. He was overjoyed. He did not allow this to appear in his face. Doctor Dolmen had caused him more worry and trouble than any of the tasks he had undertaken. He was getting some rough talk, from men who had nothing to lose, in the Golf Club and the other clubs. He was aware that he was beginning to look like a villain over Doctor Dolmen. He didn't expect to be popular in this new job, but he expected respect at least for his work. He knew in a vague way that this issue of Doctor Dolmen would haunt him for the rest of his life when he had brought it to a successful conclusion. And here was the Doctor himself providing a magnificent solution. He wasn't disturbed by the twinkling intelligence of the Doctor's eyes. The Doctor was amused at his reaction. A clever man. So he would meet him half-way.

230

'I will write you a glowing reference myself,' he said, and he rang for the secretary.

'Take this down,' he said. Suddenly he felt benevolent. He felt as if a great weight had been lifted off his shoulders. He had been a little afraid of the meeting. He knew there would be severe opposition. He would get his way, but it might leave a bad taste in people's mouths. Not that he could see why they were all so anxious over this old scarecrow, this bookworm.

Cornelius Murphy had worked for this council and his county for many years. The farmers of the county owed their present prosperity almost solely to his endeavours and advice on their behalf. He and the council didn't want to lose the services of such a man, were reluctant to part with him, and only did so because he would be getting better paid for his undoubted talents. Whoever employed him would be getting a man of sterling honesty, undeviating rectitude, giant scholarship, an ornament to his town and county. His departure from the council would leave a vacancy that could never be filled.

'Will that do?' he asked.

'Most touching,' said the Doctor. The Broom looked closely at him, but there wasn't even a hint of a smile on his mouth. 'I am very thankful to you. You have been most kind.'

'You will keep us informed?' the Broom asked, meaning, 'When can we expect your written resignation?'

'I will keep you informed,' said the Doctor. 'Nice morning. The swallows will soon be here. Good-day to you.'

He left a happy Broom behind him.

There was much agitation in the town as the day of the meeting approached. The Broom kept his secret. He waited each day for the formal resignation, but he wasn't worried. When the dismissal item came up, he could explain that the Doctor was taking up another position, and the opposition would vanish.

231

Other people didn't know this. The Broom was greeted with frowns when he came to the meeting. There was a gloom in the council chamber. Nobody could see a way out for the Doctor and they looked at this New Broom with great distaste. That was all they could do, look, because they were powerless and they knew it.

They dawdled their way through the agenda, everyone instinctively dragging out his oration as if to put off the evil moment which would have to come sometime.

It duly arrived.

The Broom cleared his throat.

'And now, gentlemen,' he started, when there was a gentle knock on the door. It opened, and to everyone's amazement who walked in but Doctor Dolmen. He was very clean, even had a new coat on, and he wasn't so burdened with books and papers as usual. He just carried an envelope.

'Gentlemen,' he said, 'forgive me for this intrusion. I will take up little of your time. I have been informed that I make up an item on your agenda today, and before you discuss it, I would be most pleased if you would read this letter.' And he placed it gently under the secretary's nose and walked out and closed the door softly after him.

The Broom was looking at the closed door in horror. The secretary was nervously wetting his lips.

'Well, come on, man, come on,' shouted Joe Muldowney. 'Read the thing.'

With frightened eyes on the Broom, the secretary read the letter with great dispassion.

This letter told them what a great person Cornelius Murphy was, to county and country, what a loss he would be if he took up another position. It practically said the council couldn't afford to lose the man's services, and it was signed with a flourish by the New Broom.

Now, over that council chamber there moved a spirit of silent laughter. The Broom knew it. He could feel it. It didn't burst into sound, but it was there, as palpable as a wind. If you had imagination you could see the ceiling of the council room rising and falling, rising and falling.

'We better skip the next item on the agenda,' said Joe Muldowney, snorting to keep in his gusty laughter.

'Passed unanimously,' said another. 'Valuable man. Should get a rise.'

Pure unadulterated glee!

'Not bad for a bookworm,' the Broom heard in a splutter from another.

'Not a bookworm,' he was thinking, realising his utter defeat; 'not a bookworm! Oh, no, not a bookworm, but a serpent. A serpent! Doctor Dolmen, serpent!' His hands were gripping the table. His knuckles were white.

Gaeglers and the Greyhound

GAEGLERS WAS ATTRACTED to the greyhound by greed. He wasn't exactly a dog lover. He'd pat stray cuddies and he'd never kick a dog, but his attitude towards them was kindly neutral, and he might never have tangled with the greyhound if it wasn't for Softshoe Sullivan.

Softshoe was one of those commission men who'd sell his grandmother, if he had one, for five per cent of anything solid. He was an excitable little man, always dressed in a soiled raincoat and a scarf to hide his lack of a collar and shoes that always seemed to be broken down or have bits cut out of the sides of them to let his bunions loose. Gaeglers accompanied him to the dog track this one night because, according to Softshoe, every race on the card was a set-up.

As you know, strange things go on at dog tracks no more than horse tracks, viz. drugs, over-feeding, under-feeding, pep-up pills, slow-down pills, or rubber bands, or all sorts of other devices well known to dog lovers. Even with all this it is nearly impossible to predict the results on account of the fellow that runs the electric hare being able to speed him up or slow him down, and then to entice or rebuff the temperamental animals, and with all, the only known fact is that the bookies always win.

Gaeglers explained this to Softshoe, just as he would to a child. He explained to Softshoe that he was gullible, and then had to explain that gullible had nothing to do with birds, except maybe

235

plucked ones, but Softshoe remained so unconvinced and so sure of his information, hopping and dancing and sweating and swearing, that Gaeglers relented.

'All right, Softshoe,' he said. 'Just this once, but if your information is not correct, I may be angry with you.'

'You can cut my throat, Gaeglers,' he said, adding generously, 'from ear to ear, if I'm not right this time.'

'All right,' said Gaeglers, 'go and wash your scarf and tidy yourself up a bit and I'll meet you later on.'

Softshoe was delighted. He hadn't many friends, mainly because he didn't wash a lot and because he was the source of false information, but Gaeglers felt a little sorry for him. Gaeglers was no snob, you know, but he was very clean and always had a shine on his shoes and a crease in his trousers. Very natty.

He was pleased to see that Softshoe had made an effort to rehabilitate himself. He had put water on his hair and applied a little polish to his shoes. They didn't take a good shine. The only part of them that took a shine were his bunions, which had got a bit of polish too.

Gaeglers laughed when he saw this and reflected philosophically that it was the effort that counted.

I needn't describe the dog-track to you. There is something very exciting about the dogs coming out of their boxes and chasing after a phoney hare. Afterwards Gaeglers told himself that he should have learned from that, a proved fact, that greyhounds must be very stupid.

The miracle of the evening was that Softshoe's information was good, genuinely good, and not only that, but very few must have known because they got good prices on five winners. It seemed almost like a sin to be taking the money from the bookies.

'What did I tell you! What did I tell you!' exclaimed Softshoe, hugging himself, counting the increasing shillings in his pockets. Gaeglers' pockets didn't jingle. He was a note man.

'Contain yourself, Softshoe,' said Gaeglers. 'The evening isn't over. We will go now and plunge a bit on the sixth.'

'It's a set-up,' said Softshoe. 'Wait'll you see.'

It couldn't last, of course. These things never do. There is always the unpredictable. A brindle bitch was to be the winner of the sixth race, and so she should have been, but a black and white dog came out of the box and ran the same as if he was drinking rocket fuel, and it was over.

'Softshoe!' said Gaeglers ominously.

'But he couldn't!' said Softshoe. 'He couldn't! He ran fair and square.' Gaeglers was benevolent. He could afford to be.

'All right, Softshoe,' he said, 'I forgive you. We will call it off now that the run is broken. That was a fast dog. Let's go back to the kennels and have a look at him.'

Softshoe was disconsolate. 'But it shouldn't have happened,' he kept saying. 'He should never have won. It's not right.'

Not only had the dog won, but he had set up a record.

They went back to the kennels. It was here that Gaeglers was really shocked. There was a man in a trench-coat talking to the owner of the black and white dog, and not only was he talking to him, but he was putting a lot of notes into his hand; and not only were they notes, but each one of them was a fifty pound note; and not only was there one of them, but there was twenty of them! Gaeglers couldn't believe his eyes. Softshoe nearly had heart failure.

The two men shook hands, and then the man in the trench-coat took the lead of the dog and away with him. The owner shouted after him, 'Man, but you have a bargain. Wait'll you see!' Then he started to wet his fingers to count the notes in his hands.

'Hello, Jack,' said Gaeglers.

'By all that's holy, Gaeglers,' said Jack, 'I hope you're not moving in on the dog business, too.' This amused him. He slapped his leg-ginged leg with his free hand and then shook Gaeglers' hand with it.

'Jack,' said Gaeglers, 'is that a thousand pounds you have?'

237

'That's right,' said Jack. 'Did you see him go? He's a great dog. It nearly broke my heart to sell him.'

'Do you mean to say,' asked Gaeglers, 'that you got a thousand pounds for one little greyhound?'

'That's right, Gaeglers,' said Jack, 'and sold him cheap but, thank God, I have a few more like him. You should start training greyhounds, too, Gaeglers,' he went on. 'I have a lovely young one at home now that will turn into a winner. He's a son of that one. It'd be good for you, Gaeglers. Get you up early in the morning and make a fortune for you if you have patience.'

'I'll take him,' said Gaeglers. 'How much?'

'Here, Gaeglers,' said Softshoe frantically, pulling at his sleve.

Jack was looking at Gaeglers.

'I'm not fooling you, Gaeglers. This will be a good dog, if you work with him. You'll get more than your money back. I'll let you have him for twenty pounds, no more, no less. I know what I'm talking about. I'd like to see you in the dog business.'

'Let's go and see him,' said Gaeglers.

That's how Gaeglers got the greyhound. He was an all-black dog with a splash of white on his chest, and a sort of hump on his hindquarters. Gaeglers didn't want to take him. He'd have taken any other of the litter in preference to him, but Jack insisted. 'You can have any of the others for nothing, Gaeglers,' he said, 'but the black one is the boy. I know. Thousand pound dogs are few and far between, but he'll be one. You'll see!'

So Gaeglers took him and called him Jet.

It's very difficult to love a greyhound. They are so lean and miserable, and when you want to pat them there's no satisfaction to your palm because they seem to be all skin and bones. They are not very good at minding babies either, if you had any babies. They have sort of cold eyes, and Gaeglers, who had never owned a dog in his life, decided that greyhounds were purely commercial propositions. He got enough information to write four heavy volumes on how to rear, feed and train the dog. He assimilated some of it, discarded the rest, ended up by thinking he knew more about it himself than any of them, and constantly in front of his eyes he saw a thousand pounds.

He'd need it.

Jet was hungry looking, but he seemed to have a tape worm. He could eat four times his own weight, and all that the food did was to press his bones against his skin. Until he became used to it, Gaeglers thought that the hump on his hindquarter was repulsive. He fed him the best wheaten bread with a little treacle, as well as two eggs a day; also chopped lamb's liver. 'A prince of the royal blood isn't better fed than him,' Gaeglers told Softshoe. 'He's costing me over a quid a week and he still looks like a dehydrated rat.'

'In another six months,' said Softshoe, 'you'll be racing him. Think of that. The thinner he is, the better he'll run. Won't he be streamlined?'

Gaeglers had a good digs with Mrs B. He paid regularly and she liked him, but Jet caused a little strain here, too. She objected a bit when Gaeglers brought him home because, as she explained, she didn't like greyhounds, and why? Because her late husband, when he'd be in a fit of the DTs, always thought that he was a greyhound, and he'd be down on all fours chasing little green men, and it was a painful recollection for her and a reflection on the dear departed. Gaeglers pointed out that this was a blackhound, not a greyhound, a different animal altogether to the one her husband had imagined himself to be, and this ameliorated her. But she never quite took to Jet, particularly since one of her cronies had talked to her about reincarnation, which she thought were flowers grown in greenhouses until it was explained to her. After that she'd say to Gaeglers about Jet, 'He's watching me! I know that dog is watching me!'

One Sunday when she went to get the leg of lamb out of the cupboard where she had put it, wrapped in paper, there was no sign of it. There was six pounds of meat on it. Nobody thought that Jet would be able to open a cupboard, so Mrs B. went out into the back and reviled the neighbours with a loud speech about how all thieves and robbers would burn in hell with the fat of stolen meat sizzling in their bellies. They had to eat scrambled eggs.

Until eggs started to disappear from the cupboard. It was the oddest thing.

Then, unfortunately, Mrs B. found eggshells on the other side of a neighbour's wall, and the government code mark on the shells agreed with the numbers she had bought, she said, so she called the young male member of the neighbour's family and she boxed his ears, roaring that he was an egg stealer, and the child's mother came out and defended her child, and things were a bit hectic around the place for a while. Gaeglers might have suspected his dog if the dog had showed any reluctance to eat his regular meals, but he didn't. He'd nearly bite the enamel off the tin as well as eating his food.

Then one day Gaeglers was coming home and as he went to the front door happened to look in the window, and there was the dog at the cupboard, his teeth bared and he opening the little catch. He shoved in his head then and came out with an egg in his mouth. Gaeglers went around the side of the house to watch him. He jumped the wall, then on the other side he cracked the egg and scooped the contents, and then went back again. Gaeglers followed him and roared at him as he reached in for another egg.

Well you should have seen the face of that dog!

Naturally Gaeglers should have beaten him – you can't talk to a dog like you would to a human being – but he wasn't up to it. He admonished him, shouted at him, and bought a new catch for the cupboard.

It was years before Mrs B. and the neighbours were reconciled.

So the time came to train the dog.

Gaeglers didn't like getting up early in the morning (who does?), but apparently you must do this, walk the dog miles in the early morning. So he made Softshoe come along, too, even if his eyes were glued with sleep. 'You got me into this,' Gaeglers told him, 'and you'll go the whole bitter road with it.'

Outside the town, when they came to a field, he'd make Softshoe go into the field and take off running as if he was a hare. It took the dog about two months to realise that he was supposed to chase Softshoe and jump on his back and knock him on his face. Softshoe didn't like this, but Gaeglers said he might as well get a laugh for his money. Softshoe complained about the dew on his bunions. Apparently dew is not good for bunions, even if it is good for the complexion. Softshoe's face was buried in the dew many times, but it didn't improve his complexion, so that's another myth shattered, as Gaeglers told him.

I personally think they made a mistake using Softshoe as a hare. After all, the dog had limited intelligence, and afterwards, if he got used to chasing Softshoe, how could you expect him to chase a real hare? So then the only thing left to do would be to mount Softshoe on the electric rail and set him going with Jet after him. This made Softshoe go pale, because Gaeglers is a queer man. You'd never know but he might do it.

Anyhow the great day came at last when Jet was as big as he ever would be and they would have to try him out on the real thing. Gaeglers borrowed an old van (when the owner wasn't looking), packed the dog and a long lead and Softshoe aboard, and set out for mountainy districts.

Near the foot of the mountains there are great boggy plains where hares abound. That's what a countryman told them. 'In there,' he said, waving his hand at a great plain about ten miles wide, 'there are more hares than midges, bad luck to them, and they eating the sheeps' grazing on them. Ye'll be tripping over them.'

Gaeglers was elated, and they set off into the plain. Well, it seems there were stacks of midges, that'd eat you down to the skeleton, but not a hair of a hare. They must have tramped fifteen miles, sinking into bogs, bitten by midges and horse-flies, and at the end of the day they were wet, squelching and thoroughly miserable. They sat on a mound to smoke a cigarette, and there almost under their feet, curled in a form, petrified with fear, Gaeglers saw the one hare.

He reached cautiously for the dog, brought him slowly between his knees, pointed his nose at the hare. This was the climax of all the sorrow, all the sacrifice, all the weary worry of the past year. Jet and a hare were, at last, face to face.

The hare got up and ran away.

'Now, Jet,' Gaegler shouted triumphantly, getting to his feet. 'After him, boy, after him! Watch this, Softshoe.'

Jet didn't move.

'The hare, you son of a bitch!' shouted Gaeglers. 'There he is! Get after him!' The hare was bounding over the horizon like a gazelle.

Gaeglers, I regret this, kicked the dog with his sodden shoe and roared at him. The dog's tail went between his legs and he moved away. Gaeglers went after him. The dog ran away from Gaeglers. He was in a fierce temper. You could have lit a cigarette off him. Softshoe ran away from the dog and Gaeglers. Gaeglers chased the dog. In a few minutes the hare, the dog, Softshoe and Gaeglers were running four directions at once over three counties.

It was terrible.

The next morning Jack was surprised to see Gaeglers on his doorstep with Jet and Softshoe.

'Jack,' Gaeglers said, 'you were wrong. This dog is no good. This dog will never be any good. This dog wouldn't catch a rabbit that had myxomatosis. He's a fraud. He has my life ruined. He wouldn't run in a fit.'

'All right, Gaeglers,' said Jack promptly. 'I'll buy him back from you. Make up what he cost you with the purchase price and I'll give it to you. He will be a good dog.'

'You're wrong, Jack,' said Gaeglers, poking him in the chest with his finger. 'This dog will never be any good. I wouldn't cheat you. Just the twenty pounds I gave you for him in the first place and he's yours. I'm out of the dog business.'

He was back the next day.

Why? Because he missed the damn dog. That's a fact. He's still a bit ashamed of this.

'No, Gaeglers,' said Jack, 'the dog is gone. I sold him to a fellow from the south last night.'

'Well,' said Gaeglers, 'that solves it. I'm well rid of him.' But it took a little while for him to get used to being without the dog. He'd wake up early in the morning when he should have been asleep.

Softshoe was very happy that the dog was gone.

Now here's the point of all this.

Some five years later, Gaeglers happened to be motoring down the south. His business had been profitable, but it was advisable for him to get back home. He wasn't taking direct routes, but going back ways where he wouldn't be too noticeable. And going through one of those by-roads in a village in the middle of the fat southern countryside, he stopped in amazement at a sight that confronted him. There, facing him on a pedestal, was the statue of a dog. The statue of a greyhound. He got out of the car at this sight and went up to look.

There was a plaque under the statue that said: *To the Memory of the Greatest Dog That Ever Raced in Ireland: Eggnog.* He walked around this statue. Listen, this dog was done in black stone with a white mark on his chest, and on his hindquarters there was a hump. And listen, Gaeglers swears this statue was grinning.

'He was a great dog,' said a voice behind Gaeglers. He turned. 'He won five thousand pounds. There isn't a dog lover around here that wouldn't raise his hat to him.' There were a couple of men behind Gaeglers gazing admiringly at the statue.

'Where did he come from?' Gaeglers asked them.

'He came from the west,' said the man. 'Where do you come from?'

Gaeglers told him.

'That's where he's from,' said the man.

Gaeglers was flooded with emotion.

Which was why he was fined ten shillings in a local court for disturbing the peace, wilful assault, and pelting mud at the statue of a noble animal.

Jack kept out of his way for years after that. He had never had the courage to tell Gaeglers that Jet was the famous Eggnog.

My own opinion is that they should have put up a statue of Softshoe Sullivan, because the dog never could have amounted to anything only for the way Softshoe coursed him.